A HODDER OMNIBUS

Why Bother with Jesus?
You Must be Joking!
New Life, New Lifestyle

Also by Michael Green

Baptism
Closer to Jesus
The Empty Cross of Jesus
Evangelism through the Local Church
Freed to Serve
How Can I Lead a Friend to Christ?
I Believe in Satan's Downfall
I Believe in the Holy Spirit
Who is This Jesus?

Why Bother with Jesus?

You Must Be Joking!

New Life, New Lifestyle

Michael Green

Hodder & Stoughton

LONDON SYDNEY AUCKLAND

Biblical quotations are the authors own rendering of the original
Greek unless otherwise specified. The following abbreviations
are used: AV (Authorised Version), LB (Living Bible), RSV
(Revised Standard Vesion).

Why Bother with Jesus? first published in Great Britain 1979
Copyright © Michael Green, 1979

You Must be Joking! first published in Great Britain 1976
Copyright © Michael Green, 1976

New Life, New Lifestyle first published in Great Britain 1973
Copyright © Michael Green, 1973

This omnibus edition first published in Great Britain 1997

The right of Michael Green to be identified as the Author of
the Work has been asserted by him in accordance with the
Copyright, Designs and Patents Act 1988.

1 3 5 7 9 10 8 6 4 2

British Library Cataloguing in Publication Data
A record for this book is available from the British Library

ISBN 0 340 67895 X

Printed and bound in Great Britain by
Clays Ltd, St Ives plc

Hodder and Stoughton Ltd
A Division of Hodder Headline PLC
338 Euston Road
London NW1 3BH

WHY BOTHER WITH JESUS?

**For those
who do not read
religious books**

Contents

To the Reader . . .

I was standing at the church door after a service when one of our church workers introduced a friend, who said, 'I believe in God – but why bother about Jesus? Could you recommend something to read on the subject?'

On the spur of the moment, I could think of nothing. And when I racked my brains subsequently, I still could not come up with a single title designed to disturb modern apathy about Jesus.

Why bother with Jesus?

It seemed to me – and it still seems – utterly astounding that so many people today can glance at the greatest life which has ever been lived and say, 'So what? Why bother?'

I want to disturb that apathy.

That is why I have written this short but trenchant book.

Michael Green

1

Why Bother with Jesus?

Ten years ago people were saying that science had proved that God did not exist and that there was very little to know beyond the physical world of the here and now. Today people are far less sure. There seems to be mounting evidence that a spiritual world exists beyond what we can merely see, touch, taste, hear and smell. Many are trying to make sense of this and are looking in all sorts of places to find some answers.

Surprisingly, in our supposedly sophisticated world, witches and black magic have never had it so good. Islam is becoming more popular in Britain and elsewhere. Hinduism has never had such an influence as it has today, along with transcendental meditation, Eastern mysticism, New Age thinking and the numerous gurus which celebrities such as Shirley MacLaine claim to follow. New religions and spiritual causes are mushrooming all over the place. It's not just the Jehovah's Witnesses and the Mormons that come round to your door nowadays: the Hari Krishna crowd may be dancing in your street. General bookshops now stock a wide range of New Age titles and the interest in spiritualism supports many specialist bookshops as well. If you take the UFO addicts and the horoscope readers into account, it is plain that we are not merely religious: we are positively hooked on the supernatural. The supermarket of gods is here with a vengeance.

But why, amid the welter of religions and superstitions which have flooded the market, should we take any notice of Jesus Christ? After all, he has had it all his own way for two thousand years. And, with all due respect to the founder of Christianity, his followers have not made a very impressive or attractive job of commending him to those who are not his fans. So long as some god or other fills the vacuum people have inside, why bother with Jesus?

The whole of this book is an answer to that very important question. But there is a preliminary answer to anyone who is wondering where to turn among the world's religions and the multitude of new cults – or even the occult.

A faith to live by has got to be true
If you go for a lovely fairy tale it will not support you in the hour of death. You will not be able to live it and teach it with conviction. Deep down inside, you know very well that it will not satisfy you unless it is true. It is well known that religions such as Mormonism, Jehovah's Witnesses and Christian Science do not pass that test. Fraud and deceit were around at their birth. However friendly their practitioners, however comfortable their teachings, they do not meet the basic requirement of truth. Jesus does. He is not merely true: he is Truth.

A faith to live by has got to be relevant
It may be true, but if it does not make any difference to ordinary life you can keep it, so far as I am concerned. A lot of what passes for Christianity does not make any noticeable difference to the Sunday congregation. People seem no happier, no kinder, no more honest or easy to live with than those who don't go to church. If church on Sundays is all that there is in Christianity, I quite agree with you; why bother with Jesus?

A faith to live by has got to be able to change lives
If it can't remove fear, especially the fear of death; if

it can't break habits that have become engrained; if it can't cleanse the conscience from guilt – then it is not what I need. You too, I guess. The glory of Jesus lies in this: nobody has ever been too bad for him to take on, and nobody who ever got into personal touch with Jesus remained unchanged.

A faith to live by has got to offer hope for society at large
If a faith is merely individual, it is petty. If it is merely social, it is impersonal. Part of the wonder of the Christian faith is that it has nerved reform, education, medical care, idealism in whole nations, as well as transforming individuals. Unlike Communism it offers the hope of a fulfilment in which all subjects of Jesus will have their share, not merely those who happen to be alive at the end. Unlike Buddhism, which offers us a future with individuality rubbed out (as we will all be absorbed into the One), Jesus promises his people that they will be for ever in his Father's house. Every individual will be there. Everyone will matter. And love, not oblivion, will be the order of the day.

A faith to live by has to appeal to everyone
If it is true at all, it must be true for all. Islam is primarily for Arabs and areas they have conquered. Buddhism and Hinduism appeal, for the most part, to the Eastern temperament. Communism appeals to the oppressed. Zen appeals to the overworked. But Jesus is the man for all races, and for all seasons. Rich and poor, Eskimo and Nubian, educated and savage: the sheer universality of the gospel is just what you would expect if it is the truth of God.

These are some of the things I would look for in a faith that will bear my weight through life and in the face of death. It must be true, relevant, able to change the lives of individuals and whole societies; it must meet the deepest needs of man, and it must be applicable with equal appeal to all men everywhere. Try that for size with other faiths and you'll see why I am an enthusiast for Jesus of Nazareth. None but he can meet all those conditions of a faith to live by. That's why it is worth bothering with Jesus.

But I can't (and don't) expect you to take my word for it. Let us look a little deeper, and I hope to show you a good many reasons, in the short chapters which follow, for bothering about Jesus.

2

Bother Because He is Real

For a great many people Jesus is not real. He is make-believe, like Cinderella. He is a folk-lore hero like Jack and the Beanstalk. Most people learn almost nothing about him in home or school these days, and their ideas of Jesus go back to a few occasions in Sunday School, to which they were packed off, protesting, while Mum and Dad read the paper in bed. Why should they bother about Jesus?

You try asking a mountaineer one day why he bothers to climb Snowdon – or Everest. He will probably reply, 'Well, because it is *there*!' That is one very good reason why you should bother with Jesus. He is there. He was a real historical person, and not a myth, a legend or a make-believe hero.

The existence of the Church shows that Jesus is real

Whatever you may think about it, you can't ignore a body of some fifteen hundred million spread all over the world who can trace their faith back to a historical figure, Jesus of Nazareth. The first Christians were all Jewish, and their religion sprang from the religion of Israel. The only basic difference was this. The Christians were sure that the great Deliverer for whom Judaism was waiting had actually come in Jesus of Nazareth. Round about the year AD 30 this new movement, called Christianity, came out of Judaism with nothing distinctive about it but the radiant conviction that the Deliverer had come. He had died on a cross and thereby, in some strange way, dealt with human badness and selfishness. He had come alive again: people could get to know him. And he was building a new society, the Christian Church.

This movement spread fast. Within thirty years there were Christians in all the main cities of the Empire, and a strange lot they seemed. A mixture of Jews and Greeks, they did not seem to contain anybody much of influence and importance, and yet they grew. They seemed very happy, very unselfish, very sure they were forgiven, very full of love for other people. This really was odd. Probably the 'love' was a bit warped: after all they called each other 'brother' and 'sister', and they were reputed to eat somebody's body and blood. Highly suspicious. So they were just the sort of people on whom Nero could pin the blame for the Great Fire of Rome, which he probably started himself in AD 64 to enlarge his palace grounds! But popular or not, the origin of the Church shows that its founder was a real person. It is impossible to explain it otherwise.

The gospels show that Jesus was real

They represent a completely new type of literature, thrown up by the new movement. Nobody wrote gospels before. There are four of them, and they were written by Jesus' followers and their associates. Much of the material clearly went the rounds by word of mouth before it was written down some thirty or forty

11

years after Jesus' death. The gospels are written from different perspectives by different men, but the figure they bring before us is manifestly the same. All of them have the spell of Jesus about them. He made such a fantastic impression on people that the normal categories of history and biography did not seem enough. They were impelled to start a completely new literary genre to do justice to this completely different man. Incidentally, in case anybody tells you that the gospels have been messed around with and embroidered as the centuries have rolled on, you might be interested to know that the manuscript tradition is far stronger for our gospels than it is for any other ancient book. Normally a thousand years or so separates the original from the oldest copy we possess. And normally there are only one or two ancient copies on which the whole text depends. With the gospels we have manuscripts going back to within a hundred years of the originals, and there are literally hundreds of ancient copies written in a dozen languages. We can be absolutely sure that the gospels have come down to us very much as they were written. They are as real and reliable as the Jesus they present.

Ancient Roman historians show us that Jesus was real

That is very remarkable when you come to think about it, because these literary Romans were very aristocratic creatures. Why should they bother about a peasant teacher who lived on the very edge of the map, in Judaea? Nevertheless, some of them did bother. Pliny was the Governor of Northern Turkey, right up by the Black Sea, in about AD 112. He wrote lots of letters to the Emperor, and they have survived. He tells us about the Christians, their numbers, their influence (sale of sacrificial victims for the pagan temples had dropped to nothing!), their worship (early in the morning, with hymns to Christ as God), their loving and harmless lives, and their regrettable unwillingness to stop being Christians when he told them to! Many of them he executed, but the movement refused to lie down and die. You can read all about it in his *Epistles* 10:96.

Another aristocratic Roman writer was Cornelius Tacitus, the Governor of the rich province of Asia Minor (our central and coastal Turkey). He writes of the way in which the Emperor Nero picked on the Christians as scapegoats for the Fire of Rome in AD 64. He tells of the incredible cruelty practised on them: some were clothed in the skins of wild beasts and torn apart by dogs, while others were covered with pitch and set alight at night in Nero's gardens. Tacitus felt sorry for them, but he did not like them. With well-bred distaste he notes:

> The name 'Christian' comes to them from Christ, who was executed in the reign of Tiberius by the procurator Pontius Pilate; and the pernicious faith, suppressed for a while, broke out afresh and spread not only through Judaea, the source of the disease, but even throughout Rome itself where everything vile comes and is fêted (*Annals* 15:44).

There is plenty of other Roman evidence that Jesus was a real person of recent date. The cities of Pompeii and Herculaneum were overwhelmed by a volcano in AD 79, and Christian mosaics, wall paintings, and inscriptions have been found there – also, in all probability, an early Christian chapel. Archaeology has also come up with a decree from the Emperor Tiberius (AD 14–38) or Claudius (AD 41–54), discovered in Nazareth, which threatens with the death penalty anyone who disturbs tombs: it looks as if this is official reaction to Pilate's report of the empty tomb of Jesus. There can be no doubt in the mind of anyone who takes historical evidence seriously that Jesus actually lived and died in Palestine under the governorship of Pontius Pilate, which ended in AD 36.

The Jewish writers also show that Jesus was real

Christianity soon became a great threat to Judaism, and there is evidence to show that the very mention of Jesus was frowned on in Jewish documents. Nevertheless, scattered through the Mishnah there are allusions like these. 'Rabbi Eliezer said, "Balaam looked forth and saw that there was a man, born of a woman, who would rise up and seek to make himself God, and cause the whole world to go astray." ' We read of his miracles, with the disparaging comment, 'He learnt magic in Egypt.' We read, too, of his death: 'They hanged Jeshua of Nazareth on the eve of Passover.' But the most surprising passage of all comes in Josephus, *Antiquities* 18:3. Josephus was an influential Jewish refugee-general, writing in Rome in the 90s, and very keen to keep his nose clean and get the best deal possible for his conquered countrymen, who were smarting under the sack of Jerusalem in AD 70. So you would not expect him to say much about a controversial figure like Jesus. What, then, do you make of this?

And there arose about this time (i.e. Pilate's governorship) Jesus, a wise man, if indeed we should call him a man; for he was a doer of marvellous deeds, a teacher of men who receive the truth with pleasure. He won over many Jews and also many Greeks. This man was the Messiah. When Pilate had condemned him to the cross at the instigation of our leaders, those who had loved him from the first did not cease. For he appeared to them on the third day alive again, as the holy prophets had predicted, and said many other wonderful things about him. And even now the race of Christians, so named after him, has not yet died out.

When you get a piece as explicit as that in an anti-

Christian writer it is pretty shattering. No wonder lots of people have attacked the text. Nevertheless, this passage is there in all the manuscripts of Josephus. Some of it may well be ironic. But there can be no doubt from this Jewish evidence that Jesus was a real historical person. And notice how we have allusions, scattered throughout this hostile testimony, to his unusual birth ('born of a woman' means 'conceived out of wedlock' in Jewish culture), his date, his disciples, his miracles (although assigned to the devil's agency!), his claims ('seeks to make himself God'), his messiahship, his death on the cross, his reported resurrection, and his continuing impact on society through his followers. That is a great deal to have gleaned from sources who, for different reasons, were so strongly opposed to Christianity. Wherever you look, then, in the ancient records, be they Christian, archaeological, Roman or Jewish, you find the same message. Jesus was real: no doubt about it. Moreover Jesus *is* real: he is still in business. And just because he is real, just because he is there, he is well worth bothering about. After all, we do not date our whole era by a myth!

3

Bother Because He is the Ideal

Are you old enough ever to have seen the legendary Pelé play football? He drew thousands to the stands whenever he played. His artistry was supreme. He was, perhaps, the greatest attacking footballer the world has ever seen. The ideal, if you like.

Soccer may not be your thing. What is? If it's

literature, would you not give a lot to spend a few hours with William Shakespeare? If it's politics, you'd learn such a lot about leadership from Augustus Caesar. We have approximations to the ideal in every walk of life, but they all have their failings, and they fade as the years pass by.

But is there anyone who is the ideal not merely for football, literature or politics, but for living? Is there anyone who has shown us what humanity is really capable of? Is there an ideal man?

Not so long ago it was fashionable to believe that we were developing towards a race of Supermen: the ideal lay before us, and close at hand. Now, in the light of increasing world famine and pressing environmental uncertainty, such optimism seems particularly dated and almost laughable. Just look at all those old *Star Trek* films to see what I mean! These days we vaguely hope, if we hope at all, that the ideal will come from some inner spiritual philosophy or New Age experience. The ideal still lies before us, or within us: but it is no longer close at hand.

Yet we are all busy looking in the wrong direction. The ideal has come. The perfect life has been lived. We are no longer able to plead ignorance of what it means to be fully human. In Jesus, the real historical Jesus, we see the heights to which man can rise. In him we see perfection.

Take the life of Jesus as recorded in the gospels. It is so superb, and yet so unexpected, that nobody could have made it up – let alone four evangelists working independently from one another! That life is perfect: there's no other word for it.

Think of the influence of that life

Wherever you look in art, music and literature you find that many of the greatest compositions have concerned Jesus of Nazareth. Think of medicine, education and humane government. There are places in the world (though very few of them) where atheist regimes are to the fore in these three areas. But in every instance the first people to bother about the bodies and minds of men, as well as their souls, have been the Christians. The ideals of Jesus have not always been followed in Western Europe. But those ideals have shaped what Europe is. This is also the case in Australia and in both North and South America. In Africa the biggest single cultural influence is Jesus, and the growth of the Church far outruns the growth of the population of that whole continent.

Think of the appeal of that life

It has fired the idealism and touched the hearts of all types of people, all over the world, all down the centuries. It has appealed equally to bosses and to servants, to soldiers and to monks, to stone-age cultures and to sophisticated professors. It has appealed to downtrodden and to prosperous alike. And it has never done so by condoning their failings or feeding their self-esteem. Always that life has challenged men and women, even as it has appealed to them. A most uncomfortable ideal: but all nations of the world and all types of men and women within them have confessed that he is the ideal. Not only has there been no better. It is impossible to conceive of any advance on Jesus of Nazareth.

Think of the balance of that life

The perfect balance between action and reflection, between masculine virtues and those generally associated with women. The mixture of gentleness and toughness, of compassion and straight talk, of gaiety and seriousness is phenomenal. Here was a man who was as much at home in a hovel or a palace, with a penitent call-girl, a truculent fisherman or a selfish governor. And, incredibly, he is always quietly in command of every situation: perfectly balanced.

Think of the inspiration of that life

The life and example of Jesus have sustained the persecuted believers during the first three centuries, acted as a beacon to the monks in the dark ages, tamed the cruelty of the Vikings, conquered the conquering Normans – just see how many churches they left all over the place! Christ was the inspiration behind the gallantry of the knights in the days of chivalry. A rediscovery of Christ led to the Reformation. In the eighteenth century the vision of Jesus, Jesus only, so dominated men like Whitefield and Wesley that the whole face of England was changed inside a generation from brutish, drunken atheism. In the days of the Industrial Revolution too little attention was paid to him and too much to profits: the bitterness in industrial relations to which this led is still with us. But even so, the trade unions were founded largely as a result of Christ and his influence and ideals. Jesus stands behind the Tolpuddle martyrs. It was he who inspired a worldwide missionary movement in the nineteenth century, which fired men to go and tell the heathen about the Saviour, even if they should themselves perish in the telling – as many of them did. It is Jesus to whom many of the Liberation movements of the twentieth century are looking for their inspiration: Jesus, the non-establishment man, the man for others, the leader who gave his own life. If you had asked Gandhi, the father of modern India, who was his model, he would undoubtedly have replied 'Jesus'. There are, in fact, signs at present that both Islam and Hinduism are looking to Jesus as in some way the ideal human being. The truth of the matter is that there are no serious competitors. Jesus is the ideal.

Is not that a very strong reason why you should bother with Jesus? He is not merely the greatest man ever, he is the ideal for everyone to follow. Wouldn't you think, then, that people would crowd round him, aching to be his followers? Just as fans crowd around a star? But they don't, do they? And they didn't when he was around on earth, either. Now isn't that a very odd thing? Does it not suggest that we are terrified by the ideal? We are afraid he might want to change some areas of our lives which are not ideal at all — but which we cling on to for all we are worth. So it is much easier, and safer, and more comfortable to turn our back on him and say, 'Why bother about Jesus? What's so special about him?'

4

Bother Because His Character is the Greatest

Coca Cola claims to be the world's number one drink. Paul McCartney is probably the most successful song writer of all time. Muhammed Ali always claimed himself 'the greatest' of all boxers. Yet difficult though it is to reach the top in business, music or sport, it is much harder in character. And this, as we saw in the last chapter, is precisely what Jesus has done. He is without doubt the greatest, noblest, most lovely character who has ever lived.

Jesus was the greatest

He was prayerful without being pious
The gospels are full of his warm, natural intercourse with his Father in prayer, and equally full of his friendship with those who never darkened the door

of a synagogue. If there had been any touch of primness, of 'holier-than-thou' about him, the ordinary people would have kept well clear.

He was vital without being hearty

There is a strong sense of movement about the gospel story which springs from Jesus himself. His straight and powerful language, his sheer energy, his commitment to individuals in need. No half measures about him. But never a touch of heartiness.

He was peaceful without being idle

Not many energetic men are peaceful. They are opposite qualities. But Jesus combined them. He was utterly at peace all the time: he called it the peace of God. No disaster, no interruption robbed him of that inner serenity. And though intense pressure led him away to rest for short periods, he was back in the battle in a short time, radiating peace.

He exuded love without sentimentality

Love that could make a prostitute weep, that could dandle little children on his knee, that could embrace the untouchables. He said that, 'Greater love has no man than this; that a man should lay down his life for his friends' (John 15:13). Well, he even improved on that astonishing goal: he laid down his life for his enemies.

He was modest and yet authoritative

On the one hand he owned no money, never looked for praise, put on no airs, acted in constant and deep dependence on God. On the other, he spoke about spiritual things as one who *knew*. 'Truly, truly, I tell you' was his characteristic way of address, and men recognised that he taught with astonishing authority although he had never been to college.

He had a genius for friendship

However, it never turned to favouritism. Time after time in the gospels you find Jesus talking to a single Pharisee, a blind man, a beggar, a lame man, a mourning widow, a Roman soldier. A tremendous variety of needs, and he cared about them all so much that each one must have felt that he was the only person that mattered to Jesus for the time being. That's quite right: he was. His friendship with the women who accompanied him, his friendship with the dozen disciples who left house and home to stay with him – this is one of the most attractive traits of character.

Jesus had a perfect character

Actually, it would not be difficult to write a whole book on the character of Jesus. It would be a long book, because every conceivable virtue known to man is there in him. I've just given a few samples.

But now I want to look at the other side. He did not merely have all the virtues, he had none of the vices. At least, I do not know of any. I have only ever heard three being suggested, and none of them hold water.

Some protest that he used violence in kicking crooked traders and cheapjacks out of the Temple when they had 'turned my Father's house into a den of robbers' (Matthew 21:13). I am not sure that I would have thought it wrong if he had used that thong of cords he had in his hands! But we are not told that he did. He just turfed them out.

The second moan is that he lost his temper with the fig tree and cursed it unreasonably. Not a bit of it. His cursing of the fig tree was an acted parable. The fig tree had for centuries been a symbol of the Jewish nation. Jesus had come to Jerusalem and found that they rejected him. He had found no fruit on the fig tree of Israel. He pronounced on it the judgment of God, and that judgment awaits us all, so we had better not be too high and mighty about it. In historical terms it took place just forty years later, when the Roman legions smashed the Holy City (which specialised in killing the prophets) to smithereens.

The third complaint I have heard against Jesus' character is that he had no sense of humour. I find that hilarious! How can anyone with a perfectly straight face tell his very smug and pious hearers that they must remove a whacking great plank from their own eye before they can see clearly to pull the tiniest speck out of their brother's eye? Can you imagine him sitting as solemn as a lord while he ticked the Pharisees off for their punctilious care in straining out any unclean thing, like a gnat, from their wine – whilst not realising that they were swallowing the biggest unclean beast in the book, a camel? Don't tell me Jesus hadn't got a sense of humour. Read the gospels and see.

Jesus had no vices

Having cleared that little lot out of the way, let me get back to the main point. And a very remarkable one it is, too. *Jesus had no vices*. Jesus never did anything wrong. The gospels never praise him; but they never give a single example of anything for which he had to say 'My mistake' or 'So sorry'. Those sorts of incidents did not take place. He told his disciples to say 'Forgive us our trespasses' each time they said the Lord's Prayer, but that was the prayer the Lord taught them – not the one he used himself. His claim was, 'I do always those things which please him' (John 8:29). He seems to have been conscious of no cloud between him and his heavenly Father. Remarkable, and all the more remarkable in one who was so quick to spot hypocrisy in the prayers of the religious, showmanship in the donations of the 'generous', lustful, murderous thoughts lurking under respectable exteriors which were very ready to condemn adultery and murder in others. How could a man as perceptive as this possibly not have apologised to God in his prayers? The only answer I can see is this. He did not say 'Sorry' for his misdeeds, *because he did not have any.* If you say, 'That is fantastic', I agree. We are talking about 'the greatest', remember? His life was not just the greatest: it was a moral miracle.

It's an interesting thing, but those who liked him and those who didn't both bore witness to his perfection of character. There's a marvellous passage in John 8:39ff where Jesus is hinting that he is older than Abraham (who had died two thousand years earlier) and that he shares the nature and the glory of God. They are hopping mad, good monotheists that they are, and rush to deal with him in the time-honoured method for disposing of blasphemers, by hurling stones at him. But Jesus gives them pause. He says 'Which of you can point to anything wrong in my life?' (v. 46). Now, surely that is asking for it. Could *you* get away with it? Of course not. Your friends, let alone your enemies, would be only too quick to point out a thousand and one things you had done wrong. But these people were tongue-tied. There was nothing to say.

Jesus was blameless

You find just the same at his trial. They try for hours to find some charge that would stick. And they fail, conclusively. They know quite well that the accusations they are rigging will not stand the cold light of day, and they give it up as a bad job. In the end they ask him if he is God's long-awaited Messiah; he says, 'That is your way of putting it,' and they give three jumps for joy and do him for blasphemy. That shows how pushed they were to find anything wrong in him. It was the same with Pontius Pilate, who three times during the most remarkable trial in history declared his prisoner innocent, and then handed him over to the execution squad. Even Pilate's wife could not get to sleep the night before, and sent a message to him while he was hearing the trial saying, 'Have nothing to do with the blood of this innocent man.' But he didn't listen: he was afraid that clemency would lose him his job. But he inwardly agreed with his wife's assessment of Jesus. So did the centurion who was in charge of the execution. So did one of the men being killed alongside him. They all unite to say with one voice: 'This man is completely innocent.'

'Ah,' you may say. 'But these folk did not get close enough to him to see the flaws.' Well, listen to some who did. Peter was as close to him as anyone, and he sums the situation up like this: 'He committed no wrong. No guile was found on his lips. When he was reviled he did not revile again. When he suffered he did not threaten, but he trusted to him who judges justly' (1 Peter 2:22f). That shows how he regarded his Master. The writer to the Hebrews was equally clear about it all. 'This is the sort of high priest we needed: holy, blameless, unstained, separated from sinners' (7:26). This is the sort of high priest God provided for us. 'He was tempted in all points just like we are; yet without sin' (4:15). John got closer to him, perhaps, than anyone else, and John has precisely the same assessment. 'If we say that we have no sin, we deceive ourselves and the truth is not in us . . . but in him is no sin' (1 John 1:8, 3:5). The evidence is identical, whatever quarter you look. And it is conclusive.

In Jesus of Nazareth you find a perfect character, the only one in all history who has never done anything wrong.

Perhaps that helps us to understand a little more the problem I mentioned at the end of the previous chapter: the way we fight shy of Jesus, whereas we would cheerfully flock round any other great man. The truth of the matter is that his life so puts ours to shame that we are deeply embarrassed. John puts it like this: 'Light has come into the world [with the coming of Jesus], and men loved darkness rather than light, because their deeds were evil' (John 3:19, RSV). That puts a rather different complexion on our 'Why bother with Jesus?' attitude, does it not? It shows that it is not only foolish, but guilty. If the light of his perfect life turns us off, then that says something very clear about our sinful lives. It indicates that a big change is needed. Jesus talked about that. Read on: we shall be coming to it.

5

Bother Because of His Offer

One of the striking differences between Christianity and the other religions is that the others all start with the assumption that God is known. Christianity does not. Jesus says that nobody knows God in the personal sense of Father except himself; and he alone can bring people into that intimate relationship (Matthew 11:27f). He then follows that up with one of the most marvellous offers that have ever passed the lips of man: 'Come to me, all who labour and are heavy laden, and I will give you rest' (Matthew 11:28, RSV).

What a fantastic offer. I find three or four heavy laden ones an enormous burden to cope with. Jesus invites all! And, in many ways, that is the heart of his teaching. It is not primarily demand, though demand is there. It is primarily offer, free offer. We have got a bit cynical about free offers, because so often they aren't free at all; there's a catch in them somehow. But the very fact that the free offer business is so widespread in the supermarkets reminds us that a genuine free gift is one of the most attractive things in the world. That is what the religion of Jesus is all about.

'See here,' he says. 'You do not know God, although

25

a lot of you are very religious. You are strangers to him.
You are, frankly, lost. Well, listen to me. God cares
about that. I know, because I know him in a way none
of you do. He is my heavenly Father. I talk to him in
the same family way as you chat to your dad.' His
special word for the Father, 'Abba', means 'dear Dad'.
It was never used between man and God until Jesus
used it. Would you not like to be in the family, and
be able to share your life with the Father like that?

'What's more,' he maintains, 'God is King. He is
King of the whole earth, but a lot of his Kingdom is
unruly and rebellious. Let's be honest about it. You
are like that, are you not? Your heart is a rebel against
him: you are too busy doing your own thing to bother
about what he wants. But with me it is different. I am
not only the perfect Servant of the King: I do always
what pleases him. But I am also the embodiment of
his Kingdom. I come with his authority to represent
him, and show in my life and teaching what God's
way of leadership is. His Kingdom is one where love
is supreme; where trust replaces suspicion, generosity
replaces hatred, and mutual service replaces bossing
people around. I want to show you the attractiveness
of life in the Kingdom. I want to teach you the law of
the Kingdom: so why not take time off now to read
my Sermon on the Mount? It is in Matthew chapters
five to seven. It will give you a bird's eye view of what
life in God's Kingdom could be like. And notice the
end bit. It is only by entering through me, by knowing
me, by building your life on me, that you will ever
discover what his Kingdom can mean for you
personally. I tell you about God's Kingdom. I represent
that Kingdom in my own life. I am the way in to that
Kingdom. So, "Come to me, all who labour and are
heavy laden, and I will give you rest." '

Jesus thought in pictures. So do most of us – which
is why we find the bureaucratic government forms so
difficult to fill in. Let some of these pictures give you
a glimpse of what he offers.

Understanding the Kingdom

'Do you want to know what God's Kingdom is like?'
says Jesus. 'I will tell you. For some it is like a ploughman slogging along, day in, day out, with his oxen,
trying to keep a straight furrow – as bored as can be.
Suddenly, one day, his ploughshare hits a box hidden
in the ground. He gets down, wrenches the lid off it,
and out cascades a heap of shimmering jewels. You
can just imagine how that farm labourer pawns all his
belongings in order to raise enough money to make
that field, with its box of treasure, his own!

'For others it is like a pearl fancier. Imagine a very
experienced merchant who has been in the pearl
business all his life, and knows a thing or two. One day
he finds a pearl which takes his breath away. For size,
brilliance and sheer perfection he has never, in all his
experience, seen anything to compare with it. He
manages to hide his excitement, haggles over the price,
and once it is agreed goes off and sells all his stock of
pearls to get it because life would not be worth living
for him if he did not possess that pearl of great price.'

There you have it. Entering God's Kingdom is like
finding treasure, like discovering the pearl that puts
all other pearls in the shade. Did you realise that?
Probably not. Like me, you may have thought it was
a matter of trying hard and doing good things and
going to church and all manner of dull and dreary
occupations. That just shows how effective the
propaganda from His Infernal Eminence has been.
Because the life that is shared with Jesus Christ is the
most joyful and rewarding and full life anyone can
possibly live. Did he not say, 'I am come that you
might have life, and have it in all its fullness' (John
10:10)? Yes, entering the Kingdom is infinitely satisfying. You may come upon it all of a sudden while
slogging along the road of life, feeling that everything
is a bit jaded and dull and a bore. You may have been
seeking it for years as you tested a variety of

philosophies, religions or drug trips. People come upon it by either path. Once they see what is offered, the shrewd ones realise it is the most important thing in the world. They are willing for any sacrifice, in order to possess it.

The King's guests

Another of Jesus' pictures puts it very clearly. Think of God as a rich king, who has decided to have the most marvellous wedding reception for his son. He does two remarkable things. First, he sends out invitations. Many of those invited turn it down: so he invites all and sundry to come to his banquet – folk from the streets, the brothels, the middle-class homes, the ghettos. That is what God is like. Willing to have anyone to his great feast of the Christian life. He makes the offer. He provides the good things. He sends the invitations. God is not the cold Judge saying, 'Go.' He is the man who throws a party and says, 'Come.'

But the second remarkable thing in the story is this. The King provides a superb banqueting robe for all his guests. They exchange it for their ordinary clothes when they come inside the door. It would be awful if the banquet were spoiled by some guests boasting in their fine clothes while others come in dirty and ragged off the streets. So God makes provision for us all to enjoy his banquet without any trace of embarrassment at the mess our own lives have been in, or of pride in our own achievements. We all come in on the level. We all wear the perfect dress of his forgiveness, his acceptance. Otherwise we don't get in at all. Actually, there is a bit about that in the story Jesus told. One man slipped in with his own clothes on, refusing the wedding robe, claiming, no doubt, that his own dinner jacket was quite good enough. And when the King came in and saw the guests, this chap stuck out like a sore thumb. So the King went and asked him why he had refused the proffered wedding garment. The man had nothing to say. Guess what happened to him? He was thrown out on his ear. God is not going to have proud people ruining his Kingdom. We enter it as forgiven people, forgiven by him at his expense and irrespective of our merits – or we do not enter at all.

Such is the amazing teaching of Jesus. Free forgiveness, free membership of God's family – the God I have neglected, and snubbed, and pretended did not exist. And that life of love and peace and joy and good relationships is a party, a real banquet. It cost him everything to prepare. It costs me nothing to accept – except my pride. For I have to take it as a gift, not dream I can earn it by trying a bit harder, going to church a bit more often, or subscribing to the Fund for Disabled Dogs.

Have you got the message? Or is it still too mind-boggling to take in? If so, listen to this. Do you remember your old mum the day she lost her engagement ring? Every drawer was turned out. Every room was swept out. Every nook and cranny was searched. And then the ring turned up! Tears ran down her face. She hugged you. She ran round to the neighbours to tell them. She was quite literally jumping for joy. Now that, believe it or not, is God's attitude to us. When we get 'lost' from him, he isn't furious with us: he doesn't say, 'Wait till I catch up with that rebel Bill.' He loves us so much that he does everything he possibly can to seek us out, draw us back, woo us to the life of love in his home that we have foolishly thrown away. And when we come back – wow! 'There is joy in heaven over one sinner that comes back' (Luke 15:10).

In a companion story which Jesus told about the runaway boy who left home, wasted his livelihood, and then began to feel the pinch, there is a similar happy ending. The boy comes back, full of fears about his reception, and finds his old dad is already out looking for him, scanning the skyline day by day to see if there is any sign of his return. He runs out to meet him, gives him a complete new outfit of clothes, and orders a great banquet and dance of celebration, 'for this my son was dead, and is alive again, was lost and is found' (Luke 15:24).

That is what God is like, so Jesus tells us. Now do you see why Christianity cannot go along with the other religions in supposing that we know what God is like? Who on earth could have supposed that God is so loving, so very generous? Who would ever have dreamed that he would welcome rebels back into his Kingdom for free, that he would adopt into his family urchins like us? But that *is* what God is like. And Jesus came to tell us. 'No one has ever seen God; the only Son, who is in the bosom of the Father, he has made him known' (John 1:18, RSV). And when a free offer of that quality and magnitude is going, I think there is good reason to bother about Jesus. Search all the religions of the world. You will not find in any of them a comparable offer.

6

Bother Because of His Claims

Who is this Jesus who says, 'Come to me and I will give you rest'? Who does he think he is?

Good question. Let's see who he thinks he is. Ask anyone you stop in the street and I'll bet he will say something like this: 'Jesus Christ? Yeah, a great guy. Good teacher. A really wonderful man.' Now examine the actual teaching of this wonderful teacher, this really great man, and you find a very different picture emerging.

He didn't lay a lot of emphasis on his teaching. Other people did, and were astonished at its originality and power. But he played his teaching pretty cool. 'My teaching is not mine but his who sent me,' he said. 'I do nothing on my own authority, but speak thus as the Father taught me' (John 8:28, RSV).

He didn't lay a lot of emphasis on his goodness. Indeed, when one man ventured to address him, somewhat patronisingly, as 'Good Master', he answered him very firmly: 'Why do you call me good? There is one good, and that is God' (Matthew 19:17). Goodness in its ultimate form does not belong to human beings, but to God. Perhaps he was trying to stretch the mind of the questioner and make him see the truth.

Examine his claims

For the truth is, according to Jesus' claims, that he is not merely a man. He is that. He was born like us, was hungry and thirsty like us, tired like us. Like us he could grieve, he could bleed, he could die. Human through and through. But something more. Not even a great prophet or a wonderful teacher or a fabulous character. Something more.

He claimed to live a sinless life
As we have already seen, he could look at an angry crowd, angry because he was implicitly claiming to share God's very nature, and ask them, 'Which of you can point to anything wrong in my life?' (John 8:46). I don't know whether that question is the more amazing – or the fact that none of them could give a reply! But in any case, no mere man could have lived a spotless life. Jesus did.

He claimed to be the way of God
Not a way, but *the* way. Not to teach the way, but to be the way. 'I am the way, the truth, the life. No man

comes to the Father but by me' (John 14:6). Or take
that claim we considered in the last chapter: 'All things
have been delivered to me by my Father; and no one
knows the Father except the Son and any one to whom
the Son chooses to reveal him.' (Matthew 11:27, RSV).
Nobody has ever made claims like that before and
backed them, as Jesus did, by a quality of life, a love,
a balance, an influence like his. No mere man ever
made such claims. Jesus did.

He claimed to give life to people
Not just to tell them about where they could get it or
improve it or deepen it, but to give life. 'I give to them
eternal life, and they shall never perish, neither shall
any one snatch them out of my hand. My Father, who
gave them to me, is greater than all, and no one is able
to snatch them out of my Father's hand. I and the
Father are one' (John 10:30). Can you imagine anyone
in his right mind making claims like that if he were
merely a man? Jesus made them.

He claimed to be able to forgive sins
On one occasion he was teaching in a house and the
people were jammed tight around him. So some bright
jokers had the idea of taking part of the roof off and
letting down one of their paralysed friends, whom they
hoped Jesus would heal. Jesus looked at the man,
swinging there on a bed with a rope attached to each
corner. It was perfectly obvious what the man's need
was. He was paralysed. But Jesus rarely did the
obvious. He said to the man, 'Your sins are forgiven
you.' Now the room was full of theologians. They were
furious. 'Who can forgive sins, but God alone?' was
their muttered question. Who indeed? That is the very
point Jesus wanted them to take in. So he said to them,
'In order that you may know that the Son of Man [his
name for himself] has power on earth to forgive sins'
– he turned to the paralysed man – 'take up your bed
and walk.' The man did just that, to the amazement

of the crowd – and the discomfiture of the theologians. Jesus claimed the power to forgive sins – God's special prerogative – and he backed that claim with mighty cures. This was not an isolated instance. We find Jesus telling a prostitute that her sins, which were many, are forgiven; a publican that he can go down to his house acquitted; or a dying murderer that he would go to heaven. We might well ask, like the theologians round the paralysed man, 'Who can forgive sins, but God alone?' (Mark 2:7). Jesus did.

He claimed the right to receive men's worship
This is really staggering, in view of his humility and his sense of dependence on his heavenly Father. No merely good man would do that. We find both Peter and Paul in the Acts of the Apostles being offered worship by ignorant pagans. Both of them immediately recoiled in horror from the suggestion. But Jesus accepted it as his due. On one occasion after a miraculous catch of fish, Peter fell at his feet and said, 'Depart from me, for I am a sinful man, O Lord' (Luke 5:8, RSV). Jesus did nothing to deter him. On another occasion, after his resurrection, Jesus saw the doubter, Thomas, collapse in a heap at his feet and worship him in the most explicit terms: 'My Lord and My God' (John 20:28, RSV). He accepted it quite naturally and merely encouraged Thomas to trust without seeing, in future. Can you think of any religious leader acting like that? Neither can I. Jesus did.

He claimed to be the judge of all mankind
Do you remember that famous story of the sheep and the goats? (Matthew 25:31–46). Jesus said that at the end of time he would divide men into two groups, as a shepherd separates sheep and goats in his flock. *Jesus* would do it! He had claimed elsewhere that the Father had committed all judgment to him. And at the end of the Sermon on the Mount he had made it clear that only if men entered through him would they get inside

the Kingdom: only if they knew him would they find a welcome; only if he was their foundation would their building stand. Is it possible to make more shattering claims than these? Our destiny will be determined by our attitude to Jesus. Of what mere man could that be said? Jesus maintained it.

He claimed he would raise people from death
There are other claims which make it clear to me that in Jesus I hear God addressing me, not just a man. For one thing he says that *he will lay down his life for the straying sheep of the world* (John 10:15). Or, to change the metaphor, Jesus will 'give his life as a ransom for many' (Mark 10:45, RSV). Who but God could do that? To give his life as a counterweight to all the death in our spoiled lives. That is too great a task for any man: if Jesus does it for the world, then he must be, as his very name suggests, 'God the Saviour' at work. Another of his claims which leaves me breathless is that *his words will never pass away*. 'Heaven and earth shall pass away but my words shall not pass away,' was his claim (Mark 13:31). It has come true. The Bible, containing his words, is the world's best seller and it is translated into far more languages than any other book. Might this not suggest that one more than man was speaking?

But the really ultimate claim of Jesus is that *he would raise men up in the last day*, and that the key to eternal life lay in relationship with him who was about to die and rise again. On his way to death he showed himself Lord of death by raising Lazarus from the tomb. That was an illustration of what his death would do. The very night before he died he encouraged his followers with an assurance that makes Socrates look pale. 'Let not your hearts be troubled. Believe in God, believe also in me. In my Father's house are many rooms. If it were not so I would have told you. I go to prepare a place for you' (John 14:1f). Even death could not shackle him.

Who is this man?

Who is this that made such claims? A sinless life, teaching that would last for ever, the power to forgive sins, to accept worship, to be the final judge of men, to give his life as ransom for us, to raise us up at the last day. Who is this? He comes to us not merely as a man, not even the greatest man who ever lived. Not as a great teacher, or a wonderful healer. He comes to us with the authority of almighty God, his heavenly Father. He shares his Father's nature, his Father's power, his Father's finality. He is not merely man, but a chip off the divine block. When we meet him we meet the human face of God. That's why we need to bother with Jesus.

7

Bother Because He Loves You

She holds you tight and murmurs in your ear, 'Honey, I love you.' Marvellous. It makes you feel very good. But will it last? Or is it a passing feeling that may be gone tomorrow and by next year may be murmured into somebody else's ear? We have almost forgotten what real love is like nowadays, because we are so hooked on the emotional feelings that go with it.

Real love is tough. Real love is lasting. Real love is unselfish. Real love hates to see blemishes in the beloved. Real love can put up with anything. Real love is willing to suffer for the loved one. Real love is willing to die for him.

That is the sort of love Jesus Christ has for us lot. And it is not because he finds us attractive. He doesn't.

Has it ever struck you how petty, how repulsive, how foul we must look to the perfectly sinless eyes of Jesus? He loves us not because he finds us attractive, not because we deserve it, but simply because he is love. Listen to the way the New Testament stresses it, time and again. 'God so loved the world that he gave his only Son that whosoever believes in him should not perish but have everlasting life' (John 3:16). 'God shows his love for us in that while we were still sinners Christ died for us' (Romans 5:8, RSV). 'God is love. In this is the love of God made manifest, that he sent his Son to be the remedy for the dirt of our sins' (1 John 4:8f). And an exiled Christian leader, John, condemned to the mines in the island of Patmos, is full of praise for the love that has met him and changed his life. 'Unto him who loves us and has freed us from our sins by his blood . . . to him be glory and dominion for ever and ever' (Revelation 1:5). But perhaps the most moving expression of what it means to be reached personally by that love of God is found on St Paul's lips, 'The Son of God loved me, and gave himself for me' (Galatians 2:20). It is a marvellous thing to be loved. It somehow purifies you, it ennobles you, it makes you carry your head high. You want everyone to know about it. Your heart sings. Someone has thought you worth loving. And that is one of the most marvellous things about the Christian life. The Lord himself has thought you and me worth loving.

But how do you *know*? And how do you know he loves *me*? Those are the burning questions. Mercifully the New Testament gives a clear answer to them. We do not have to remain in doubt or suspense about so important a matter.

The symbol of Christianity

What is the most important mark or symbol of Christianity? The cross, of course. And that cross gives us the answer to our problem. It is an answer that the most profound thinker has never got to the bottom of, but it is an answer which can be perfectly clear, in outline, to a child. That nanny who wrote the famous hymn 'There is a green hill, far away' for her children, had got the message very clear:

> He died that we might be forgiven
> He died to make us good,
> That we might go at last to heaven
> Saved by his precious blood.
>
> There was no other good enough
> To pay the price of sin;
> He only could unlock the gate
> Of heaven and let us in.

Yes, the cross of Jesus Christ is the proof, the unanswerable proof, of how much he loves us. He loved us enough to be mocked, despised, betrayed, given the cat-o'-nine-tails, and nailed alive to a ghastly great chunk of wood before being hung up amid the flies and the heat and the agony to die a lingering death in excruciating pain. When I look at Calvary I can have no doubt that he loves me, with a love stronger than death.

The message of Christianity

But why did he go there? What was the point? Could he not show his love in some less gruesome way? Yes, perhaps he could. But he did not go to the cross simply to show us how much he loved us. That was part of it, and a most important part of it. Like a magnet it has drawn folk to Jesus ever since. But there was more to Calvary than that. He had a job to do on that terrible gallows.

To describe that job very bluntly, he went there to save us. We needed saving so badly that no other way was possible. That's an old-fashioned word, but we still use it. If you were washed over a weir in a river, you would need saving. If you were in a burning house, you would need saving. If you were broke with a massive debt on your hands, you would need somebody to step in and save you. That is the sort of rescue the New Testament has in mind when its writers say that Jesus saved mankind on the cross. He saved us from drowning in the alienation into which we had slipped, away from God. He saved us from being destroyed in the burning house of our own selfishness. He saved us from the enormous debt of our failures before God when we had nothing to pay with: he stepped in, and paid it himself for us.

You say, 'I still don't see it.' Right, let me turn you to the simplest and most profound explanation of the cross and its meaning that I know. It comes in the first letter of someone who was there on the edge of the execution crowd that first Good Friday, Simon Peter. Why did he die, Simon? You ought to know. 'Christ once suffered for sins, the just for the unjust, that he might bring us to God' (1 Peter 3:18). That is why. On the cross he suffered unspeakable agonies. Why did he bother? *To bring us to God*: that was his supreme purpose in coming to this earth at all. What was in the way? Our sins, of course. Our selfishness, lust, hate, greed, meanness, pride and all the rest of the horrid things in our lives. They acted like a great wall between us and God. We couldn't see to the other side. We didn't even know for sure if there was another side, and if anyone was there. But on the cross Jesus suffered to get that sin wall pulled down. He achieved it by allowing the wall to fall on himself. *The just for the unjust*: that was it. He, the just one, took the place of us the unjust, paying our debts, bearing our load, serving our sentence. He did it so that we could be well and truly forgiven by God without for one moment denying his justice. It was all fair: the Lord himself had borne the penalty in our place. And he did it *once*, i.e., once for all. It never needed to be repeated.

The wonder of Christianity

Once you see that, it takes your breath away. Did he love me that much? Yes, Calvary proves it. What, me? Yes, you. He loved you that much. 'The Son of God loved me, and gave himself for me,' sings Paul, the rebel turned disciple. He never ceased to wonder at it. Can you blame him? Isn't your own heart beginning to thrill at the thought that the Maker of the heavens and earth should love you enough to go to those lengths to save you from the results of your own stupid selfishness?

That sets us free. It puts a new song in our mouth and a new spring in our step. The Son of God loved me and gave himself for me. What a value that sets on little me. What a Lover the Lord must be. And I can be sure that I am forgiven because the thing has been settled once and for all on that cruel – yet utterly glorious – cross.

You will notice that I have not attempted to give any human illustrations of what happened on that cross. There aren't any. For a love which sacrifices itself not for its friends but for its enemies has no parallel in our world. You will find that no analogy of a sea captain going down with his ship or a mother sacrificing herself for her baby compares with it for one moment. You will not find anything in the other religions that remotely compares with it. It is utterly and gloriously unique. There is nothing in the whole wide world like the love of God for sinners. That is why you should bother with Jesus. He loves you so much that he was willing to go through all that for you. Can you look him in the eye, as he stretches out his nail-pierced hands to you in welcome, and say, 'Why should I bother about you?'

8

Bother Because He Conquered Death

If Jesus was just a marvellous person who lived a long time ago and loved us enough to go to a peculiarly unpleasant form of death – then it might be permissible to ignore him. After all, we have to look to the future, not be bound by the past. But if he rose from the grave, that puts things in an entirely different light. It means that one man has broken the death barrier. One man knows from personal experience what is on the other side. One man is qualified to guide us over the chilly flood of death. One man, unlike all others before and since, has been 'defined as Son of God by the resurrection' (Romans 1:4). If that is true, then there is no possible excuse for ignoring him. If that is true, he towers above all other religious leaders, healers and teachers of mankind. Who else has risen from the dead?

But is it true? Did he leave that tomb on the first Easter Day? It is, at first sight, most unlikely. Dead men are not in the habit of leaving their graves. But wait a moment. Any dead men we know about have all succumbed to the human disease of sin and failure. We do not know what would happen when a perfect example of the species died. There haven't been any, apart from Jesus! We are in no position to say that he could not have broken the bands of death. So we had better examine the evidence. And the evidence that he rose is very strong indeed. So strong that although attempts have been made to crack it ever since the first century, no single alternative explanation has ever survived for long. They simply don't bear critical investigation. If you are interested in following this up, you might care to look at a leading lawyer's assessment, Professor Sir Norman Anderson's *The Evidence for the Resurrection*. Or, if you don't like lawyers, see what a journalist made of it in Frank Morrison's *Who Moved the Stone?* I've had a go at it myself in *The Day Death Died*. There is obviously not space to go into the details here, but the broad outlines can be stated very simply.

First, let us get it quite clear that Jesus was dead. Dead beyond any shadow of doubt. He was certified as dead by the centurion in charge of the execution squad. He was recognised as dead by Pilate, the Governor (who gave permission for a friend to bury his body). And the crowning proof is that when a spear was thrust into his side under his heart in order to make sure he was dead, out came what an eyewitness called 'blood and water' (John 19:34ff). Obviously the scientific explanation of this was unknown to men of those times, but the diagnosis is clear. Dark blood and light serum came from the body of Jesus, and the separation of clot from serum in the blood is the strongest medical proof that the patient is dead. So don't swallow any of the 'swoon' theories which imagine that Jesus was not quite dead but recovered in the cool of the tomb! He was dead, all right. But did he stay that way? Consider four factors.

Consider the rise of the Christian Church

It began at the first Easter, when the followers of Jesus were dispirited, scattered and crestfallen. Their leader, from whom they hoped such great things, had met an untimely and disgraceful end. What could have turned them into a force which rocked the Roman Empire? They had one answer for it. That, 'This Jesus, whom you crucified, God raised up, and we are witnesses of it' (Acts 2:32). Moreover the Church had three things

41

from the start which underline this conviction that Jesus was risen. They had two sacraments: baptism and the Lord's Supper. In baptism the believer went down into the water and up the other side – this symbolised his union with Jesus in death and resurrection. In the Lord's Supper they not only recalled his death with gratitude but exulted in his risen presence as they 'broke bread with gladness' (Acts 2:46). Neither sacrament would have been conceivable had the resurrection of Jesus not lain at the very foundation of their belief. It was the same with the third innovation, Sunday. Christians are from the outset found keeping the first day of the week special, instead of the seventh, as the Jews had done. Why? Because God's work of new creation in raising Jesus from the dead on the first day of the week seemed to them even more significant than his completing the work of creation and resting on the seventh day of the week. Once again, you see, the resurrection is absolutely central.

Consider the empty grave of Jesus

On all sides it is agreed that the tomb was empty on the first Easter Day. If it were not, the Jews could very easily have silenced the Christians when they first began to preach the risen Jesus. They could have said, 'Far from being risen, he is decaying in the grave round the corner.' But much as they would have loved to say this, and so nip the new movement in the bud, they were not able to say anything of the sort. By the way, the fact that they could not produce the body proves that the Jews had not moved it. The Romans hadn't, either – otherwise it could have been produced when the Christian Church began to prove a threat to the peace (which it did within a few weeks). This really only leaves the disciples as possible grave robbers. But the longer you think about the possibility the more incredible it appears. Even if they could have got through the guard that was posted on the tomb, I can't see that they would have been willing to be torn limb from limb for what they knew quite well was a fraud. You cannot possibly explain the sense of joy and confidence and power which radiates from the New Testament on the assumption that the early Christians were hypocrites, pretending Jesus was alive when they knew he was not. I do not know anyone who has studied the evidence who regards that as a possible explanation. Very well, then, if the body of Jesus was not removed by either his friends or his enemies, that leaves only one possibility. It is that God raised him from the dead, just as the amazed and triumphant Christians claimed.

Consider the appearances of Jesus

He did not leave us with an unexplained empty tomb. For forty days he appeared to his disciples on a variety of occasions in a variety of locations. And that disproves at once the view that these appearances might have been hallucinations. You don't get the same hallucination happening to lots of different people of different temperaments in different places. On one occasion he appeared to over five hundred people at once, most of whom were still alive to vouch for it when Paul mentioned the fact in his first letter to the Corinthians (1 Corinthians 15:6).

Consider the changed lives of his followers

1 Corinthians 15:5–8 has a most interesting and very early list of those who met with Jesus after his resurrection. The list originates within two or three years of the event itself, and was already fixed in the tradition before Paul became a Christian on the Damascus Road in the mid-thirties AD. It relates that Jesus rose from the dead and appeared to Peter, then to the Twelve, then to five hundred believers, then to

James and last of all to Paul. Think of the transformation which that resurrection brought about! Peter changed from being a mercurial turncoat to a man of rock, on whose courage and witness the early Church was founded. You can hear the joy of the resurrection bursting out in his first letter: 'Blessed be the God and Father of our Lord Jesus Christ! By his great mercy we have been born anew to a living hope through the resurrection of Jesus Christ from the dead' (1 Peter 1:3, RSV). The Twelve, who had forsaken Jesus at his hour of need, now stand up courageously for him in front of Jewish leaders, Roman governors, and ordinary sceptical people in the streets. The five hundred, who had presumably known Jesus in Galilee, are now turned from a dispirited rabble into a humble, joyful, confident Church. James, who along with Jesus' other brothers, had been very dubious about him while he was alive (what brothers wouldn't?) now becomes a believer after it is all over. Why? The New Testament tells us why: 'He appeared to James' (1 Corinthians 15:7). So James turned from sceptical brother to fearless leader of the church in Jerusalem, eventually to suffer martyrdom for the brother he had once laughed at. And Paul, well, everyone knows about Paul. The greatest opponent of Jesus was converted into the greatest disciple. Why? 'Last of all . . . he appeared to me.' When you consider honestly and soberly the change in the lives of these men, and the way they all put it down to the resurrection, then I think you will agree that we have strong evidence that the resurrection did in fact take place.

The rise of the Church, the empty tomb, the resurrection appearances, the changed lives of his followers form our strands into a single rope. All the evidence indicates that Jesus did in fact rise from the dead. That is why his followers were convinced he was more than man. That is why they thought him worthy of worship. That is why they were so confident. That is why they spread so rapidly. And that is why millions of Christians all down the ages and all across the globe have been able to add their testimony to the fact that Jesus rose from the dead. *He lives, and they know it!*

All in all, this adds up to a very powerful reason why you should bother with Jesus. If he rose from the dead, he is the Son of God. If he rose from the dead, he is alive and you can have dealings with him. If he rose from the dead, he can guide you in this life and the next – the only person in the world qualified to do so. It would be well to bother about him while there is time.

9

Bother Because He Can Change Your Life

The evidence for the resurrection of Jesus does not end with the first century. Indeed, one of the most remarkable proofs of its truth is this. Unlike most historical events, which become more uncertain the further you are from them, the conviction that Jesus rose and is alive has grown down the centuries. Now you can meet not a Peter, a John, a Paul and perhaps five hundred Christians who could assure you that he is alive and in business, but millions all over the world. They can do so partly because of the historical evidence, but mainly because they know him. Not know about him, mind you: *know him*. There's a world of difference between the two.

When I *know about* someone he is just a flat, historical figure to me, whether he is alive today or whether he

45

lived long ago. But he springs into three dimensions the moment I get to know him. First we are introduced; then we spend time together; then we become friends; then we get to know one another in depth.

Change in others

It is rather like that with Jesus. For years I knew about him in a flat, historical sort of way. And then one day I came to see that if he rose from the grave (which I vaguely believed) he was alive, available, and I could come to know him. So I asked him to make himself real to me. I asked him to become my friend, my intimate. I asked him to set to work changing me by his transforming friendship into what I ought to be. From that day onwards, and it is more than thirty years ago, I can honestly say that I do not just know about Jesus. I know him.

In one way, things haven't changed much since he walked this earth. Then he used to change men's lives as they came into close contact with him. Think of James and John, those 'sons of thunder' as they were nicknamed, hot-tempered and bloodthirsty couple that they were. And then read the first letter of John and see the love of Christ simply flowing from it. You will appreciate what a genius Jesus was at changing character for the better.

Or look at Mary of Magdala, not only a prostitute but possessed by demons: she had been deep into the occult. Jesus changed her whole life. She became pure and loving, an absolutely devoted follower of his, and first witness of the resurrection. Or think of James and Jude, two of the brothers of Jesus, who did not think much of their famous brother while he was around, but came to discover who he was after the resurrection and both wrote letters in the New Testament declaring themselves his slaves!

That life-changing pattern continued once Jesus left this earth, and his Spirit came to live inside the hearts and lives of believers. The Spirit enabled Jesus to do in many lives what he could do, during his lifetime, only in the few that he met: transform them. Indeed, the whole purpose of the Spirit in the lives of Christians is to make them like Jesus. He gradually changes us into Christ's likeness as we live close to him (2 Corinthians 3:18 is a wonderful verse about this). The change in the early Christians is striking. They were not 'nice, respectable folk, who enjoyed going to church on Sunday'. They were 'immoral . . . idolaters . . . adulterers . . . sexual perverts . . . thieves . . . greedy . . . drunkards . . . revilers . . . robbers'. 'Such were some of you,' writes Paul (1 Corinthians 6:9f, RSV). 'But you were washed, you were sanctified, you were justified in the name of the Lord Jesus and by the Spirit of our God.' That is the supreme glory of Jesus: taking lives that have been spoiled by selfishness and sin, and transforming them so that they begin to shine with light borrowed from his own character. That is what the Christian life is all about. The living, risen Jesus still changes lives.

Think of some of the well-known people of our day. Sportsmen and women, rock stars and media celebrities are among those who have discovered that Jesus is alive and well. Many Members of Parliament, Congressmen and Cabinet Ministers freely acknowledge that faith in Jesus has been the most life-changing factor in their whole career. Others courageously follow Jesus Christ in the highly professional world of soccer or pop music: it shows in their speech and behaviour.

Change in you

But it is not just the well-known people that Jesus is interested in. I think of a lovely man I know, a labourer, who found Jesus when he was in prison. So did his wife while waiting for him to come out. It made a big difference! Prison reminds me of another ex-con, a car thief, whom I know well. He found Christ while in Reading Gaol. Guess what he is doing now? He's a vicar!

I think of the scores and scores of agnostic students each year in Oxford, where I used to work, who came to find in Jesus Christ a living, challenging friend and guide. And you can always notice the difference he makes. A new joy, a new concern for other people, a new ability to break with bad habits, a new delight in prayer, a love of the company of other friends of Jesus, an unselfishness that was not there before. It does not matter what background people come from. I think at the moment of a cultured Japanese, a rich Muslim from Turkey, a gentle Hindu, a gangster in prison for life, a prostitute, many middle-class kids, a carpenter, an able Jew. Jesus has made room for all of them. He is the man for all seasons and the man for all types.

Because he is alive, you can talk to him – once you have been introduced. You can enjoy his company, and that makes such a difference to the loneliness which comes to all of us from time to time. 'I am with you always' is his promise (Matthew 28:20, RSV).

Because he is alive you can ask him for his help when the pressures are on and when temptation seems irresistible. 'Greater is he who is in you than he who is in the world,' says the Good Book (1 John 4:4). And it's true. You can prove it for yourself. Just say, 'Lord, help me' – and he will.

Because he is alive you can come back to him when you have done something you could kick yourself for. You can say, 'I've been a fool. So sorry.' And, 'If we confess our sins, he is faithful and just to forgive us our sins, and cleanse us from all unrighteousness' (1 John 1:9, AV).

Because he is alive you can meet him in the lives of other Christians and recognise the changes he is making there, rejoice in them, and learn from them.

Because he is alive you can entrust your job, your marriage, your future to him. As Peter puts it with admirable simplicity: 'Throw all your worries on him. For it matters to him about you' (1 Peter 5:7).

Because he is alive even retirement and old age need not terrify you. You need never retire from his employment. He will not scrap you when you are grey-headed. And when one day you have to die, he will whisper to you, 'Be of good cheer. It is I. Be not afraid.'

Living with Jesus like this cannot fail to transform your life. And isn't that what you really want, at any rate in your better moments? Then what's all this about 'Why bother with Jesus?' He is the very one you need if you are going to be the man or woman you could be – and were meant to be. Don't turn down the chance of a lifetime.

10

Bother Because You Need Him

'I don't need Jesus Christ,' do I hear you say? 'He's just for weak characters who need a crutch in life.' Really? Then let me ask you a question or two.

Being honest

Do you know a lot of love in your life?
Sex, sure. But lasting love? A love that puts up with you when you are being impossible? A love that makes your family a joy to enter? A love which grows as you and your partner get older? A love that overflows to other people in a free, unjudging acceptance? If you haven't got a lot of that in your life, you need to bother about Jesus. For he can provide it.

Do you find yourself really fulfilled in life?
Many people think that happiness is the result of
getting more and more money and possessions. Have
you found that doesn't satisfy? Others think that if
only you get fame or power or achieve your ambitions,
that will automatically make you happy. Have you
discovered that isn't true, either? Happiness is a state
of mind. Happiness is more or less independent of
your outward circumstances. St Paul wrote, as he lay
chained in prison, 'Rejoice in the Lord always, and
again I say, rejoice' (Philippians 4:4). Could you do that
if you were in prison? If not, you need the one who
can bring joy like that. It is Jesus.

How about your relationships?
Do you find that you actually do what you set out to
do – treat everyone as you would like them to treat
you? Are you even-tempered, thoughtful, kind, giving
people the benefit of the doubt? If you find that
question hard to answer, ask your wife or husband,
your secretary, your workmates or schoolfriends or
business colleagues. We seem to be a lot better at
relating to things than to people these days. People
are so much more unpredictable! If the whole area of
relationships is one where you are weak, you need to
get acquainted with the expert in the subject, Jesus.
He tells us that his new commandment for us is to love
one another. He also tells us that he can provide the
love within us. It is the first and choicest of the fruits
produced by his Spirit, once he is allowed to take root
in us.

Are you troubled about the future?
Or look at it another way. Do you not find *the whole
question of the future* exceedingly perplexing? It makes
no difference whether you are in a union or in management, a girl wondering whether to get married (and
reckoning that one in three marriages pack up; will
hers?) or a boy wondering what to do when he leaves

school (and perhaps having to start off by joining the dole queue). On any showing, life is difficult, and decisions are harrowing. Is there not something to be said for having the personal guidance and care of the one who has been this way before us, and knows every snag, every problem? He holds the future in those hands of his. I do not promise you easy answers if you entrust yourself to him. In many ways problems get harder. But the joy of having this loving, understanding friend to share them with is something I would not trade for a million pounds.

Do you have any failings?

I wonder if you have any *weaknesses* that get you down time and again? Or are you perfect, like William Weddell, Esq., whose imposing monument stands in Ripon Cathedral? 'To the memory of William Weddell, Esq. of Newby, in whom every virtue that ennobles the human mind was united with every elegance that adorns it, this monument, a faint emblem of his refined taste, is dedicated by his widow.' We laugh when we see something like that. We know that human beings are not like that. We aren't, ourselves: far from it. Do we not need the Master-carpenter of Nazareth to get to work on the rough wood of our lives and carve in us something of his own lovely character?

Are you at peace about your life?

There are two other areas which are not often spoken about these days, and yet every man, woman and child on this earth needs them: *a forgiveness that wipes out the past, and a life that lasts into the future.* I have yet to know anyone who has not got a skeleton or two rattling around the hidden cupboards of his life. And the doctors, the psychiatrists, and the 'snap-out-of-it' brigade cannot get rid of it for us. There are things we have done which we would give anything not to have done: there are guilty acts in our own lives, which we ourselves did *and meant to do*, but of which we are now

51

deeply ashamed. We feel dirty as a result of them, and we do not know how we can get spring-cleaned. That is one of our basic needs. And there is an equal need as we live through our three score years and ten. Life seems endless when we are teenagers. It seems very short in our fifties. And by the time we are seventy-one, we realise we are living on borrowed time. Can this life be all there is? Deep down we feel it can't be. And yet how can we be sure about anything beyond it?

Jesus Christ is the only one who can meet these two most universal of all needs. His death on the cross wiped out our sins. When he looks at the very things we feel we can never forget, and can never forgive ourselves for, he says, 'Your sins and your iniquities I will remember no more (Jeremiah 31:34) . . . Happy is the man whose transgressions are forgiven and whose sin is covered (Psalm 32:1) . . . There is no condemnation for those who are in Christ Jesus (Romans 8:1) . . . He has once suffered for sins, the just for the unjust, that he might bring us to God (1 Peter 3:18).' Where else do you get an offer like that?

Eternal life

The whole purpose of his coming to earth was to make eternal life a possibility for us. Eternal life does not start when you are dead. It starts before you are dead, or else it does not start at all. 'This is eternal life, to know the only true God and Jesus Christ whom he has sent,' said Jesus (John 17:3). St John put it with great simplicity: 'He who has the Son has life, and he who does not have the Son does not have life' (1 John 5:12). Eternal life is not an added *quantity* of life, but a new *quality* of life — such as a young man senses when he get his first motor-cycle, or a young woman on her wedding day. A new dimension to living seems to have opened up. That is how it is when Jesus Christ comes into our lives. Eternal life begins then, and carries on through death for ever, in the company of the Lord we love.

OK, then, if you don't want eternal life and don't see the need for forgiveness, I can understand you saying, 'Why bother with Jesus?' That is your decision. He will respect it. He never forces himself on anybody – that is not love's way. But if, in addition to the need for moral strength, deep satisfaction, a life full of love, his guidance, and the ability to develop really caring relationships with others, you are aware of these two great needs of forgiveness and eternal life, I can tell you one thing. Nobody will be able to give them to you but Jesus. If you don't bother about him it will be pointless to bother about them.

11

Bother Because He Calls You

The idea has got around that to be a Christian is a soft option. Incredible! It just shows how good the Enemy's propaganda machine is. As a matter of fact, only the people with courage, the folks who are prepared to swim against the current, are to be found among the committed followers of Jesus Christ. They may be little old ladies, or tough business executives, navvies or newspaper men, but they all need moral courage if they are going to stand up and be counted among the friends of Jesus. He never offered us an easy time. He had a tough one, and he warned us that we would, too. We would have to love him better than father or mother or home or job. We would have to be unashamed of him in any company. We would have to be prepared to stick out as unmistakably as a city on a hill top. We would have to be in a minority. We would have to go the way of the cross in some form or other. It would not be easy to follow Jesus. It never has been and it isn't today.

The challenge

So let's get out of our heads, for good and all, the 'Come to Jesus and everything in the garden will be lovely' sort of approach. If you have ever heard preachers talk like that, forget them. That is not the authentic article, but a sugary imitation of genuine Christianity.

Listen to the first recorded words of Jesus:

> Jesus came into Galilee, preaching the gospel of God, and saying, 'The time is fulfilled, and the kingdom of God is at hand; repent, and believe in the gospel.'
>
> And passing along by the Sea of Galilee, he saw Simon and Andrew the brother of Simon casting a net in the sea; for they were fishermen. And Jesus said to them, 'Follow me, and I will make you become fishers of men.' And immediately they left their nets and followed him. And going on a little farther, he saw James the son of Zebedee and John his brother, who were in their boat, mending the nets. And immediately he called them; and they left their father Zebedee in the boat with the hired servants, and followed him (Mark 1:15–20, RSV).

There are lots of interesting things in that short story. Notice how Jesus strides on to the scene and takes these tough fishermen by storm. They would not follow just anybody! He must have convinced them that he did indeed bring God's Kingdom in his own person. They must have seen him as 'good news' – for that is what 'gospel' means. Do you think of Jesus that way? And the Jesus who brings good news of all that God's kingly rule can mean in human lives tells them that time is up. They need to decide for him or against him. Are they going to repent, and change their self-centred attitude, or not? Are they going to trust him, or not? Will they or will they not launch out on a life following him, entrusting themselves to his sure hands for all that the future may bring? Will they rate him higher than their job, higher even than their family and their workmates?

Such was the challenge then. We all know what they did about it. But the challenge still comes to us now. Jesus says to you, who have got this far in the book, 'The time is fulfilled.' Time is up. You have hung around long enough. You may only know a little about him, but you know enough to entrust yourself. It is a matter of the will. How about it?

The response

'But what am I supposed to do?' you may ask. Nothing very complicated: just something very tough. He says, 'Repent.' That means, have done with all you know to be wrong. It doesn't mean you have to give it up before you enlist in his cause: you can't. That's what you need a Saviour for. But it does mean you must be willing for him to cut out all the diseased parts of your life. He is the skilled surgeon. You can trust him not to hurt you more than is necessary, and only to remove what is hopelessly diseased. You don't have to rustle up lots of crocodile tears about how wicked you are. You simply have to let go and let God. Say to him, 'Jesus, come and clean me up. I really want it, whatever it costs.'

Surely that is hard enough? No, there is more to come. Nobody said it was going to be an easy ride. From now on it is the Kingdom of God that is going to control your life, remember? Very well, the King has got to come first. Before those 'nets' of yours: all the things your life is taken up with. Before the 'boats': all the possessions that seem so important. Before the

'hired servants': all the folk who might laugh at you.
Before 'Zebedee': all those nearest and dearest to you,
who might not like the change of direction. Are you
willing to put him first? If not, keep clear of Jesus. He
is not the one for you. He is looking for revolutionary
characters who will pledge their all in his cause. He
gave his all for us . . .

'OK,' you say, 'I am prepared. At least, I think I am.'
Fine. Then the next step is simple, but it is very
difficult. Simple because a child can do it. Difficult
because it takes the humility of a child to get round
to doing it. Jesus says, 'Believe in the good news.' Do
you feel you believe in it already? Wait a moment. The
good news is first and foremost bad news: it tells us
that without Jesus we are hopelessly lost. Do you
admit that? Do you recognise that your good deeds are
not enough to win God's favour? That you can't earn
it by going to church or giving your money to the poor?
You enter the Kingdom through a very narrow door.
That door is near a cross. And on that cross hangs one
with a filthy burden on his back. As you look, you see
to your horror that the burden is made up of all the
wrong things, wrong thoughts, wrong attitudes,
wrong words, wrong habits of which you are guilty.
He looks straight at you, as he hangs there, and says,
'Do you believe in the good news? I hang there for you.
I bear your burdens so that you may never be choked
by them. Will you accept a free pardon – because I
have taken your place?' To say, 'Yes, Lord: thank you
so much,' is very simple, but incredibly humbling.
Nobody has ever yet entered the Kingdom any other
way. No exceptions will be made for you. You come
on your knees, you come crying for pardon, you come
with tears of gratitude in your eyes, if you 'believe in
the gospel'. Do you? If so, just kneel down now,
wherever you are, and thank the Lord for what he has
done to make you accepted. Entrust your whole life
to him in glad response. Remember, it is for keeps.
He will not abuse your trust.

What next? These moments pass, do they not? What about that future – spent with Christ? Well, the first disciples had to learn an important fact. They were disciples: that word means 'learners'. They put their 'L' plates up. And so must you. As a matter of fact, you keep them up for the rest of your earthly life. You will never 'pass your test' and become independent of your Instructor. He will sit alongside you in the front of your car for the rest of life's journey now that you have let him in. He knows the perils and the problems of the route. He is infinitely experienced. He says, 'Follow me.' How do I do that? Two ways spring to mind at once.

First, *find out his instructions*. There is a perfectly adequate manual in the front of the car. The Scriptures show you all you need to know about the journey, and give you his instructions on how to finish it successfully. Read that manual. There are modern translations of it, like the Good News Bible or the New International Version. There are Bible-reading helps like the Scripture Union. But if you want to follow his instructions you simply must, yes *must*, study that driving manual.

The other thing, of course, which those first disciples realised is that *you do not follow him alone*. It is a 'together' thing. They were called together. They followed together. They came to love and trust each other, because they had Jesus as their common Instructor. You need Christian people if you are to follow Jesus properly. Go and find some. Tell them what you have done. And ask them to help you on your way. Public worship is a 'must'. So is some informal gathering with one person or a group of people with whom you can let your hair down and voice your hesitations, problems and hang-ups. You're going to need something like that, especially in the early days. Go looking for it straight away.

Jesus has the same purpose in store for us as he had for these first followers. 'I will make you become

fishers of men.' We are far from that when we come
to him all raw and fresh. He has a lot of work to do
on us as we put up our 'L' plates and begin to follow
him. But his intention is that we shall bring other
people to bother about him, and know him and love
him. His strategy is to work through people like us to
win people like us. Simple, isn't it? And effective. If
we let him, that is. Some people say, 'I couldn't
possibly talk about religion to my friends.' You aren't
being asked to. Religion is bad news. Jesus is good
news. Tell them what you are beginning to discover
in your Friend and Boss, Jesus. And since it is to be
a lifelong occupation, the sooner you start the better.
Go and tell someone today if you have entrusted your
life to Christ. You don't necessarily need to pick the
most hostile sceptic in your circle of friends. But you
do need to open your lips right away. Secret disciples
are no use to Jesus. They never achieved much in
the fishing business. Jesus depends on your
recommendation among your friends. And there's
another side to it: typical of him. When you pluck up
courage to speak about him, however falteringly, he
gives you a great sense of assurance that you do belong
to him, and that his Holy Spirit is at work in you.
That's the point of Romans 10:9, 10 and Mark 13:11.
They are good verses. Look them up!

Taking the plunge

Are you still wondering whether to take the plunge?
Then let me remind you of one striking thing about
this little passage in Mark, chapter one. Jesus did not
say, 'Just you follow me and you will have a
marvellous time.' Jesus did not say, 'Just you follow
me and I will give you lots of desirable things.' Jesus
did not wheedle them and say, 'Please, please, come
and follow me.' He commanded them to do it. No
nonsense about it. He had already, we must believe,
shown them who he was, and what he could do for

them. He has certainly not left *us* in doubt on these things. Now he says, in effect, 'Get on with it. Decide. Not because of what you will get out of it. Not because you will have an easier time: you won't. Not because I plead with you (although I do). But come and follow me because that is the only possible right response to my love, which has gone to such lengths for you. Come and follow me because there is no other way you can find life and bring it to others. I do not merely advise you. I do not cajole you. I, your Lord and your God am willing to be your Saviour and your Friend. I command you. I tell you. Come, follow me.'

Will you?

12

Get Big by Bothering

A celebrated London employment agency once made the proud boast that it got big by bothering. There is a lot in that. Growth does not happen by accident in business: nor does it in the Christian life. You only get big by bothering.

Now the New Testament certainly expects us to get big. But one part of us that should not grow is our head! You will not need a larger size in hats the longer you go on with Christ. Quite the reverse. The more time you spend in his company the more you will see yourself in your true colours, and the more you will realise that any progress is to be credited to him not you. Simon Peter learnt that from painful personal experience. The man who had thought he could never fall away from Jesus denied him three times the night when Jesus was arrested. He writes later, with feeling,

'Clothe yourselves, all of you, with humility toward one another, for "God opposes the proud, but gives grace to the humble." Humble yourselves therefore under the mighty hand of God, that in due time he may exalt you' (1 Peter 5:5f). No, the areas in which we grow big are quite different.

Grow big by eating

However old you are when you come to faith, you then become a spiritual babe. Just as the baby longs for its bottle, so the new Christian will long for 'the pure spiritual milk, that by it you may grow up' (1 Peter 2:2, RSV). Spiritual milk includes Bible reading, and it helps no end to get some system like the one produced by the Scripture Union, obtainable from a local Christian bookshop, and to find some Christian friend who can read it with you a bit and give you some help. But spiritual food is wider than Bible reading. It includes prayer – and here again we shall need help. It includes the Holy Communion: Jesus left us a meal to remember him by, and we need it regularly. In it we not only remember that we owe everything to his body broken and his blood shed for us: we also feast with the risen Lord, and we look forward to being with him when this life is over.

Grow big by trusting

'We are bound to give thanks to God always for you brothers, because your trust is growing all the time' (2 Thessalonians 1:3). The new believers in this northern Greek city were learning to trust the Lord whom they could not see. They trusted him to build them up in love for other Christians, to teach them, and to see them through hard times. They trusted him with their problems and their need for guidance. And this is how they grew in confidence and in experience of the Lord. 'Commit your way unto the Lord. Trust

also in him. And he will act' said the Old Testament
(Psalm 37:5). The Thessalonians began falteringly to
exercise this trust: and so can you. It is a great way
to grow.

Grow big by sharing

Christianity is not a solo trip. It has to be done in a
team. God is not interested in changing individuals
alone. He wants to show what he can do in a community who trust him. The New Testament puts this
point in various ways. Here are a couple out of the
same letter, written to Christians in what was then the
leading city of Turkey, Ephesus. You people, says the
apostle, are like limbs in a body. You need to grow
and to keep pace in your growth with one another,
so that the whole body is co-ordinated. 'Speaking the
truth in love, we are to grow up in every way into him
who is the head, into Christ. From him the whole
body, joined and knit together by every ligament,
makes bodily growth when every part is working
properly, and builds itself up in love' (Ephesians
4:15ff). Isn't that a marvellous picture of our need for
a close, supportive Christian fellowship? He put it in
a different way in chapter 2:21. Christians are seen not
as limbs in a body this time, but as stones in a building.
And, as he watches, he seems to see 'the whole
structure joined together and growing into a holy
temple for the Lord. You, too, are built into this temple
and together become a place where the Holy Spirit
lives.' (How about that for privilege? Doesn't it put a
new perspective on our mutual relationships as
Christians? We grow by being together. It can't be
done on our own.)

Get big by growing fruit

In Colossians 1:10 Paul longs that the Colossians may
lead a life worthy of the Lord, learn to please him in

everything they do, and bear fruit in every good work, while they increase in the knowledge of God. Fruit-bearing is the natural outcome of growth, and so it is when the Holy Spirit is planted in the soil of our lives. 'Fruit' is used in the New Testament mainly to indicate change in our character and the conversion of other people to faith in Jesus: these are the qualities God longs to see in his followers who are growing.

None of these aspects of growth happens by accident. You have to actually get a Bible out, you have to go to church, you have to start praying if you mean to grow big by eating. You have to commit problems and temptations to the Lord, if you want to grow big in faith. You have to get stuck in with other Christians if you are to grow up into one body, one building. If you are going to bear fruit, you have to ask the Holy Spirit to transform your character; and to take your courage in both hands and open your mouth to speak. These things require attention. But then growth always does. You get big by bothering. Don't be a dwarf Christian, will you?

You only get big by bothering . . .

YOU MUST BE JOKING!

POPULAR EXCUSES FOR AVOIDING JESUS CHRIST

This book is affectionately dedicated to all the jokers who have tried out on me the excuses I deal with in the text!

Acknowledgments

The author and publishers wish to acknowledge copyright material from:

Gordon Bailey, SOL Publications, Box 356, Birmingham

Roger McGough, © Roger McGough, 1967 Penguin Modern Poets 10, Corgi Publications, Random Century House, Vauxhall Bridge Road, London SW1

M. B. Yeats, Miss Anne Yeats and the Macmillan Company of London and Basingstoke for a quotation from 'Death' (The Collected Poems of W. B. Yeats)

Contents

Preface

The stimulus to write this sort of book came from Friedrich Hänssler, the head of Hänssler-Verlag, publishers. The idea and title emerged as I lay in bed in Durban with meningitis under the care and imaginative friendship of Dr. John Hill. The chapter headings came from the many jokers who have tried them out on me. Valuable suggestions came from Tony Collins of Hodder and Stoughton. The typing came from my overworked secretary Anne Johnson.

TO ONE AND ALL, THANK YOU.

I

From the Author ...

I F I HAD called this 'Foreword' or 'Preface' you would have skipped it, in all probability. But I want you to read it. It is quite important, and it shows what the book is about.

A STARTLING AGREEMENT ...

In recent years I have had the opportunity of travelling widely in Europe, Asia, Africa, North America and Australia. I have had the chance to discover the basic attitudes to life adopted by ordinary people of every conceivable variety of

background, colour and education. You would expect these attitudes to differ enormously; and on most subjects, of course,
they do. But on one subject there is startling agreement. When
it is a matter of what men think about human nature and religion, man's origin and destiny, the possibility of forgiveness or
life after death — then people tend to come up with the same
answers, whether they hail from Paramatta or Portsmouth.
Such agreement looks at first sight, to be very encouraging:
when the United Nations can rarely agree about anything at all,
it is amazing that men all over the world should tend to think
alike about the basic questions of our existence. However, I am
not very impressed by this apparent unanimity.

... BUT SHALLOW

For one thing it is shallow. When you broach the question of religion, and a fellow replies 'Oh, but all religions lead
to God', ten to one he knows almost nothing about his own
religious background, still less about any other. When he says,
'I'm not the religious sort', you can be fairly confident that he
has made no investigation whatever into whether or not there is
a religious sort, and, if there is, what it is like. When he says,
'Jesus was just a marvellous teacher but no more', it is unusual
to find that he has ever examined the claims Jesus made, or the
evidence supporting those claims. When you hear a person say,
'I do my best — no man can do more', of one thing you can be
certain: he does not do his best (which of us does?) but he hasn't
the honesty to admit as much. So do you see why I am not all
that impressed by these parrot cries which come up, as regular
as clockwork, whenever I begin to talk about God? They are so
shallow. They simply show that people, on the whole, are content not to *think* about the really important matters of life and
death. 'Oh, I have no time for religion,' says a prosperous
business man who spends an hour a day keeping up with the
Stock Market. But if there is a God, if there is a heaven, if there
is forgiveness, what an appallingly short-sighted attitude! The
man who invests shrewdly and carefully in his stocks and shares

may be pathetically naïve and incompetent when it comes to investing in life.

. . . AND ESCAPIST

There's another reason why I am not impressed by the common responses about religion which I meet everywhere I go. They are not only shallow, betraying an absence of thought: they are also evasive, betraying an unwillingness to face up to the evidence. Many of the things people come out with, when you ask them their fundamental attitudes to life, boil down to something like the answers I examine in the chapters which follow. And the trouble is that they are not only shallow but dishonest. The man who says, 'It doesn't matter what you believe so long as you are sincere', would never dream of applying that motto to any area of life other than religion. He may think he's being straightforward when he comes out with a statement like this, but he isn't really. What he means is that he is not going to take the trouble to investigate the truth of Christianity or of any other religion — maybe because he doesn't think it important enough, maybe because he fears he would get exposed, or challenged, or involved. Although he sounds so fine and liberal-minded, he is likely to be an escapist at heart.

You see, then, why I am not satisfied to find such widespread agreement about fundamental beliefs? The agreement is unthinking and escapist. It is an agnosticism which does not want to know in case the answer should prove costly or inconvenient. So right at the outset of this little book, I am going to ask you to be different.

A PLEA FOR HONESTY

Will you stand out from the crowd, and think for yourself? Will you have the courage to examine the evidence and ask yourself how sound are the assumptions about God and meaning, life and death, with which you have lived so far? Will they bear the weight of your life and future? After all, these *are* the basic issues. It makes an enormous difference if there is a God

or not; if he has revealed himself or not; if he will accept us or
not; whether we have a future after death or not. It simply will
not do to hide our heads in the sand, repeat our parrot cries, and
refuse to see how they stand up to critical examination. The
Old Testament has some trenchant things to say about people
'who make lies their refuge; and the rain shall sweep away the
refuge of lies' (Isaiah 28:15, 17). Could your refuge be like
that? A famous insurance company has as one of its selling
gimmicks the picture of a roof, and the phrase 'Refuge for
Life'. Well, have you got a roof that will keep the rain out? The
New Testament (Matthew 7:24f) records the contrast between
the man who built the house of his life on the rock and the one
who built on sand: the rain and the wind and the floods assail
both houses, but only the house on the rock can withstand the
onslaught. Could it be that you are building on sand?

I have collected here a number of very common assumptions
about the most important issues in life. You may recognise one
or more of them that you share. Very well, why not begin with
that chapter, and ask yourself if the assumption is well
founded — or mistaken? Let me, for my part, come clean at the
outset. To my mind these assumptions sound good, but they
won't do. They are dangerous fallacies, and offer no proper
foundation for life. Time and again when folk have brought
them forward I have felt (or said!) 'You must be joking!' Will
you, too, come clean at the outset? Lay aside prejudice; examine the evidence; and be prepared for change should you
become persuaded that your assumptions won't hold water.
These matters are of critical importance to all of us. There
really is no excuse for shallow thinking or evasive action as we
look into them together.

'I'm not the religious sort'

THE RELIGIOUS SORT

'NO, VICAR, GO and talk to someone else. I'm afraid I'm not the religious sort.' That is very often said, and I have a lot of sympathy with it. There is something creepy and sanctimonious, something effeminate and wet about that phrase 'the religious sort'. I think of business men in black ties at the funeral of one of their companions trying to imitate 'the religious sort' for half an hour, and then emerging breathless from the

funeral to the open air in order to light up a cigarette and return
to normality. I think of a country church with six people in it
along with the vicar, not to mention a bat or two, while the men
of the village meet across the green in the pub for a cheerful
evening in each other's company. Church? Not for them, thank
you; they're not the religious sort. Or the mind strays, perhaps,
to some ceremonial occasion in a great cathedral: the trum-
peters, the taperers, the choir, the candles, the expensive robes,
the perfectly rendered service which nobody seems to
mean — all of this evokes the response, 'I'm not the religious
sort'. Or take two very different examples of 'religion'. One
comes on the radio with the daily service and a handful of
singers who may sound professional and bogus: canned religion
is not attractive at the best of times. The other comes in a great
stadium where the evangelist is urging people to come to the
front for counselling: that can seem a mere playing on the religious emotions — and 'I'm not the religious sort'.

HYPOCRISY?

Why do we so strongly dislike 'the religious sort'? Is it not
because we have almost come to regard religion and hypocrisy
as the same thing? There is a very long history of this. In
Isaiah's day back in the eighth century B.C. men were offering
God all manner of sacrifices, but their hearts were far from
him. In Jesus' day the scribes and pharisees gained the reputation for being hypocrites. Many of them must have been absolutely genuine. Some, however, were seen to make long prayers
in order to impress; to give ostentatiously so that everyone
should think how generous they were; to make a great show of
their biblical knowledge in order to shame others. Piety outside
and corruption inside is a revolting mixture. Jesus had to
accuse some of his hearers of being just like that: they reminded him of the white sepulchres which were such a common
sight on the hills set against the deep blue of the Sea of Galilee.
They looked marvellous from the outside: but inside they were
foul and full of corruption and dead men's bones.

The link between religion and hypocrisy did not die in the first century. Think of the hypocrisy in those very religious days of the Victorian era: the immorality that flourished, the exploitation that went on alongside meticulous religious observance. And, rightly or wrongly, there are many who suspect hypocrisy in the high churchgoing figures among the whites in Rhodesia and South Africa, and among the middle class in America. Could this be a sort of insurance policy to preserve the regimes against the inroads of black power and Communism? I do not know. But what I do know is that many people assert very forcefully that they are not the religious sort because they hate hypocrisy, and they feel that somehow it is tied up with religion.

BEGGING?

Closely allied to this is begging. None of us like seeing beggars. It makes us feel uncomfortable; indeed, we feel 'got at'. But organised religion bears the image of the beggar. How many churches do you pass with a notice outside inviting you to save this ancient building? How many cathedrals do you go into with a notice inside telling you how much per minute it costs to run the place? Then there are the fêtes, the whist drives, the door to door collections, the stewardship campaigns and all the other money raising gimmicks. The churches always seem after your cash. And we are very wary of folk who are after our cash. Let's make it crystal clear that we are not the religious sort.

I take the force of all this. Indeed, that is why I said at the outset that I have a lot of sympathy with people who say they are not the religious sort. But all the same I think they are wrong.

CLEARING THE AIR

First, let me clear the air and have a look at those justifiable objections to the religious sort which have just been raised. It is true that a lot of bad things have been done in the name of religion. So they have in the name of medicine, but that does not mean we don't go near a doctor. A lot of good things have been done in the name of religion, too: but that by itself does not make it true. There is only one proper question for men of integrity: is the religious account of the world and man true? If it is, then I want it, however many bad things have sheltered under its umbrella. I shall want to throw out into the rain the bad things, but not to take down the umbrella.

It is perfectly true that some expressions of religion border on the nauseating — always remembering that what is nauseating to one man is meat and drink to another. I personally get switched off very fast indeed by B.B.C. services and cathedrals. Others get annoyed by prayer meetings, evangelistic rallies or good old Anglican Matins. I have no doubt that there is a great deal of insincerity in church circles, and I have no doubt that illicit psychological pressure is exerted by some evangelists. But once again, back to the basic facts. Did they or did they not happen? Was Jesus or was he not the Son of God? Did he, or did he not rise from the dead? If he did, then I can afford to be broadminded about types of religious expression I personally dislike. If not, then the whole lot is rubbish, a type of escapism for which I have no time at all.

As for hypocrisy and money grabbing, these need not detain us long. Just because there are counterfeit coins about, that does not stop you using money, does it? Indeed, were there no good money, nobody would bother with making counterfeit. So the existence of hypocrisy in religious circles is no reason for rejecting religion. It rather suggests that there is a genuine article as well as spurious copies. Take a good hard look at Jesus in the Gospels. There is not a sniff of hypocrisy about him. He was the first to denounce it in others. And it is with Jesus that we are concerned. Following him means following the one who denounced hypocrisy and would have no part in it at all. Just because some of his followers have failed to live up to that, it does not stop you having a go.

On the money-grabbing issue, I think the church has deserved its appalling image. It does give the impression that it is always out for money. It should rather proclaim that it has found great treasure in Jesus Christ, and that unlike most treasures, this one is for free. Jesus was always impressing upon people that entry into the Kingdom of God, or the Great Supper or friendship with himself (all three add up to the same thing) was absolutely free, for black and white, Jew and Gentile, prostitute and Pharisee alike. Free. But he also made it plain that life within the kingdom was costly. It might cost you all you have, just as it cost him all he had. So the church is right to say to its members that they owe Christ a proportion of their time as well as their money and their talents. The church is wrong to ask those who are not its committed members to act as if they were. To them the free generosity of Christ's acceptance of any man who comes to him should be the main message that gets through. If that message is not being heard, it is not because Christ has changed his attitude, but because the church is being unfaithful to his teaching and example. So if this matter of money has been bugging you, forget it. Jesus is the one we are concerned with. And he never went round taking collections from folk who dropped in for the odd funeral. He never put a collecting box outside the Nazareth synagogue begging non-members to prop it up. If the church does not follow his example, so much the worse for the church. Don't let it stop you finding the most wonderful person in the world, Jesus himself.

Having, I hope, cleared the air, I now want to ask some pertinent questions of any who are hiding behind this 'I'm not the religious sort' motto.

IS THERE A RELIGIOUS SORT?

First, let me ask you, can you honestly say there is a religious sort? Don't pretend it is comprised of the effeminate, the retired and the addle-headed. I think round some of the people in our own parish church: a leading gynaecologist, a factory worker, a librarian, a horticulturalist, a garage owner, a builder, an architect, an engineer, a man who has been finding God in prison, a lawyer, an atomic scientist, a university teacher, a man on the dole, literally hundreds of students, the majority of whom are studying scientific subjects, members from Iran and India, Sri Lanka and Rhodesia, South Africa (black and white) and U.S.A., Canada and Sweden, Germany and Hong Kong, Japan and Australia, Kenya and Uganda, Sudan and Nigeria and so on. The diversity of their attitudes, their backgrounds, their educational attainments, their temperaments, their ages, their interests, their *everything*, is so vast that it would be ridiculous to class them all as the religious type. These Christians are not just one type: they are all types — extrovert and introvert, tough and weak, old and young, black and white. Their diversity has only one unifying factor, but that factor is strong as steel: Jesus Christ. Here is an example of the sort of thing I have in mind. I had a letter a few days ago from a correspondent working with *Time Magazine*. The writer tells me that he was treasurer of the Oxford Humanist Society in 1964, and was converted in 1966 largely through conviction of the Holy Spirit's presence in the life of my predecessor as Rector of St. Aldate's. He is deeply involved in the work of the church in Hong Kong at present, and is not only experiencing a deepening maturity in his own life but is also leading numerous other people to the Christ he used to reject but who is now his living Lord. Can you say that such a man was the religious sort? Can you say that the first disciples of Jesus were the religious sort? Perhaps a mystic like John was, but what of rugged, hard-swearing fishermen like Andrew and Peter? What of freedom fighters like Judas Iscariot and Simon the Zealot? What of money grabbing tax collectors like Matthew? What of the drunkards and homosexuals at Corinth who became Christians? What of the thieves and magicians at Ephesus? It is ludicrous to suppose that the people who first followed Jesus belonged to the religious sort. The Jews, in fact, had a word for the religious sort; and another, far from complimentary, word for the ordinary folk, 'the people of the land'. All Jesus' first followers came from this latter group: all were the non-religious sort.

A NON-RELIGIOUS FAITH

Don't let your dislike of religion keep you away from Jesus. In a very real sense he came to destroy religion. The German martyr, Dietrich Bonhoeffer, was not playing with words when he coined the phrase 'religionless Christianity'. That is precisely what Christianity is. It is not an attempt by good-living men to please God and win a place in heaven. It is God coming in his love and generosity to seek folk who would never seek him, holding out his arms to them on a cross, and saying, 'Come to me, and let us share life together'. Not a religion, but a rescue. That is why the earliest Christians were so keen to stress that they had no temple, no altars, no priests. They had no religion in the normally accepted sense of the term: hence the Romans called them 'atheists'. Instead they had a Person, who knew them, loved them, and never left them. Nothing could separate them from his loving presence. So prayer became not a ritual but converse with a Friend. Worship was not a ceremony for Sundays but the natural outpouring of love and adoration to the Saviour by his people when they met together. They needed no churches, for where two or three were gathered together in his name, he was in their midst. They needed no priests, for Jesus had opened immediate, equal access to God's presence for every one of them. Christianity, properly understood, is the most earthy of faiths: it does not separate the secular from the sacred, but keeps the two firmly together. The Lord is as interested in what I do at eleven o'clock on Monday in my daily work as he is in what I do at eleven o'clock on Sunday in a church service.

Yes, Christianity is for non-religious people. It is not going too far to say that if you insist on being religious you will find Christianity hard, almost impossible. You will find it almost impossible to *become* a Christian, because your 'religion' will get in the way: you will feel that somehow you are better and more pleasing to God than your irreligious neighbour, and that is just what the pharisees felt — and what kept them away from Jesus. And you will find it almost impossible to *be* a Christian:

because once again your 'religion' will get in the way: you will feel that the Christian life depends on your religious observances, and not on the Lord. You will be inclined to keep a little religious corner in your life for God and not allow him to have the whole thing. You will definitely find it much harder to become and to be a Christian than the man who is not 'the religious sort'.

THE MATTER OF TRUTH

And now a few other questions for the man who is not religious. *Are you concerned about truth?* That is a vital question. Do I hear you say, 'Of course I am'? Very well, then you and the Christian are interested in just the same thing. Jesus claimed, 'I am the truth'. He claimed, in other words, to be ultimate reality in personal, human terms. If you are interested in what is ultimate and what is real, then you cannot remain disinterested in Jesus. You may examine his claims and dismiss them as untrue: what you cannot do if you maintain a deep concern for truth, is to pay him no attention, shrug your shoulders and say, 'I'm not the religious sort'.

THE MATTER OF COURAGE

Next question: *have you the courage of your convictions?* I met an atheist at a discussion group recently, an able man doing doctoral studies in physics. When we were talking personally at the end of the meeting I asked him if he had ever read one of the Gospels with an open mind, willing to respond to Christ if and when he was convinced by what he read. His reply surprised me, but on reflection I think it may be true of many others. He said, 'I dare not'. What a remarkable admission! Here was a man used to assessing material, making judgments, committing himself to theories in physics on the ground of the evidence; yet he was afraid to do the same with the New Testament material in case it should convince him and draw him to the Christ he was evading. Surely, if he had the courage of his atheistic convictions, he should have been quite willing to read the Gospels. It would give him first-hand material to make fun of with his believing friends. But no. He did not have the courage of his convictions.

The next question is very similar: *dare you take your stand with a minority?* Jesus warned potential disciples to sit down and count the cost of what following him would mean. Were they prepared to stand with 10,000 men against an opposition force of 20,000? If not, they would have to make humiliating peace terms in double quick time. It is not pleasant to admit you are wrong about the basic issues of life and death. Not easy to join the despised Christian company. Not easy to stand being mocked at work for your allegiance to Christ. Not easy to allow Christ to affect your morality. Of course it is not. Jesus never said it would be easy. He said that following him meant death as well as life. Death to the old way of living, then accepting new life, new power, new standards from the Lord. All this is very tough. Many people dress up their cowardice in quite other terms, such as indifference — 'I'm not the religious sort.' But cowardice it remains. The man of Nazareth is too demanding, too uncompromising, too loving, too upright for the soft and compromising, the lazy and those who like to go with the crowd.

THE MATTER OF FULFILMENT

Another question I would like to ask the man who is not interested in religion: *do you want to find fulfilment?* Jesus once described the Kingdom of God as finding treasure. Imagine a farmer ploughing his field, drearily, monotonously, without any special expectations. Then his ploughshare hits a box. He investigates, and finds to his amazement that the box is full of diamonds and rubies. Whose heart would not beat faster at such a discovery? That, Jesus implied, is what discovering God's kingdom is like. For the kingdom is brought to us in the person of the king; and the king is Jesus. Really, then, it is nothing to do with 'religion' and its demands and observances.

The Christian life is concerned with relationships. First comes the restoration of our relationship with God: then the restoration of our links with others, as the basic harmony brought by Christ spreads outwards. Relationships are among the most precious things in life. Yet too often they are spoiled by selfishness, racial prejudice, jealousy or pride. Jesus Christ unites people, and brings harmony where once there was discord: and that spells fulfilment at the deepest level of all.

I think of a painfully shy student who found a living faith in Christ his first weekend at the university. Within six weeks he had opened up like a flower and was relating with far greater freedom to others. I think of a couple whose marriage was on the point of breaking up, when both partners were brought to faith in Jesus. The new relationship with Christ brought them closer together than ever before, and their marriage is now strong and happy. I think of a soldier, loathed for his big-headedness and rudeness, whose whole attitude to others changed radically when he allowed Jesus Christ to take control of him. I think of two schoolboys who could not stick each other, until both of them found Christ in the same summer holidays: thereafter relationships were on a completely new plane (I should know, for I was one of the boys). This same Jesus draws together those whom every pressure in the world is driving apart. He does it in Northern Ireland, as genuine believers (as opposed to the 'religious sort', be they Protestant or Catholic) meet across the border at nights and pray for one another, support each other's widows and tend each other's wounded. He does it in the Middle East as he brings together in one Christian fellowship the political irreconcilables, Jews and Arabs. He does it in South Africa, between white, coloured and black believers: I have seen it time and again with my own eyes. But I know no other force on earth that can do the same. Jesus is treasure indeed: for he brings fulfilment to all our relationships, once we allow him to repair our relationship to God.

THE MATTER OF DESTINY

There is one other question I would like to ask the man who
is not interested in religion: *are you interested in your future?*
What man is not? Our education, our aspirations, our
qualification seeking, our hunger for promotion is all geared to
this end — securing a better future. But what when we have got
it? Is there not an emptiness at the top? Money does not satisfy
permanently, nor does sex, nor does fame; nor does manipu-
lating others. And many of the people at the top know it. The
actress Raquel Welch put it well in the *Daily Express* of
October 31st, 1972:

> I had acquired everything I wanted, yet I was totally mis-
> erable ... I thought it was very peculiar that I had acquired
> everything I had wanted as a child — wealth, fame and ac-
> complishment in my career. I had beautiful children, and a
> life style that seemed terrific, yet I was totally and miserably
> unhappy. I found it very frightening that one could acquire
> all these things and still be so miserable.

After all, what is life about? Are we bound for extinction, or
is there some life beyond the grave? If you are really concerned
for your future, you can scarcely avoid considering the matter
of final destiny. Pascal put it at its most entertaining when he
suggested that the after-life is like a wager: if you believe in
God you are at no disadvantage in this life, and at considerable
advantage in the next. If you do not believe, but find in the next
that there *was* a next, you are most unfortunate! But to be
more serious; what sense is there in shutting your eyes to the
one person who is well attested as having broken the grip of
death, and having come back to tell us not only that there is an
after-life, but how to get there? In business or commerce it
would be accounted sheer folly to go for short-term gains and
neglect capital appreciation — or depreciation. Yet that is just
what the man does who takes no thought for life after death. He
goes for short-term goals, and takes no account of the fact that

his capital, his life, is depreciating towards zero, when it could, if rightly invested, appreciate indefinitely. Christians assert, not just on the basis of documents written 2,000 years ago, but on the basis of continuing world-wide experience, that Jesus of Nazareth has broken the ultimate barrier in our universe: death. They may be right; they may not. That you must decide after investigation. But to shrug off the whole issue with 'I'm not the religious sort' is sheer folly if you think at all seriously about your future.

FAITH HAS TWO SIDES

Sometimes people say 'I'm not the religious sort' with a touch of wistfulness, rather as they say 'I wish I'd got your faith'. My answer to that is simple. You can have my faith. Faith is nothing other than trust; and trust, to be any good, must have two sides to it. First, there needs to be good evidence of trustworthiness; then there needs to be genuine commitment. It is as simple as that. You have faith in Rolls Royce engines when you fly in a jet, do you not? That means that in your opinion Rolls Royce engines are reliable; it also means that you are prepared to entrust yourself to their trustworthiness. So it is with Christianity. You need first to be convinced that there is a God, that he cares about mankind, that he has revealed himself in Jesus Christ, and that it is possible for you to get in touch with him. Then you need to entrust yourself to his trustworthiness.

In the pages that follow we shall be considering the various topics in a progression which will, I hope, help you both to appreciate the trustworthiness of God and also encourage you to entrust yourself to it. Then you will have my faith. Then you will be able to say 'I'm not the religious sort, but I think I have discovered the key to the universe.'

3

'You can't believe in God these days'

GOD IS OUT OF FASHION

Despite the opinion polls, which show that the majority of people in Western countries (not to mention the overwhelming majority in the East) do believe in God, it is amazing how often you hear the question of the Almighty dismissed in a single sentence, 'Oh, you can't believe in God these days.'

Very understandable in a way. We live in a very busy age, and many of us have neither the time nor the inclination to

enquire into abstruse subjects which do not directly concern us.
But what if there is a God who made us, loves us and will judge
us? Well, if that is the case, as Dr. Jowett, famous head of an
Oxford college once put it, 'It is not what I think of God, but
what God thinks of me that matters.'

Again, the idea of God has been so abused in the past that we
tend to shy away from it. God has been portrayed as the man in
the sky with the big stick. We have been told to be good and to
do the right thing because God would judge us if we offended.
God's will has been found a very useful tool for keeping people
in their places:

> The rich man in his castle,
> The poor man at his gate;
> God made them high and lowly,
> And ordered their estate.

A whole system of social and racial oppression has been founded on that view of God (a verse from the hymn 'All things
bright and beautiful', now generally omitted). Indeed, God's
will is something which certain people in certain ages have
claimed to be so sure about that they have engaged in religious
wars, like the Crusades, or religious persecutions, like the In-
quisition, to press their point. God has, furthermore, been used
as a sort of plug to fill gaps in scientific knowledge: even
Newton postulated God to keep the universe and its laws going.
But as scientific knowledge has grown, the gaps have shrunk
and God with them.

For all these reasons God is out of fashion. As *Time Magazine* headlined on its cover in April 1966, *God is Dead*! But it
is difficult to be sure about these things. Perhaps there is as
much fashion as there is reason about it all, for in December
1969 the headlines of *Time Magazine* were asking, *Is God
Coming to Life Again?* After all, you get no justification for
religious wars or inquisitions in the Bible. You do not find this
handbook of Christianity maintaining that you should do good
in case God should punish you for your failures. God is no-

where used in the Bible to plug the gaps in human knowledge: rather, he is portrayed as the source and sustainer and goal of the whole universe, including man and his knowledge. Perhaps we ought to look a little more closely at this claim that you can't believe these days. What is so special about these days that makes it harder for us to believe in God than it was for our fathers?

THE PROBLEM OF SCIENCE

First, there's the astonishing success of science. In the past fifty years the whole face of the world has changed. When my father was a boy there were no cars, no aeroplanes, and most people never moved more than a few miles from their own village. The change to space travel, nuclear technology, and the global village has all happened in his lifetime. No wonder men are confused. Science would seem to have won the day. No wonder many people pin all their hopes on it, and discard the idea of God. Sir Richard Gregory wrote his own epitaph:

> My grandfather preached the gospel of Christ.
> My father preached the gospel of socialism.
> I preach the gospel of science.

In point of fact, there is no battle between an informed belief in God and the assured results of science. The fathers of modern science, men like Kepler, Galileo, Copernicus and Bacon were earnest believers in God. They saw God's revelation in Scripture and in the natural world as complementary. Kepler, for instance, asserted. 'The tongue of God and the finger of God cannot clash.' The Cavendish Laboratory in Cambridge has inscribed above its entrance: 'The works of the Lord are great, sought out by all who have pleasure therein.' And, contrary to the belief of many, there is a high proportion of believing Christians among the leading scientists of the world.

But doesn't evolution rule out the possibility of a Creator? Far from it. The theory of evolution sets out to explain how varied forms of life have developed from more simple forms over millions of years. Belief in a Creator sets out to explain the great Mind behind all matter. There is no contradiction between the two. Interestingly enough, the Bible account of God's creation tells us something of the One who created, and something of why he did it. But it does not set out to tell us how. The world may have originated in a big bang or in a steady state; our first parents may have been developed from a collateral stock with monkeys or they may not. This is not a matter on which the Bible has anything to say. What it does say is that behind the creature lies the Creator, and that we are not only 'of the dust of the ground', and part of the physical universe, but are also in some sense infused with 'the breath of life' and made in the Creator's image. No discoveries in the realm of how life developed can repudiate that claim. If man discovers how to create life in a laboratory that would not put God out of business. It would simply show that when brilliant minds take matter (with real living matter to copy, incidentally) and arrange it in a very special way, a living particle may come into existence. In other words, matter arranged by intelligent minds can produce life. Exactly what Christians have always claimed for God. If we discover the secret of life, we shall merely be thinking the Creator's thoughts after him.

There is nothing in the scientific method that can either demonstrate God's existence or disprove it. But, for what it is worth, the basic presupposition of the scientific method strongly supports the existence of a Mind behind matter. It is axiomatic for all scientific enquiry that there is order and purpose in the physical world. Why should this be if the world sprang from chance and chaos? There are very few pure materialists around these days, for it is abundantly obvious that analysis of physical laws and chemical constituents cannot explain human behaviour, reason, emotion, wonder, speech, morals and worship. 'There are more things in heaven and earth than are dreamed of by your philosophy': these words of Shakespeare are applicable to the man who tries to make scientific materialism the only arbiter of truth. There is nothing in scientific procedure, still less in the theory of evolution, that need embarrass any believer in God the Creator.

THE PROBLEM OF SUFFERING

Second, there's the ghastly problem of suffering. Not that it is greater than ever before, but it seems greater. It is brought into the living room every night on T.V. How can there be a God if he allows all this pain and anguish in his world?

I do not want to minimise this problem for one moment. It is by far the strongest argument against the existence of God. But suppose for a minute that the problem of pain drives you to reject God's existence and to imagine that either some monster rules our destinies or that the stars are in charge of our fortunes, how does that help? You may have got rid of the problem of evil and pain (though you still have to live with them) but you have replaced them with a much bigger problem; how you get kindness and humanity, love and unselfishness, gentleness and goodness in a world that is governed by a horrid monster or uncaring stars. No, that way does not help.

As a matter of fact the Christian has a greater insight into the insoluble problem of suffering (and it remains insoluble, whatever philosophy of life you take up) than anyone else. For the Scriptures teach us that God is no stranger to pain. He did not start the world off and leave it callously to its own devices. He does not willingly afflict us, and take delight in torturing us. The very reverse. He cares so much about the agony and pain of this struggling world of his that he has got involved in it personally. He came as a man among men. He lived in squalor and suffering; he knew thirst and hunger, flogging and heart-break, fear and despair. He ended his life in one of the most excruciating ways known to man. Let nobody tell me that God doesn't care! Let nobody claim that the boss doesn't know what life is like on the shop floor!

Take a long hard look at the cross. Through that cross God is saying to you that he does care about pain. He cares passion-ately and selflessly. He cares so much that he came to share it.

He is for ever the Suffering God. The cross tells me that God loves me even in the midst of pain and suffering; when everything looked at its blackest Jesus was still the supreme object of his Heavenly Father's love. More, through that cross I can vaguely discern another truth: that God uses pain. He turns evil into good. For it was evil, real evil, that crucified Jesus. And yet by the way he took it he overcame evil; he turned hatred to love in some at least of his persecutors. He gave an example of innocent, uncomplaining suffering which has inspired men ever since, and enabled men like Bishop Wilson to win the hearts of some of the men who tortured him in a Japanese prison camp in the Second World War by means of his courage and spirit. And what makes such overcoming of pain possible? Not merely the cross of Jesus as an example to follow. One needs more than an example in the midst of agony. There was something else about the cross which has rubbed off on Christians ever since. It is the sense of victory. On the first Good Friday Jesus died with a cry of triumph on his lips: triumph over pain and hatred, suffering and death. And that was not the end. He rose from the chill grip of the tomb on the third day. From that moment onwards he enjoys the power of an endless life. Christians are people who have put their trust in him, come to know him, and begun to taste the power of his risen and endless life. How is it that the early Christians could look cheerfully at death in the arena from wild beasts and gladiators or being roasted on a grid? Simply because they were convinced that evil and pain had suffered a crucial defeat through what God did on that cross of Calvary and the resulting resurrection. Even death was a defeated foe. So they came to look on suffering not as an unmitigated evil, but as an evil which had been conquered by their suffering and triumphant God; an evil which he could even use to discipline them, to refine them, and to equip them for further usefulness and deeper Christlikeness. And the suffering but victorious God, the sinless but sinbearing God, has given on the cross of Christ a trailer of his future film. They could safely leave him to give fuller light on it all in the life to come, knowing that it would be a further explanation of the mystery of the cross, where, in the very midst of history, God showed that he cared about pain, shared it, and overcame it. To be sure, the Christian need not be worried that suffering in the world makes belief in God impossible these days. It is only belief in a suffering God that stops us from either becoming totally callous or going out of our minds at all the suffering which afflicts our world.

THE PROBLEM OF MEANINGLESSNESS

Third, there's the problem of meaninglessness. Never before in the history of mankind has there been such a widespread belief that in the end nothing matters; we came from nothing and we go to nothing. No values are implanted in us because there is no God to implant them; no part of the human frame survives death, because there is no eternity. Meaning has disappeared from life. More money, more leisure, yes: but don't talk to us about meaning in life, because there isn't any. A leading modern painter, Francis Bacon writes:

> Man now realises that he is an accident, that he is a completely futile being, that he has to play out the game without reason. Earlier artists were still conditioned by certain types of religious possibilities, which man now, you could say, has had cancelled out for him. Man can now only attempt to beguile himself for a time by prolonging his life — by buying a kind of immortality through the doctors ... The artist must really deepen the game to be any good at all, so that he can make life a bit more exciting.

What in fact the artist has done is to bring home this meaninglessness to every level of society. It comes through the films and the pop music. It is everywhere. Take David Crosby's song *If only I could remember my name*:

> I thought I met a man who knew a man who knew what was
> going on

I was mistaken — only another stranger that I knew.
I thought I'd found a light to guide me through the night and
    all its darkness
I was mistaken — only reflections of a shadow that I saw.
I thought I'd seen someone who seemed at last to know the
    truth
I was mistaken — only a child laughing in the sun.

Running to sex seems to be the way out of meaninglessness: but
no. This extract from the sex novel *Naked as the Wind from
the Sea* is typical:

> Everyone is confused after our last catastrophe. We are
> like ants whose stack has been taken away: we run around in
> all directions with the straw and want to build a new one. But
> they've taken away our meaning. All we can do is to struggle
> with our straw just the same . . .

Now if you are eaten up with this philosophy of meaninglessness, of course you won't find any sense in God talk. But
it is a chicken and egg situation. The philosophy of meaninglessness is an attempt by modern existentialists to draw the
full consequences from atheism. Deny God, and then see if you
can make sense of everything else. And the fact is that you
can't.

But try it the other way around. What if there is a God?
Then the world is not a mere fluke; it is the result of his creation. Man is not rubbish, but God's deputy on this earth. History is not bunk, but God's story struggling for expression
through all the follies of mankind. Life is not meant to be
understood simply in terms of the three score years and ten, but
as a training ground for being with God for ever. No longer
need we be torn between the very obvious order and purpose in
nature and the purposelessness, the meaningless lostness which
modern man finds in his heart. If modern man will return to the
Creator of order and purpose in nature, he will begin to find
order coming through in his own life, and a sense of purpose in
co-operating with the Creator in the management of his world.

THE PROBLEM OF PROOF

The fourth problem is the matter of proof. 'You can't prove God,' they say. Perfectly true. You can't. But you can't prove that your mother loves you, either. In fact, there are precious few things that you can prove, and they are by no means the most interesting things in life. To prove a thing really means to show that it could not be otherwise, a very final form of certainty. You cannot prove that the sun will rise tomorrow. You cannot prove that you are alive. You cannot prove the link between cause and effect which runs through every action we do. You cannot prove that you are the same man you were ten years ago. The philosopher, David Hume, attempted to prove the link between cause and effect and between himself as he then was and himself ten years previously, and he failed. Failed utterly. Proof is only applicable to very rarefied areas of philosophy and mathematics and even here there is debate. For the most part we are driven to acting on good evidence, without the luxury of proof. There is good evidence of the link between cause and effect. There is good evidence that the sun will rise tomorrow. There is good reason to believe that I am the same man as I was ten years ago. There is good reason to suppose that my mother really loves me and is not just fattening me up for the moment when she will pop arsenic into my tea. And there is good reason to believe in God. Very good reason. Not conclusive proof, but very good reason just the same. Let me outline to you why I believe it is much harder to reject the existence of a supreme being than to accept it.

1. THE FACT OF THE WORLD

Look at the fact of the world. So far as we know at present, this planet is the only part of the universe where there is life. What accounts for this world of ours? Whether we go for the 'Big Bang' theory or the 'Steady State' theory, we are driven to ask *why* it should be so? The world must have come from somewhere. It will not do to reply 'It is just one of those things.' It will not do to assign the whole thing to chance. If the world is due to chance, how is it that cause and effect are built into that world at every turn? It isn't very rational to suppose that chance gives birth to cause and effect! And it isn't very rational to argue that the world which is based on cause and effect is itself uncaused. Huxley once said, 'The link between cause and effect is the chief article in the scientist's creed.' If you think hard enough, science itself drives you back to believe in a Creator.

2. THE FACT OF DESIGN

Look at the fact of design. At every level the world of nature shows evidence of design. Think of the focusing equipment of an eye, of the radar of a bat, of the built-in gyroscope of a swallow, of the camouflage of a nesting pheasant. Or think of the perfect harmony of the laws of physics. Reflect on the marvel of conception and birth. At every point there is evidence of a great Designer. Even John Stuart Mill, a strong opponent of Christianity, came to the conclusion at the end of his life that 'the argument from design is irresistible. Nature does testify to its creator.' Einstein, too, spoke of his 'humble admiration for the illimitably superior Spirit who reveals himself in the slight details which we can perceive with our frail mind.' After Einstein had propounded his theory of relativity, and after its general acceptance following the Michelson–Morley experiment, the experiment was repeated and gave different results. But nobody doubted the relativity theory! Everyone assumed (rightly as it turned out) that the results must be due to experimental error, because the theory was too good, *too rational*, to be false. In other words, the physicists themselves were operating on the assumption of design in the universe, however much they might have claimed to be following merely experimental results.

Very well then, if there is design in the world, where did it come from? Not from us: we don't lay down the laws of nature or design the development of the foetus in the womb. It looks very much as though a Designer is at work.

Long ago Paley developed the argument by means of a watch. It runs something like this. 'See this watch? Well, in the old days people used to believe that a watchmaker had made it. The cogs, the pinions, the glass and numbers all bore the marks of intelligent design. But now we have grown out of that sort of thing. We know that a watch has gradually evolved. There is no design about it. Natural selection has slowly eliminated all elements that are irrelevant to watches. The metal has coalesced, the glass has grown over, the cogs have gradually developed, and last of all the strap grew.' Put like this it is not difficult to see how ridiculous the argument is; the man who advanced it would be ignored, if not hastily hustled into a mental hospital! Yet precisely the same argument is advanced about the world itself by sane men who think they are being both reasonable and avant-garde. To attribute marks of design to blind evolution makes no more sense in the case of the world than it does in the case of the watch. Paley's argument has been attacked on the ground that God is not a watchmaker. True, but Paley never said he was. God is far more than a watchmaker, if he is God at all. But he is assuredly not less! The argument from design is extremely persuasive, and to say with Jean-Paul Sartre, 'This world is not the product of Intelligence. It meets our gaze as would a crumpled piece of paper . . . What is man but a little puddle of water whose freedom is death?' is to shut your eyes to one of the clearest indications that there is a Creator God who has not left himself without witness. 'The heavens declare the glory of God and the firmament shows his handiwork' remains true: so does the Bible's assertion 'The fool has said in his heart, "There is no God." ' (Psalm 19: 1, and 14: 1).

3. The fact of personality

Look at the fact of personality. It is one of the most remarkable phenomena in the world. The difference between a person and a thing, between a live person and a dead one, is fundamental. When Sartre, in the quotation given above, denied that the

world was created by Intelligence, he was not only insulting his
Maker but his own power of reasoning. He was saying, in
effect, that there was no reason to believe what he was saying!
The fact is that we are not mere robots; there is more to us than
that — human personality. Some thinkers are so reluctant to
believe this that they have advanced the improbable creed of
materialism, seeking to reduce everything in life to what can be
measured scientifically. In other words, other people are mere
blobs of protoplasm: so am I. I have no future, no real existence. I think I am a conscious, rational being who can mix with
others like me. But no. Science knows nothing of rationality
and consciousness, of personality and sociability. It deals only
with molecules and magnestism, elements and electricity,
things which can be counted and measured. I have no place in
such language, and if that is the ultimate language of reality,
then I cannot describe myself, and am driven to the conclusion
that I do not exist. Not very plausible. But the alternative is
disturbing. It suggests that my personality cannot be explained
simply in terms of its physical components. I am more than
matter. Very well, but how come, if there is no God? Does a
river run higher than its source? Of course not. Then how do we
get human personality out of the inorganic matter which is the
brute stuff of which our universe is entirely composed, in the
atheist view? Can rationality and life spring from chance and
non-being? No, the fact of human personality is another impressive pointer to the God who created a man in his own
image. This is not to say that God is restricted to a personality
like ours: but it is to say that the ultimate source of our being is
not less than personal.

4. THE FACT OF VALUES

Look at the fact of values. We all have them, but they are very
hard to understand if there is no God. After all, you don't
expect to find values knocking around in molecules! Matter
does not give rise to morals. So modern Godless man is confused about where his values fit in. That comes across clearly in

The Who's record *The Seeker*, 'I've got values, but I don't know how or why'. We value life — but why should we if life really springs from chance? We value truth — but why should we if there is no ultimate reality? We value goodness — but what is that doing in a world derived from plankton? We revel in beauty — but there is nothing in it, since it too springs from the chaos in which our world originated. We value communication — but the universe is silent. Yes, we have our values, and they do not accord very well with the atheist's picture of the world, sprung merely from chance, matter, and millions of years to allow for extensive development. I do not find much basis for value judgments there.

But what if there is a Creator God? Then life is valuable because it is his greatest gift, hence the infinite value of every individual. Truth matters because it is one aspect of God, the ultimate reality. Beauty and goodness are likewise two of the 'faces' of God, and every good action or beautiful sight is an inkling of the good and beautiful source from which they come. Best of all, we do not inhabit a silent planet: God has spoken and revealed himself, to some extent at least, in the world, in its design, in values and in man. When we communicate it is not vain jabbering but a God-given ability, entrusted to us by the great Communicator himself. Those are two basic attitudes to values. I know which makes more sense to me. John Lucas, the Oxford philosopher, develops this argument clearly and simply:

> I want to do well. But it is impossible to do well unless there are values independent of me by which my performance can be assessed. I cannot want to do only what I want to do, or I am denying my nature as a rational agent. I must want to do what is worth doing, and what is worth doing is so not because I want it, but because independently of my desires, and whether I wish it or no.

The existence of values is a pointer to God which it is hard, indeed, to evade.

5. THE FACT OF CONSCIENCE

Look at the fact of conscience. That's a pointer to God if ever there was one. Your conscience doesn't argue. It acts like a lawgiver inside you, acquitting you or condemning you. It doesn't say, 'Do this because you will gain by it' or 'Do it because you will escape trouble that way.' It just says, 'Do it.' It is a most remarkable pointer to the God who put it there. Oh, of course it is not the voice of God straight and simple. It has been warped by all sorts of things, your environment, your rationalisations, your disobedience. But equally certainly conscience can't just be explained away as the pressure of society. It was not from any pressure by society that Newton and Wilberforce conscientiously fought for the liberation of slaves, or Martin Luther King championed the cause of the blacks. Their action was carried out in the teeth of opposition by society, and so it has always been with every moral advance.

Despite the diversity of human cultures the world over, there is actually remarkable agreement on the essential values to which conscience points: the general condemnation of murder and theft, of adultery and lust, of hijacking and hate. There is universal agreement that peace is right and war is wrong; that love is right and hate is wrong — however little men manage to carry it out in practice. And it is conscience that points us to this difference between right and wrong, and the claim that right has upon us. C. S. Lewis summed it up like this:

> If no set of moral ideas were better than another, there would be no sense in preferring civilised morality to Nazi morality. The moment you say one lot of morals is better than another, you are in fact measuring them by an ultimate standard.

Even Bertrand Russell, who during the earlier part of his life fought tooth and nail against the idea of an ultimate distinction between right and wrong, said, towards the end of his life, 'To love is right, to hate is wrong.' But how does he get such moral absolutes in what he claimed is a Godless world? It doesn't add up. You do not locate principles of conscience in a chance collection of atoms, which is all the world consists of if you remove the possibility of a Creator. No; morality, conscience, the difference between right and wrong are important indicators of a God who is interested in what is right and good and true. He is no blind force, no abstruse designer, but a personal God, so concerned with what is right that he has built a moral indicator into each one of his creatures.

6. THE FACT OF RELIGION

Look at the fact of religion. Man is a religious animal. In the sixth century B.C. philosophers in Greece poured scorn on religion, and invited men to grow up. Religion continued. And so it has done everywhere in the world ever since. The Russians sought to abolish religion after the Revolution in 1917. They failed. They tried again with violent persecution under Stalin. They failed. It is the same in China. Man is incurably religious. He is going to worship either God or a pseudo-god, but worship something he will, even if it is something very physical like his material prosperity or something very abstract like the idea of progress.

There is one fact about man that has distinguished him from his first appearance on earth. It marks him as different from all other creatures. That is, he's a worshipping animal. Wherever he has existed there are the remains, in some form or other, of his worship. That's not a pious conclusion: it's an observed fact. And all through history and prehistory when he's deprived himself of that he's gone to pieces. Many people nowadays are going to pieces, or they find the first convenient prop to tie their instincts on to. It's behind the extraordinary adulation of royalty. It's behind the mobbing of T.V. stars. If you don't give an expression to an instinct you've got to sublimate it or go out of your mind.

Such is the conclusion not of a philosopher or priest, but of a novelist, Winston Graham in *The Sleeping Partner*. He's right, isn't he?

These are some of the facts that, taken together, not only make belief in God reasonable, but make it very hard indeed rationally to deny his existence. They point to a God who is skilful, skilful enough to design the courses of the stars and the development of a foetus. They point to a God who is the source of human personality, and therefore not less than personal however much he may transcend all that we mean by that word. He is the ultimate source of our values: life and language, truth, beauty and goodness find their ultimate home in him. He is so concerned about right and wrong that he has furnished each of his creatures with a conscience. And he wants us to know him and to enjoy him, to worship and to live in his company — hence the universal religious instinct of men through history and throughout the world.

But he still remains the Unknown God. How are we to discover any more about him? Perhaps all religions lead to God. Let us examine that possibility in our next chapter.

4

'All religions lead to God'

AN ATTRACTIVE THEORY

UNTIL A FEW years ago comparative religion was a study for the handful of experts who busied themselves in such an odd subject. Now it is replacing the study of theology in universities all over the Western world and has a firm niche in religious instruction in schools. The reason, of course, is that we have at last woken up to the fact that the world is a global village, and the influx of Asians, Indians, Arabs and Pakistanis into Britain has meant that the problem of other religions has landed on our own doorstep. What are we to make of these other faiths? Presumably they are all much of a muchness. Presumably they are all pathways to God, and you might as well take your pick.

Such a view has immense attractions. It avoids the black and white choice and sees everything as a shade of grey. It is essentially tolerant, and tolerance is a very fashionable virtue. It is modest, and does not make strong pretensions for your own particular religion. It seems admirable common sense. We take the views of everybody, and try to build up an Identikit picture of God. And some extremely significant people and organisations back it up. For example the saintly Indian leader Mahatma Gandhi said, 'The soul of religions is one, but it is encased in a multitude of forms . . . Truth is the exclusive property of no single scripture . . . I cannot ascribe exclusive divinity to Jesus. He is as divine as Krishna or Rama or Mohammed or Zoroaster.' The Hindu mystic Ramakrishna used to speak of himself as the same soul that has been born before as Rama, as Krishna, as Jesus or as Buddha. The Roman Emperor Severus hedged his bets by having in his private chapel not only the statues of the deified emperors, but those of the miracle-worker Apollonius of Tyana, of Christ, of Abraham and of Orpheus! A very contemporary attitude, as this song of Quintessence makes plain:

> Jesus, Buddha, Moses, Gauranga,
> Draw me deep in the sea of your love
> Jesus, Buddha, Moses, Gauranga,
> Oh maya, oh maya, oh maya.

A very common view then — but it won't do, for two compelling reasons.

IT'S ILLOGICAL

It is a lovely sentimental idea to suppose that all religions are basically one, and that they all represent variations on a common theme. But unfortunately it flies in the face of all the evidence. How can all religions lead to God when they are so different? The God of Hinduism is plural and impersonal. The God of Islam is singular and personal. The God of Christianity is the Creator of the world. The divine in Buddhism is not personal and is not creative. You could scarcely have a greater contrast than that. Christianity teaches that God both forgives a man and gives him supernatural aid. In Buddhism there is no forgiveness, and no supernatural aid. The goal of all existence in Buddhism is *nirvana*, extinction — attained by the Buddha after no less than 547 births. The goal of all existence in Christianity is to know God and enjoy him for ever. The use of images figures prominently in Hinduism: Judaism prohibits making any image of God. Islam allows a man four wives; Christianity one. Perhaps the greatest difference of all lies between the Bible, which asserts that nobody can save himself and make himself pleasing to God, try as he will; and almost all the other faiths which assert that by keeping their teachings a man will be saved or reborn or made whole or achieve fulfilment. Nothing spells out this contrast more powerfully than the Buddhist story which starts off so like the parable of the Prodigal Son. The boy comes home and is met by the father, and then has to work off the penalty for his past misdeeds by years of servitude to his father. The principle of *karma* (cause and effect, paying off your guilt) is poles apart from grace (free forgiveness when you don't deserve it a bit).

I do not at this point want to evaluate different religious faiths. I just want to show how utterly illogical it is to say that they are all pointing in the same direction. It is as foolish as to say that all roads from Nottingham lead to London. They do nothing of the sort, and it is not helpful in the least to pretend that they do. They lead to radically different goals. Extinction or heaven; pardon or paying it off; a personal God or an impersonal monad; salvation by grace or by works. The contrasts are irreconcilable.

The trouble is that today's tolerance has reached the point where it is no longer a virtue but a vice. It is a cruel casualness to truth. It is no kindness to anyone if we tell everyone that their views are as true as anyone else's. We are simply displaying our cynicism, as if we said to a blind man sitting on the edge of a precipice, 'It doesn't matter which way you move. All paths lead to the same goal.'

Lesslie Newbigin, Christian bishop in Madras, has been forced to examine very carefully the difference between Christianity and other faiths. How could he help it, living in the midst of a Hindu culture? He puts it like this in his remarkable book, *The Finality of Christ*. The great divide among religions, he maintains, is their attitude to history. Most religions are like a wheel. 'The cycle of birth, growth, decay and death through which plants, animals, human beings and institutions all pass suggests a rotating wheel — ever in movement yet ever returning upon itself.' The wheel offers one way of escape from the meaningless, repetitive movement it generates. That is to take a spoke — it cannot matter which one — and travel along it to the hub, where all is at rest, and where you can observe the ceaseless movement without being involved in it. This is the way of most religions: 'dispute among the different "ways" is pointless; all that matters is that those who follow them should find their way to that timeless, motionless centre where all is peace, and where one can understand all the endless movement which makes up human history — understand that it goes nowhere and means nothing.'

The other great symbol is not a wheel but a road. This is the view of Judaism and Christianity. Newbigin expresses it thus:

> History is a journey, a pilgrimage. We do not yet see the goal, but we believe in it and seek it. The movement in which we are involved is not meaningless movement; it is movement towards a goal. The goal ... is not a timeless reality hidden behind the multiplicity and change which we experience. It is yet to be achieved; it lies at the end of the road.

That is the uniqueness of the Christian claim. God has intervened in history. The history of the Jewish people, the birth of

Jesus, the cross and the resurrection are milestones along that road which ends in heaven.

Not only, then, is it illogical to suppose that all religions lead to God: it is impossible.

IT'S IMPOSSIBLE

There are two reasons why it is impossible for us to find God through whatever religion you care to name. The first is because of the nature of God. If there is a God, then he is the source of both man and his environment. He is the Lord over all human life.

> Have you not known? Have you not heard? Has it not been told you from the beginning? It is he who sits above the circle of the earth, and its inhabitants are like grasshoppers ... Whom did he consult for his enlightenment, and who taught him the path of knowledge and showed him the way of understanding? Behold, the nations are like a drop from a bucket, and are accounted as dust on the scales; behold he takes up the isles like fine dust (Isaiah 40: 21ff).

That is the God we are talking about. How can we possibly climb up to him? How can the cup understand the potter who made it? It cannot be done. Man cannot find out God however hard he searches. Religion, all religion, is bound to fail.

As we have seen, we can have a go at it. But how far does it get us? The facts we considered in the last chapter get us a little way along the line, but only a very little way, and they amount to not much more than conjecture. The fact of the world indicates an outside cause. Design in the world suggests this cause's intelligence. The fact of human life suggests that this cause is not only intelligent but personal. Conscience indicates his concern about right conduct, and values like truth, beauty and goodness may have their origin in him. The fact that no nation in the world has lived without belief in God suggests that God wants man's worship.

But so what? He remains the unknown God. You can get so far by inference, but no further. After that you need to hear from him, or meet him — or both. The creature cannot possibly discover the Creator, unless he chooses to disclose himself. That is one reason why all religions are bound to disappoint. And as a matter of fact that is precisely what they all do.

Christopher Mayhew published a book some years ago, entitled *Men in Search of God*. In it, representatives of various world religions gave their account of their religious experience, and their search for God. Not surprisingly, none of them claimed to have found him. Gordon Bailey puts it epigrammatically in his little poem *If*.

> If
> all religions
> lead to God
> how come
> most of them,
> having been given
> a thousand years at least,
> haven't yet
> arrived?

If by 'religion' we mean man's search for the divine, it is bound to fail. What we need is not to compare the chinks of light that each of us may have grasped, but for the day to dawn. We need not a religion but a revelation. And that is precisely what Christianity claims to be. A revelation from God. Unlike other holy books, the Bible does not bring us the story of men in search of God; it tells us about the God who comes in search of men.

No through road

There is a second reason why religion will never win through to God. Not simply because of the nature of God, but because of the nature of man. The Bible gives a pretty unflattering picture of man, but one that is uncomfortably near the mark. It tells us several unpleasing truths.

For instance, it informs us that we are not the earnest lovers of God that we would like to suppose: on the contrary, we are 'enemies in our minds by wicked deeds'. We do not have that heart of gold which we like to think we have: on the contrary 'the heart of man is deceitful above all things and desperately sick'. It tells us that we are not impartial in our search for the truth: on the contrary, 'men suppress the truth in unrighteous living'. We do not follow every gleam of light that comes our way: on the contrary, 'men love darkness rather than light because their deeds are evil' (Colossians 1: 21, Jeremiah 17: 9, Romans 1: 18, John 3: 19).

There seems to be a basic twist in human nature which makes us incapable of welcoming the best when we see it. More often than not we want to get rid of it, because it shows us up. One of the more pathetic illusions of humanism is that men are all good folk at heart, and given decent environment, decent working conditions, plenty of money and secure employment they will all be good citizens, and the heart of gold will shine out. What rubbish! If we are all good folk at heart why does the crime rate go up every year along with our prosperity? (In London it has increased twenty fold in the last fifty years, and in a recent survey ninety per cent of London youngsters under sixteen admitted they had at some time or other engaged in theft). If we were all good folk at heart, how we would flock to the best person there has ever been, Jesus Christ. But anyone who has had any experience in evangelism, in bringing others to share in the joy of the Christian life, knows what a battle generally ensues before the person in question finally gives in to Christ. I have seen 'good' men sweating with the intensity of their struggle to keep clear of the Light of the world. Francis Thompson knew what he was talking about in that poem of his, *The Hound of Heaven*, which begins:

> I fled him down the nights and down the days
> I fled him down the arches of the years

> I fled him down the labyrinthine ways
> Of my own mind, and in the mist of tears
> I hid from him, and under running laughter.

The very fact that we hide from him shows that we are self-centred creatures at heart, just as the Bible says we are. And we have another closely allied problem. There is something wrong with our will. We don't seem to be able to live up even to our own occasional efforts after high standards. How long do your New Year resolutions last, for instance? How long does that peace and goodwill of the Christmas period continue in your office? Or how many times have you given up smoking? Jesus put his finger on the trouble when he said, 'Whoever does wrong becomes a slave of wrong.'

No wonder Paul comes to the conclusion that the Old Testament had reached before him, as he draws to the end of his shattering indictment of contemporary pagan and religious society. 'There is none righteous, no, not one. There is none that understands and seeks after God' (Romans 3: 10, 11). The myth is exploded. We are not honest seekers after God. Most of us, most of the time, are only too thankful to keep out of his way. All men are disqualified, whether they come from the so-called Christian West, the Communist bloc or the mystic East. None have arrived at God, both because he is too great for any of his creatures to pierce his incognito; and because his creatures are too twisted, too self-centred to want to. The greatness of God and the sinfulness of man are two massive barriers to our supposing that all religions lead to God. They do nothing of the sort. No religions lead to him.

ONLY ONE HOPE

There is only one hope, and that is the possibility of revelation. We cannot reach God, but there is no reason why he should not reach us. That is a consideration which escaped the celebrated Herbert Spencer, a leading agnostic. He maintained, sensibly enough, that no man has ever been known to penetrate with his finite mind the veil which hides the mind of the Infinite. He concluded that the Infinite could not be known by the finite, and that agnosticism was therefore secure. Not at all. There is no reason why the Infinite should not make himself known to the finite, and the Bible gives the account of the only faith which claims that he has done precisely that.

A REVELATION

Suppose for a moment you were God. The people you had made have turned their backs on you. They do not want to share their lives with you. They want to go their own way. What are you to do? You might start with a likely individual, and work on him and his descendents. God did that: the likely individual was called Abraham. He trusted God, obeyed him, and became the father of the Jewish nation. But that nation strayed away from the path Abraham had trodden. What was to be done? Perhaps a time of hardship in a foreign and oppressive country might make them come to their senses? That is what Israel's time in Egypt was all about, and later on the medicine had to be repeated in the Babylonian exile. You might raise up prophets to call the people back to yourself. God did just that, too. 'Listen to the words of my servants the prophets,' says the Lord, 'whom I sent unto you, rising up early and sending them . . . but you have not listened.' Finally, if you cared enough, you might come in person, for a sort of summit visit, after your staff had sufficiently prepared the way. That, too, God did at the first Christmas. The way was as prepared as it could be. The Jewish nation after two thousand years of history was passionately persuaded that there was one God, and no runners up. The Roman Empire had secured peace throughout the known world. The Greek language was universal, and its culture pervasive. The stage was set for the maximum impact of God's personal visit. And so the one called Jesus ('God the rescuer'), or Emmanuel ('God is with us'), was born. The God who had over many centuries and in many different ways spoken through his prophets to the people, had at last spoken a clear,

final and decisive message, not through a prophet but in the
person of his Son. At long last men could see that God is, God
speaks, God cares. No longer is he the unknown God. 'No man
has seen God at any time, but the only begotten one, himself
God, has made him known' was how one eyewitness summed
the matter up (John 1: 18). Jesus shows us in terms of a human
life what God is like. That was the first purpose of his coming
to our world, to bring us the revelation of God without which
we would still be fumbling vainly in the dark.

A RESCUE

His coming had a second purpose, as well, closely linked with
the first. For when mankind saw that perfect life of uprightness
and love, the highest and the best imaginable, they nailed him
to a cross. He was too uncomfortable. His was too blazing a
light. The natural instinct of mankind who likes living in the
dark was, and is, to extinguish that embarrassing light. They
did not succeed, of course. 'The light goes on shining in the
darkness, and the darkness did not quench it,' but they had a
jolly good try. Do you see what happened? The coming of Jesus
did not merely show us what God is like. It also showed up
what man is like. 'Men loved darkness rather than light because
their deeds were evil,' wrote St. John; and if you want com-
mentary on that verse ask yourself what would happen to the
circulation of the Sunday papers if they started recording acts
of virtue rather than deeds of vice! There you have clear evidence that men love darkness rather than light. So we human
beings need something more basic even than a revelation from
God. We need a rescue by God.

Not only our understanding but our will is at fault. Jesus
came to rectify both. He showed us what God was like by his
incomparable life. He put us right with God by his sacrificial
death. That is why the cross is the symbol of Christianity. It is
the most important achievement of the whole of his life, indeed
in the whole of history. There Jesus, the God-man, took responsibility for all the evil of mankind. 'He suffered for sins,

the just for the unjust, so as to bring us to God,' said one
eyewitness (1 Peter 3: 18). 'Herein is love, not that we loved
God, but that he loved us, and sent his Son to be the remedy for
the defilement of our sins,' writes another (1 John 4: 10).
Another New Testament writer cries out in exultation, 'There
is now no condemnation for the man who is united to Christ'
(Romans 8: 1) because 'God sending his own Son in the likeness of human flesh, and as a sin offering, condemned sin in the
flesh [i.e. of Christ].' Wherever you look in the New Testament
you find the same truth, however variously it is expressed. In
the pictorial language of the Book of Revelation you find it put
like this: 'I saw a great multitude, whom no man could number,
of all nations and kindreds and peoples and tongues stand
before the throne and before the Lamb, clothed with white
robes, and palms in their hands, saying with a loud voice "Salvation belongs to our God who sits on the throne and to the
Lamb" ' (Revelation 7: 9, 10).

NOTHING LIKE IT

The symbolism is plain. These people from every background
in the world are praising God in heaven, and thanking him for
his rescue operation that covers the scruffy clothes of their fancied goodness with the perfect white robe of Christ's righteousness. As the writer goes on to say a few verses later, 'These are
they who have washed their robes and made them white in the
blood (i.e. the death) of the Lamb (i.e. Jesus, willingly
sacrificed for them).' A rescue operation indeed. Where else in
the religions of the world do you hear of a God who undertakes
salvation for his people by personally bearing responsibility for
their wickedness and allowing it to crush him?

But even that is not all. The God who has revealed himself
and rescued us has done it for a purpose. Amazingly, he wants
to relate to us. That is where the resurrection comes in. He is no
dead figure in a history book, two thousand years out of date.
He is alive, and we can have dealings with him. I remember
vividly the day when this truth became a reality to me. I asked

the Risen One to come and live in me. He has done so. I have
not found God. I could not if I wanted to, and I would not have
wanted to anyway, so self-centred was I. But he has found me.
He came to earth to reveal himself to me. He died to remove
the beastliness of my wrongdoing. He lives, and is at work
changing my life from the inside. And all this I find to be very
good news.

No other faith does anything remotely like this. No other
faith claims to. Christianity is quite distinct from other religions. It is not a case of man in search of God but of God in
search of man. Not a religion at all, but a revelation and a
rescue.

It is at this point that two important questions arise.

'IF YOU ARE RIGHT ABOUT JESUS, ARE OTHER RELIGIONS ALL WRONG?'

By no means. The God who made the world, the God who
revealed himself in Christ, has not left himself without witness
in the world. Every good thought, every gleam of light, every
word of truth to be found in any religion, and in atheistic philosophies like Marxism as well, is part of God's self-disclosure.
All truth is God's truth, and has its focus in the one who
became incarnate. So Christians welcome truth wherever it is
found. As you look into other faiths you will find an enormous
amount that is true and worthy, that is moral and good, as well
as much that is not. But you will not find anything that is good
and true which cannot be found in Christ. You will not hear
from them about a God who cares for you enough to die for
you, to rise from the grave as a pledge of your future, and to be
willing to come and share your life with you. You will not find
in any other faith a revelation of God in fully personal terms, a
rescue of man from his self-centredness and sin, and the offer
by this God to come and indwell the life of every man, woman
or child who welcomes him.

It is not that Christians are narrow-minded about other
faiths. But if Jesus is, as the resurrection asserts, God himself

come to our rescue, then it is crass folly to reject him. And this is something that we can investigate for ourselves. We are not dealing with myth and legend, such as makes it impossible to know when Buddha lived (estimates vary between 1000 and 500 B.C.) or details of his birth (there are 547 birth stories). We are dealing with history. Christians claim (and there is plenty of documentary evidence to support the claim) that Jesus of Nazareth rose from the dead on the first Easter Day in A.D. 30 or 31 and launched the Christian community. His scattered followers did not expect it. To begin with they did not believe it. But they were driven to do so by their experience of the risen Jesus, and once they were convinced, nothing could silence them. For they had discovered the key to life. They did not claim merely that a corpse has been resuscitated. That would not have done much good. They believed that Almighty God took our nature as the man Jesus, that he suffered and died, *and that death could not hold him*! His resurrection says 'Yes' to his claim to be the Way, the Truth and the Life. The resurrection vindicates his claim to deity. In the risen Jesus God confronts us with shattering directness. He offers us total aid; but he demands of us total obedience. It is splendid to have an interest in comparative religion. But the more you know of others the more you see Christianity to be unique. And the key to Christianity is the resurrection.

I have investigated the reliability of the resurrection with some care in a little book *Man Alive*, and we shall be looking at the evidence more briefly in Chapter 9. But the point is this. Christianity is a historical religion. It claims that God has taken the risk of involving himself in human history, and the evidence is there for you to examine with the utmost rigour. The facts will stand any amount of critical examination. No book on earth has been subjected to such prolonged and detailed scrutiny by some of the best minds in the world over many hundreds of years as the New Testament. Examine the evidence for yourself, and do not rely on second hand opinions from those who believe the Christian story or from those who reject it. This is the most important issue you will ever have to

decide. Did Jesus rise from the dead or not? If not, then there
will be time enough to look to all the other faiths in the world,
to see what help for living can be found in them. But if he did
rise, and you are persuaded of it, then that settles for you the
question of which religion. Christ can no longer appear to you
just as a very fine man. Although fully human he somehow
brings God to you. And as God he claims your loyal obedience.

The second question that commonly arises at this point is
this.

'IF YOU ARE RIGHT ABOUT JESUS, ARE ALL NON-
CHRISTIANS INEVITABLY LOST?'

Here again the answer is No. It is certainly not taught in the
New Testament that all who have not heard of Jesus Christ are
inevitably lost. The whole Bible makes it plain that men will be
judged by God with utter fairness and they will be judged by
their response to such light as they have had. In a famous passage of his Letter to the Romans Paul maintains resolutely that
God has no favourites. 'When Gentiles who do not have the
Law do by nature what the Law requires, they constitute a law
over against themselves (even though they do not have the
Law). They show that what the Law requires is written on their
hearts, while their conscience also bears witness and their
conflicting thoughts either accuse or perhaps excuse them, on
that day when God judges the secrets of men by Jesus Christ'
(Romans 2: 14, 15). He means that heathen nations who do not
have God's revelation in the Scriptures still have a knowledge
of right and wrong; their moral sense acts as law-giver and
judge within them, and either commends or condemns them for
what they do. God is absolutely fair. But Paul goes on to show
that this breath of opportunity does not much help. For pagan
and Jew alike have failed to keep God's holy law, or even their
own relative standards, the inner law of conscience. No man,
therefore, can be reconciled with God on the grounds of his own
goodness and sincerity; for no man's goodness and sincerity are
perfect — far from it, in fact. Paul's solemn conclusion of that

whole passage in the first three chapters of Romans, where he surveys the moral records of religious and pagan world alike, is this: 'every mouth shall be stopped, and all the world shall be found guilty before God' (3: 19). And that is the backcloth against which he sets forth the joyful news that what no man can do for himself, or for anyone else, God has done for all who will trust him, be they religious or pagan by background. He has made it possible for us to be accepted in his beloved Son, Jesus Christ.

Christ died 'not for our sins only', says the New Testament, 'but for the sins of the whole world'. He died so that men of faith in Old Testament days could have their accusing record wiped clean. Now Abraham and the others did not know how God would find it possible to accept sinful men like themselves. They just trusted him when he made it clear to them that they were accepted. We, with our greater perspective, know that Abraham was saved because of what God in Christ was going to do for him on that cross of Calvary. It would seem consistent, therefore, with God's gracious activity, that those who have not heard of Christ in centuries since Calvary could also wake up on the other side of death to find themselves accepted with God, if they have really repented of their sins and cast themselves upon the mercy of God. For did not Jesus teach us that his heavenly Father is accustomed to give to everyone who asks, and to open the door to everyone who asks? The condition of asking, of seeking, of knocking, of repenting in self-abandonment and despair at our own goodness — that is the human side. But God's side has been made plain at the cross. He is prepared to accept any man of any tribe at any time into his heavenly kingdom.

It has sometimes been thought that to admit this would be to cut the nerve of missionary endeavour. But this is not the case. Many a missionary has gone to a place where the gospel has never been preached. He has spoken of the love of God for sinners. The response from one or two of his hearers, but by no means all of them, has been to say, 'We have been looking for something like this all our lives. We gladly repent and surrender our lives to the God who has so loved us. But, oh, why did you not come and tell us this before?'

It has sometimes been thought that to admit this 'wider hope' is to let us off the hook of deciding for Christ or against him. But nothing could be further from the truth. The heathen in a pagan land, who repents and believes the first time he hears the gospel, has been searching for years. He is in a very different situation from the careless Western churchgoer who says, 'What about all those who have never heard the gospel? Surely all religions lead to God?' in order to avoid commitment of any sort. Such a man is frivolous. He has no excuse for rejecting the Light of the world, Jesus. For the evidence lies open to him in the Scriptures, which he can buy for a few pence. He is surrounded by Christian believers who know from first hand the experience the truth of what is written in those Scriptures. He is without excuse if he does not follow the lead of the Scriptures and the men who have found the truth, in coming to Jesus in the surrender of faith and obedience.

There is one category of people who, the New Testament tells us, will be lost. It is not those who have never heard. It is those who have heard and said 'No'. Such were many of the Pharisees in the time of Jesus. He sadly had to say of them, 'You search the Scriptures, because you think that in them you have eternal life. But you would not come to me that you might have life.' And when in his second letter to the Christians at Thessalonica Paul speaks of the possibility of hell, he does so in the terrifyingly simple terms of 'everlasting destruction from the presence of the Lord', and he asserts, following his Master, that it awaits those who, having heard the good news of God's rescue, 'obey not the gospel of our Lord Jesus Christ' (2 Thessalonians 1:9). Let us make sure we do not belong to their number.

5

'Jesus was just a good man'

OURS IS A questing generation. We won't take anything on authority, and if an opinion is old it is probably wrong! We want instant truth, instant relevance. Old dogmas such as the Church's view that Jesus of Nazareth was divine simply don't turn us on any more. And yet we remain fascinated by Jesus. Books about him continue to pour from the presses despite the soaring cost of paper and printing. Films about him are box office successes. Rock operas such as *Jesus Christ Superstar* and

Godspell get top world ratings. He certainly has not lost his appeal. But we aren't quite sure what to make of him.

David Essex, who played Jesus in *Godspell,* was asked why he thought there was such a vogue for religious musicals. Did it say anything about us as a generation? He replied, 'I think it does. We all went through a period of trying to find a complete mystic experience. Lots of people tried drugs and lots of people tried Eastern religions. Then we found that that didn't work, so consequently we went back to Christianity, but in a kind of new way. We identified in Jesus a *different* kind of man, a kind of Che Guevara figure, if you like, that wasn't political.'

I find that helpful. Jesus was, on any showing, a great man, a good man, a fabulous teacher, heroically dedicated. But so have others been. David Essex begins to put his finger on that special quality about Jesus when he says 'a different kind of man'. Let's get back to the New Testament documents and look a bit closer at that difference — and then see whether the easy solution 'Jesus was just a good man' will carry conviction or not.

1. HIS CHARACTER WAS DIFFERENT

Different from any man who ever lived. That character has dominated the world in the two thousand years since he walked the narrow streets of Nazareth. To be sure, Mohammed has had profound influence, and so has Socrates. But nothing like Jesus. Jesus has captured the heart and mind and allegiance of peasant and king, of intellectual and illiterate the world over, all down the centuries. It makes no difference whether you go to the Naga tribesmen in the hill country of India, or the warlike Masai in Kenya, black and white in Southern Africa and the U.S.A., the men of Fiji and of Finland, of Singapore and Sebastapol. Everywhere there are Christians. Wherever the message of this man Jesus has been proclaimed, some men of every tribe and culture and background and intellect have turned from their own ways to follow him. This has brought opposition, often persecution. It has meant self-sacrifice and ostracism. But that has not stopped people succumbing to the spell of Jesus.

You could, I suppose, say the same of Lenin or Mao. At least, nearly the same. They have a tremendous following in certain parts of the world. Their followers have often gained in material prosperity, in living standards, and in a goal to live for. But the appeal has been to one class of person only. Mao brings hope to the oppressed worker, but offers nothing but doom to the bourgeois. Jesus too offers hope, justice, and love to the poor, but he also reaches the rich and disillusioned. He changes them, to be sure; but he does not threaten them or require of them the rejection of their class. Moreover the philosophy behind a Lenin or a Mao has a lot of envy and hate about it, a lot of ruthlessness in the pursuit of ideology, and a terrifying indifference to truth. Where do you find, in the whole history of mankind, a character that has dominated and appealed to men of every generation and type, and in so doing has transformed them for the better? Nowhere but Jesus. That one solitary life is without parallel. Do you know that anonymous piece entitled 'One Solitary Life'? Here it is:

He was born in an obscure village, the child of a peasant woman.

He grew up in still another village, where he worked in a carpenter's shop till he was thirty. Then for three years he was an itinerant preacher.

He never wrote a book. He never held an office. He never had a family or owned a house. He didn't go to college. He never visited a big city. He never travelled two hundred miles from the place where he was born. He did none of the things one usually associates with greatness.

He had no credentials but himself.

He was only thirty-three when the tide of public opinion turned against him. His friends ran away. He was turned over to his enemies and went through the mockery of a trial. He was nailed to a cross between two thieves. While he was dying, his executioners gambled for his clothing, the only

property he had on earth. When he was dead he was laid in a
borrowed grave through the pity of a friend.

Nineteen centuries have come and gone, and today he is
the central figure of the human race and the leader of mankind's progress. All the armies that ever marched, all the
navies that ever sailed, all the parliaments that ever sat, all
the kings that ever reigned, put together, have not affected
the life of man on this earth as much as that ONE SOLI-
TARY LIFE.

If Jesus was just a good man, I wonder what it was that made
his life so different? David Essex called him 'a kind of Che
Guevara figure that wasn't political'. Che is a marvellous parallel . . . and contrast. Son of a rich family, himself a highly
educated banker and doctor, he gave himself to the cause of the
underprivileged in Bolivia. Like Jesus before him, 'though he
was rich, yet for your sakes he became poor . . .' Like Jesus, he
led a movement of radical opposition to the corrupt existing
regime. Like Jesus, he was betrayed and killed. Like Jesus, he
evoked the admiration and dedication of a worldwide band of
followers. But there the similarity ends. Unlike Che, Jesus did
not preach or practise hatred and violence against his foes:
rather, love. Unlike Che, he did not take up arms. Unlike Che,
he was not tricked to his death, but went to it in the dignity of a
voluntary choice. Unlike Che, he does not remain dead and
gone, with nothing but his memory and ideals to cheer his followers. For Jesus lives, as we shall see in Chapter 9, and it is
highly significant that in the past couple of years or so there has
broken out a Christian revival in Bolivia, in which over 60,000
people have turned from the shadow to the reality, from Che
Guevara to Christ. There is, you see, something different about
him.

2. HIS TEACHING WAS DIFFERENT

Nobody ever taught like this. That was the conclusion of the
soldiers sent to arrest him. St. John tells us that when the Phari-

sees asked them why they had not obeyed orders, they replied 'No man ever spoke like this man' (John 7: 46). He taught them, says the earliest evangelist, as one who had authority, and not like the teachers of the day. These men would prop up their opinions by endless references to teachers before them who had held the same view — rather like the acres of footnotes in modern scholarly books about God. Jesus prefaced his teaching with the remarkable formula, unknown in all literature, 'Truly, truly I say to you.' Who was this 'I' who spoke with such authority? Who was this man who spoke so much about the Kingdom of God, and calmly announced that he was bringing it in? 'Until John, it was the law and the prophets,' he once said. 'Since then, it is the good news of the Kingdom of God.' In other words, his forerunner, John the Baptist, marked the end of the old era: he inaugurated the new. This accounts for the note of urgency which runs through those remarkable parables of his. The farmer who has been sowing and tending his seed now has to harvest the crop: if he lets the moment pass, the crop is lost. The pearl fancier who finds the best pearl he has ever seen, or the ploughman who turns up a bag of buried treasure in a field — for both zero hour has arrived: they must go for it even if it means gambling their whole capital. The generous house-holder has spread his banquet and invited all and sundry; to make excuses at this juncture, to refuse the invitation would be disastrous — it would mean final exclusion from the party. No wonder that the whole countryside was agog at teaching like this. There was nothing comparable in the religious history of the world.

You only had to compare Jesus' teaching with the Old Testament to get the message. Now, don't get me wrong. Jesus took the Old Testament as his Bible. He believed that it was inspired by God, and was therefore decisive both for himself and his hearers. But still he can contrast his teaching with it, not as black against white, but as fulfilment over against promise. 'I have not come to abolish the law and the prophets, but to fulfil,' he claimed (Matthew 5: 17). And he proceeded to show what he meant. 'Your goodness has to be better than that of the religious leaders,' he maintained — and explained that many religious men make a show of their piety in order to impress men; they give to be praised by men; and they pray to be seen by men. Secret prayer, unseen generosity, unostentatious religion is the order of the day for the follower of Jesus.

Or take the matter of murder. 'You have heard that it was said to the men of old, "You shall not kill; and whoever kills shall be liable to judgment." But I say to you that everyone who is angry with his brother without cause shall be liable to judgment' (Matthew 5: 21). Jesus is not abolishing the Old Testament law of manslaughter. He is fulfilling the principle behind it, for he is showing how God hates the evil thought of uncontrolled fury no less than the bitter outcome in murder. Again, he takes the famous maxim from the Old Testament, 'An eye for an eye and a tooth for a tooth' and adds, 'But I say to you, "Do not resist one who is evil." ' (Matthew 5: 38). Is he repudiating the Old Testament principle? Not at all. He perceives the principle that lay behind it (that of limiting revenge to the equivalent of the wrong done) and fulfils that principle by allowing love to banish revenge altogether.

This matter of love was hard enough to fulfil, even to the folk you liked. So the Old Testament had said, 'You shall love your neighbour,' and to it the scribes had enthusiastically added what the Old Testament did not add, 'and hate your enemy'! To this Jesus brings an undreamed-of fulfilment, a new thing in the history of thought, an ethic which is the most difficult and the most powerful in today's world as it was then: 'But I say to you, Love your enemies, and pray for those who persecute you, just as your heavenly Father does' (Matthew 5: 43).

If you want more of this, turn to the Sermon on the Mount in Matthew chs. 5–7. But the point is clear enough. Though Jesus built on God's revelation in the Old Testament, he taught a fulfilment of what had been foreshadowed there which was breathtakingly new, completely lucid, intensely profound, and as relevant now as it was then.

Now I ask you. Where can you find anything in the teaching of Jesus that does not strike you as truth? Where can you find anything that strikes you as error? How do you account for the fact that no ethical advances, no teaching of how men should behave towards their fellows has emerged in the centuries since then which represent any advance on the Man of Nazareth? Where did the man get this fantastic teaching from? He had an answer: 'My teaching is not mine, but His that sent me' (John 7: 16). Could he be right? Did he come from God? Could this account at one fell swoop for his authority, his simplicity, his depth, his world-wide appeal? If you reply, 'Of course not: he was just a very impressive teacher,' I want to ask you a question or two.

Why did he strike contemporaries and subsequent generations as so utterly different from other teachers? How is it that he got all this learning without having been to college? How is it that, unlike other great teachers such as Socrates and Mohammed, his teaching fits all men everywhere? How is it that nobody has dreamed up any moral advances since his teaching? What was there in his heredity and his environment to account for this unique teacher, and the remarkable fact that no greater has ever looked like emerging? Yes, there was something different about this teacher. Perhaps it was not so strange when he took over the old Jewish saying 'When two or three busy themselves over the Law of God, the glory of God shines upon them' and replaced it with 'Where two or three are gathered together in my name, there am I in their midst' (Matthew 18: 20). Perhaps he *was* different.

3. HIS BEHAVIOUR WAS DIFFERENT

Time and again he told doubters not to believe him unless his behaviour bore him out. His works, as he sometimes called them, had to match his words. And they did. Exactly. How sublime to be able to tell the story of the shepherd who goes out at night and braves danger to seek one lost sheep — and carries on until he finds it. But more sublime still to go and live it out by loving a Simon Peter even when he denied knowing him, and deserted him in his moment of greatest need. It is marvellous to find Jesus talking of the love his Father has for all men irrespective of their merits; love which, like the rain and sunshine, falls on all alike. It is even more marvellous to give the favourite's portion at a supper party to the man you know is just about to betray you, and then to kiss him on the cheek as he does so! It is one thing to say 'Blessed are the poor', and quite another to be happy in poverty, as Jesus was. One thing to say 'Bless your enemies', and quite another matter to cry 'Father, forgive them' as cruel soldiers nail your bleeding body to a cross. But that is the way Jesus behaved. His actions matched his teaching.

That is something that has never been equalled. Socrates, Plato, Moses, Confucius, and in our own day Martin Luther King, Pope John, or Billy Graham taught wonderful things and men have hung on their words. But never did any of these great men actually manage to carry out all they taught. In all of them there has been consciousness of failure. Indeed, this is one of the surest marks of greatness — to recognise that one's object exceeds one's reach, the goal lies far beyond the achievement. And growth in greatness always carries with it growth in humility. Talk to any truly great individual, and he will tell you how ashamed he is of his failures and of his mistakes. The most famous saints are always most conscious of wrong within.

But Jesus was different. He taught the highest standards that any teacher has formulated, and he kept them. He really did. There is remarkable unanimity on this matter. It is interesting to note how united the opposition to Jesus is about his innocence. Three times in the account of the trial before Pilate, the governor pronounces his innocence. Pilate's wife sends a message to the courtroom to the same effect. The Jewish leaders cannot find an accusation which will stick, and so they have to get him to incriminate himself by admitting to be the Messiah. Even the traitor Judas confesses that he has betrayed innocent blood. Even the brigands crucified with him recognised that he had done nothing wrong. Even the man in charge of the crucifixion was driven to exclaim, 'This man was innocent.'

Quite an impressive bunch of testimony from the Opposition benches. Jesus was different.

Perhaps still more impressive is the testimony of his friends. The more we know someone, the less inclined we are to entertain any exaggerated claim on their behalf: we know them too well. But not in Jesus' case. John knew him intimately. Yet he could call Jesus 'the true Light which gives light to every man', and could assert, 'If we say we have no sin we deceive ourselves ... but in him there is no sin.' Peter could call him 'the just one' in contrast to us 'the unjust', and could be so overcome by the quality of Jesus' life that he fell at his feet on one occasion and asked him to depart from a sinner like himself. Paul calls Jesus the sinless one; the writer to the Hebrews spoke of him as just the one we need, 'holy, blameless, unstained, separate from sinners'. In short, every strand of the New Testament, written as it was by those who knew Jesus or knew of him well, is quite clear on this matter: his life was perfect. It was a moral miracle. His life was different from other men's, and showed theirs up.

This is precisely what we seem to find in Jesus' own allusions to his behaviour. We never find him having to apologise. We never find him having to admit he was wrong. And this from the man who was so shrewd in spotting hypocrisy in others! There are several occasions when we are given the substance of his prayers; but never once do they betray any shadow of consciousness of guilt. He tells us to pray 'Forgive us our trespasses', but significantly he does not seem to need to do so himself. Fascinating. Unique. Here is a person of the most refined spiritual insight who can say of his heavenly Father, 'I do always those things that please him' (John 8: 29). Here is a man who can turn to an angry crowd furious because he was claiming that he was one with God, and with childlike innocence can ask them, 'Which of you can convict me of sin?' (John 8: 46). I do not know which is the more remarkable: that he could ask such a question — or that he could not be faulted by the crowd!

Whichever way you look at it, that life was unique. He alone of all the people known to history has come down to us with a clean sheet. No mud slung at him has stuck. His behaviour was blameless. What other man has behaved like that? Even for one day? Very well then, will it do simply to say 'Jesus was no more than a fine teacher'? Isn't that a very shallow assumption, in the light of a life that was so staggeringly different?

4. HIS ABILITIES WERE DIFFERENT

You cannot disentangle Jesus from miracle. Scholars in the last century spent endless ingenuity on the quest of a non-miraculous Jesus. In the end it was an acknowledged failure. Because every strand in the evidence about Jesus shows him as different from other men: through him God acted in a way impossible to understand on the assumption that he was just a good man. The miracles begin at his birth: he was God's Son, according to Mark; God's Word and agent in creation, according to John; the full repository of the Godhead according to Paul (whilst none the less being 'born of a woman'); the one who came into the world without the agency of a human father, according to Matthew and Luke. The miracles continue in his ministry: miracles of healing, or exorcism, nature miracles (such as the feeding of the multitude from a handful of loaves, and his walking on the sea in a storm), and supremely his raising from the dead Lazarus, the widow of Nain's son, and Jairus' daughter. Last of all came the greatest of all miracles, his own resurrection from the grave — not just to a further span of life but to a new quality of life over which death has no power. Such is the testimony of the New Testament: a Jesus who was different, in view of the powers at his command. In the first three Gospels these miracles are actually called 'acts of power' in the original Greek. But St. John's Gospel shows the true significance of the miracles when he calls them 'signs'. Signs of who Jesus is. Signs of what he can do for men. The one who fed a multitide can feed the hungry soul. The one who opened blind eyes can do the same for men blinded by pride and prejudice. The one who raised the dead can bring new life to someone who is dead spiritually and morally. The miracles were never done for selfish purposes; never to show off. They were evoked by Jesus' compassion for human need, and they were intended both to show that the long awaited Messianic kingdom had begun, and also that Jesus was the liberator who could unlock the various chains of man.

It is fashionable to laugh at the miracles. Such things could not happen. But why not? The laws of nature do not forbid them. A 'law of nature' is simply the name we give to a series of observed uniformities; this is the way things happen. But if a contrary instance is well attested, the scientist will widen his so-called 'law' to embrace both the uniformities and the exception to the rule. In the case of Jesus there is lots of strong contemporary evidence that he was the exception to the rule. If he was just a good man, that would be astonishing, perhaps meaningless. If he was different, if he was in some way God himself coming to disclose himself to us within the limitations of human form — then perhaps it is neither so incredible nor so meaningless that he should perform miracles.

At all events the evidence is overwhelming, and it is not all contained within the pages of the New Testament. You will find the earliest Christian apologist, a man called Quadratus, writing early in the second century:

> But the works of our Saviour were always present (for they were genuine): namely those who were healed, those who rose from the dead. They were not only seen in the act of being healed or raised, but they remained always present. And not merely when the Saviour was on earth, but after his departure as well. They lived on for a considerable time, so much so that some of them have survived even to our own day.

I find it intriguing that this, the only passage of Quadratus to have survived, should be devoted to drawing out the implications and establishing the truth of the miracles. It shows how confidently the early Christians could look to the miracles of Jesus as a pointer to his being more than man, to his being different.

But there are traces of his miracles in Roman and Jewish sources as well. Justin Martyr, writing his *Apology* about A.D. 150, can say with casual confidence, 'That he performed these miracles you may easily satisfy yourself from the *Acts* of Pontius Pilate.' It was the same with the Jews. We find them in the Gospels unable to deny the miracles of Jesus, but taking the only way out — attributing them to the devil. In the Acts of the Apostles we find Jews attempting to use the name of Jesus as a potent spell in exorcism: later on this continued, so much so that the writers in the *Mishnah* (Jewish law code) have to forbid Jews to heal in the name of Jesus! And the Tractate *Sanhedrin* tells us that Jesus 'was hanged on the eve of the Passover because he practised sorcery and led Israel astray' — a plain reference to his miracles.

Clearly, this man was different . . .

5. HIS FULFILMENT OF SCRIPTURE WAS DIFFERENT

Strikingly different. It hit the first disciples between the eyes. So much so that they found themselves writing like this: 'this was done in order to fulfil the words of the prophet Isaiah . . .' and the like. It is a recurring theme in the New Testament. Now this is very remarkable. The first followers of Jesus, being Jews, had the highest reverence for the Scriptures of the Old Testament. Yet there were manifestly incomplete sides to them. Those Scriptures spoke of a day when God would judge the earth. They spoke of a king of David's stock whose dominion would be endless. They spoke of all the families of man being blessed in Abraham, the man of faith who had started the nation of Israel. They spoke of one like a Son of Man coming to the Ancient of Days, and receiving a kingdom that would never be destroyed, together with power, glory and judgment. They spoke of a prophet like Moses arising among the people whose teaching would be unparalleled. They spoke of a Servant of the Lord whose suffering would be intense and whose death would carry away the sins of the people. They spoke of a Son of God whose character would measure up to that of his Father. This coming one would fulfil the role of prophet, of priest and of king for ever. He would be born of David's lineage, but of a humble, despised family. His birthplace would be Bethlehem. He would both restore the fallen in Israel and be a light to the Gentiles. He would be despised and rejected by the very people he came to rescue from their self-centredness. He would die among malefactors, and his tomb would be supplied by a rich man. But that would not be the end of him. He would live again, and the Lord's programme would prosper in his hands. When he saw all that would be accomplished by the anguish of his soul, he would be satisfied. For he would have forged a new agreement between God and man by his death; indeed, his death would open up the possibility of ordinary men and women having the Spirit of God come and take up residence within their lives.

All of this came true with Jesus. Not some of it: all of it. There is no example in the literature of the whole world where the prophecies made centuries beforehand in a holy book were fulfilled in a historical person in this way. It amazed his followers, but it convinced them. They came to see in him, the humble carpenter of Nazareth, the fulfilment of these ancient prophecies. He was born in Bethlehem of David's stock. His teaching showed him to be the prophet like Moses. He was the Suffering Servant of the Lord whose anguish on the cross brought pardon for all who would believe, as Abraham had believed. He was the one who would restore the fortunes of Israel and open the way of faith up to the Gentiles. He had established this new covenant between God and man, sealing it with his blood. His death had made the ultimate sacrifice, and no priesthood was ever to be needed again — for he had once and for all reconciled men to God by his own self-offering. His kingly rule would be for ever; veiled now, but apparent when he came to judge. His Spirit was already at work in the transformed lives of the disciples.

In the centuries that followed, this argument from prophecy

had an enormous impact. Many distinguished pagans were won
to faith in Jesus by the way he fulfilled the prophecies made in
these writings of an Old Testament which seemed so much
older and so much nobler than their own writings of Homer and
Plato. And many still are. As Professor Moule, one of the leading New Testament scholars in England, puts it:

> The notion of the 'fulfilment' of Scripture in a single indi-
> vidual, a figure of recent history, and he a condemned and
> disgraced criminal, who claimed to be the coping stone of the
> whole structure, and the goal of God's whole design, was
> new. And it was the Christian community which first related
> together, round a single focus, the scattered and largely dis-
> connected images of Israel's hope. It was utterly new for
> images like 'Messiah', 'Christ', 'Son of God', 'Son of Man',
> 'Suffering Servant' and 'Lord' to be seen as inter-changeable
> terms all relating to one figure (*The Phenomenon of the New
> Testament*, p. 16).

That figure *was* different.

So different that we find the New Testament writers attributing to him titles and activities reserved for God himself in
the Old Testament. For instance, in Isaiah (41: 4, 44: 6,
48: 12) God calls himself 'the First and the Last', but in the
New Testament this title is applied to Jesus (Revelation 1: 11,
2: 8, 22: 13). 'I am' is the special name of God (Yahweh,
usually known as Jehovah) and it is too sacred to be pronounced, so that the Jews used the word Adonai, Lord, as a
substitute. But we find claims to be the 'I am' coming on the
lips of Jesus; notably the fantastic claim of John 8: 58, 'Before
Abraham was, I am.' So much so that when asked, at a crucial
stage in his trial, whether he was the Messiah, Jesus replied, 'I
am, and you shall see the Son of Man sitting at the right hand
of power and coming with the clouds of heaven' (Mark 14: 62.)
This produced so savage a reaction in the high priest and his
colleagues because it appeared to be a claim to personal deity
on the part of Jesus.

Again, who is it in the Old Testament who is the Shepherd of his people? God, of course. 'The Lord is my Shepherd,' begins that most famous Psalm 23. But Jesus calmly uses the title of himself, 'I am the good Shepherd'; and other New Testament writers such as Peter and the writer to the Hebrews speak of him as 'the chief shepherd' and 'the great shepherd'. They had got the message. Perhaps the most remarkable function of God in the Old Testament was to create the world. 'In the beginning, God created the heaven and the earth' is, after all the opening sentence of the whole Bible. But listen to Paul: 'By Christ were all things created in the heavens and upon earth . . . all things have been created through him and for him' (Colossians 1: 16). Listen to John: 'He was in the beginning with God: all things were made through him, and without him was not anything made that was made' (John 1: 3).

Clearly, this man was different. No good man fulfilled all the strands of ancient scriptures, themselves penned over a thousand years, as this man did. Perhaps his contemporaries were right in believing he was one with God.

6. HIS CLAIMS WERE DIFFERENT

If you have read the Gospels, you may well have been struck by a remarkable contrast. On the one hand Jesus is a humble, self-forgetful figure, healing the sick, teaching the people, befriending the outcast. He is no academic theologian, but a horny-handed carpenter whose words are full of hard-headed wisdom and earthy illustrations. He has no money, no settled home, no vote, no rights. On the other hand he makes the most fantastic claims, and many of them are almost casual, throw-away remarks. For example, he takes it for granted that he is entitled to man's worship, the worship due to God alone. When Peter falls at his feet in adoration after a fishing expedition and says, 'Depart from me, for I am a sinful man, master' (Luke 5: 8), Jesus does nothing to stop him. When Thomas falls at his feet after the resurrection and exclaims, 'My Lord and my God' (John 20: 28), Jesus does not rebuke him — except for needing the evidence of his eyes to come to that conclusion. No good man would do that. Indeed we have examples in the New Testament of two good men, Peter and Paul, who found themselves being worshipped by ignorant pagans, and they reacted violently against it, telling them to worship God alone. Jesus seems to have taken such worship as his due.

Watch him deal with a woman taken in adultery, or a man sick with paralysis (John 8: 1ff, Mark 2: 1ff). 'Your sins are forgiven you,' says Jesus, and in the case of the paralytic he gave a visual demonstration of the fact — the man got up at Jesus' command and walked! Now what are we to make of a claim like that? The Pharisees knew very well what to make of it. 'Who is this that forgives sins?' they asked. 'There is one who forgives sins, God.' That is precisely the point. Jesus was laying implicit claim to do what God does, to forgive men their sins. Indeed, when Mary is told that her baby must be called Jesus, the explanation of the name is brought out like this: 'for he shall save his people from their sins'. In the Old Testament (Psalm 130: 8) this task for forgiving sins is specially, and naturally, said to belong to God alone. Here, right at the start of his life, Jesus takes on the job. The implication is obvious. In Jesus we meet someone who is different. He is no merely good man.

What are we to make of this? C. S. Lewis puts the challenge with his customary force.

There is no halfway house, and there is no parallel in other religions. If you had gone to Buddha and asked him: 'Are you the son of Bramah?' he would have said, 'My son, you are still in the vale of illusion.' If you had gone to Socrates and asked, 'Are you Zeus?' he would have laughed at you. If you had gone to Mohammed and asked, 'Are you Allah?' he would first have rent his clothes and then cut off your head. If you had asked Confucius, 'Are you heaven?' I think he would probably have replied, 'Remarks which are not in accordance with nature are in bad taste.'

This man was different. He was no merely great teacher.

Listen to Lewis once again:

> The things he says are very different from what any other teacher has said. Others say, 'This is the truth about the universe. This is the way you ought to go.' But he says, 'I am the Truth and the Way and the Life.' He says, 'No man can reach absolute reality, except through me. Try to retain your own life and you will inevitably be ruined. Give yourself away and you will be saved.' He says, 'If you are ashamed of me, if, when you hear my call you turn the other way, I will look the other way when I come again as God without disguise. If anything whatever is keeping you from God and from me, whatever it is, throw it away. If it is your eye, pull it out. If it is your hand, cut it off. If you put yourself first you will be last. Come to me, everyone who is carrying a heavy load, and I will set that right. Your sins, all of them, are wiped out. I can do that. I am Re-birth, I am Life. Eat me, drink me, I am your food. And finally, do not be afraid, I have overcome the whole universe.' That is the issue.

Yes, that is the issue. What are you going to make of it? In the light of his character and teaching, his behaviour and miracles, his fulfiment of prophecy and his astonishing claims, what are you going to say? He backed the whole thing up with a death such as the world has never seen, and, unlike any other person before or since, a resurrection from the grave. (I shall deal with his cross in chapter 8 and his resurrection in chapter 9.) It was the way he died and the way he rose that supremely convinced the first disciples that the man Jesus was nothing less than God. 'He was declared to be Son of God, powerfully, through the resurrection from the dead,' wrote Saul or Tarsus, once such a doughty opponent of the Christian faith, but now convinced by that death and resurrection that Jesus' claims were true.

Take a long, cool, look at the evidence I have brought before you in this chapter. Read any one of the Gospels with an open, enquiring mind. And then if you still say, 'Jesus was just a good man,' I shall say, 'You must be joking.' That is the one thing he cannot be. That is the one thing the men on the spot never thought of calling him. They were terrified of him: they believed him: or they hounded him to death. But nobody patronisingly said of him, 'What a splendid preacher we had in the synagogue last Sabbath. You must come along and hear him some time.' Jesus does not present himself to us as the best example of the human race, for our edification. He comes to us from beyond the human race, as God himself, hastening to our rescue. He expects of us, indeed demands of us, not our admiration but our allegiance, not our patronage but our hearts. He has the rights of God Almighty over us. And he can make all the difference of God Almighty within us, once we allow room for him in the lives he has given us.

Do you know Gordon Bailey's poem *The Lord Jesus Christ*? This is what he wrote after he had made room for Christ in his life:

> When he said
> 'I am the Way'
> he was claiming
> that only he could lead
> man to God.
>
> When he said
> 'I am the Truth'
> he was claiming
> universal and exclusive rights
> on the ability to reveal
> God to man.
>
> When he said
> 'I am the Life'
> he was claiming
> to be that quality of existence
> sacrificed for and sought by
> men and gods.

He also claimed
a supernatural birth,
an impossible death, and
a miraculous resurrection.

His claims mean that he is either
utterly insane,
undeniably evil, or
uniquely everything he claims to be!

6

'It doesn't matter what you believe so long as you are sincere'

ATTRACTIVE, BUT WRONG

Lots of people seem to believe this. And it is certainly a very attractive position to hold. For one thing it is eminently tolerant; and tolerance is just about the only virtue that has escaped the corroding cynicism of our day. It sounds a very liberal and enlightened creed, for it means that everyone will win the race; everyone will get prizes.

There is another reason for its appeal. At a stroke it removes the problem of seeking the truth, the embarrassment of being challenged by it. And that is very agreeable. After all, we are so busy these days we have little time to examine the different religions of the world, and we have no desire to have our lives unmasked by the truth when we find it.

What is more, this view that it doesn't matter what you believe so long as you are sincere has the great advantage of giving voice to our deep-seated disgust at insincerity. It is always a blow when a man or a country loudly professes one thing and then promptly does another. A classic example of this insincerity was given not so long ago by Haile Selasse, Emperor of Ethiopia, who claimed the most ancient continuous empire in the world. Temporarily deposed when the Italians invaded Ethiopia in 1935, he was restored in 1941 partly through the good offices of the South African Government. In gratitude, he vowed eternal friendship to them — and subsequently founded the Organisation for African Unity, one of whose prime targets many consider has been the destruction of the existing structures in South Africa! He professed to be a liberator of his people, but two thirds of the population were kept in serfdom. He claimed to uphold justice and fair play, but he and a small nobility retained most of the best land in the country. For all his professed love of his people, he was content to ship enormous loads of Ethiopian gold overseas, while hundreds of thousands of his countrymen die of starvation and cholera. The man was insincere. And he was toppled from power. We cannot help feeling that this was right and proper. 'He had it coming to him,' we say, because sincerity is very important, and no matter how broadminded we are, we cannot stand a man who is two-faced.

Insincerity is bad in individuals. It is worse in a whole country. I heard on the radio, the morning I wrote this chapter, some extracts from the South African Ambassador, Mr. Pik Botha's speech to the United Nations when he was seeking to avoid South Africa's expulsion from the world body. He claimed that his country did not discriminate against a man simply on the grounds of his colour. The effrontery of such a claim, the sheer insincerity of it, is breathtaking to one who, as I was at the time, lives in South Africa and sees daily the discrimination all around him. But what about the African nations which were hounding South Africa for racialism at the United Nations? Is there no racial discrimination in Kenya between the Kikuyu and the Luo? Or in Burundi as the Tutsi slaughter the Hutu? Or in Uganda where the Asians were unceremoniously bundled out of the country simply and solely because of the colour of their skin? Insincerity stinks wherever it is found.

But perhaps the worst kind of insincerity is the religious sort. The corruption of the Czarist church in ninteenth century Russia, or of the Coptic church in Ethiopia today is positively sickening. In the last century in England thousands of working men went to church in order to keep in with the bosses, not because they were believing Christians. We have no time for insincerity like that. And when occasionally one hears of a church organisation charging excessive rents from the poor, or a bishop running off with a barmaid, we feel swindled and let down. We say, 'It doesn't matter what a man believes so long as he is sincere.'

But, attractive though it is, it will not do. If you tell me that you believe it, I shall conclude — you must be joking. Here are three good reasons why I can't accept it.

LIFE TEACHES US THAT SINCERITY IS NOT ENOUGH

A moment's reflection will show what a ludicrous creed it is! We would never apply it to matters we consider important, would we? Take politics, for instance. What politician would accept for a moment that it does not matter what you believe so long as you are sincere? That would obliterate the difference between Monarchist and Republican, between Socialist and Capitalist, between Nationalist and Progressive. On that view it would be impossible to censure Russia's invasion of Czechoslovakia. On that view you could whitewash Hitler's ruthless slaughter of six million Jews in pursuit of *Herrenvolk* policy! No, in politics it matters enormously what you believe.

We would never apply this argument about sincerity being enough to economics, say, or to examinations. Who could suppose that it doesn't matter what firm you invest your money in so long as you sincerely believe that it is sound? Who would maintain that it does not matter what you believe when you write an examination? You can put down sense or nonsense; it makes no difference, so long as you are sincere! As we all know to our cost, you can be very sincere and very wrong.

Actually, you'd never get to work in the morning if you operated on this sincerity principle. No matter what earnest beliefs you held about the public transport system, you would miss your train and fail to reach your destination if you took no notice of the timetable but continued to maintain that it does not mattter what a man believes so long as he is sincere.

Pause to reflect on it for a moment. The outlook we have been considering is not merely ridiculous, but cruel. Just think of applying it to advising a crippled man when to cross a busy road: 'It doesn't matter what you believe about the speed and frequency of cars. Just carry on sincerely towards the other side, and you'll be all right!' Liberal and tolerant though it seemed to begin with, this outlook turns out to be cynical and cruel. Under the guise of charity this maxim hides a callous indifference to truth. It is little short of criminal.

Yes, life teaches us unequivocally that it matters enormously what we believe. We need to be sincere: we also need to be right.

THE BIBLE TEACHES US THAT SINCERITY IS NOT ENOUGH

Now, you may or may not be inclined to take the Bible as a final authority about God. But you must at least recognise that it is the most significant book in the world, has done more than any other book to change the world for good, remains the world's best seller, and was composed over a period of some fifteen hundred years. So it may be worth listening to. It may well embody perspective and wisdom, for it comprises a very broad spectrum of human history and experience. What does it have to say on whether sincerity is enough?

Take, first, a man like Abraham, the father of the Jewish nation. If you were to ask him whether sincerity was enough, he would reply 'Far from it. I was sincere when I lived in Ur of the Chaldees. But God called me out. I believed him, and obeyed. God promised to raise up a family and indeed a nation out of my loins, when both I and my wife were too old to have children. I believed him — and here is Isaac my son to show you how much belief matters. Why, the whole latter part of my life has been based on the conviction that what you believe is fundamental to what you do and what you are.' What Abraham became in virtue of his faith in God is graphically summarised in Hebrews 11: 8–19 (if you find the longer account, starting in Genesis 14, too much to cope with).

Noah would never have agreed for a moment that it doesn't matter what you believe so long as you are sincere. No doubt his neighbours were very sincere in thinking they were all right. But Noah's sincerity was of a different stamp. It sprang from his belief that God had called him to build an ark in which those who took refuge would be safe from the waters of the flood. Belief led to action.

Naaman, the great Syrian general, was a stickler for sincerity. He sincerely believed that Elisha the prophet would come out to him 'and stand and call on the name of the Lord his God and strike his hand over the place and heal the leprosy'. He sincerely believed that if washing in a river was to be the prescription, the cool, clear waters of his native Abana and Pharpar would do every bit as much good as Israel's muddy Jordan. He was sincere, but wrong. If he had not admitted as much and changed his attitude, he would never have been healed.

The night of the Exodus, when the escape of the Israelites from Egypt cemented them fully into a nation, was another case in point. You will recall the story. Only those households who sacrificed a lamb and splashed some of its blood above the doorpost of their home were spared the death of their firstborn. Only they left Egypt unharmed. If a father had said, 'Oh, it doesn't matter about that silly old blood on the lintel. Let's get a good night's sleep in preparation for the journey,' he might well have been sincere, but he'd have been wrong, his firstborn son would have been dead, and there would have been no Promised Land for him.

The New Testament attitude is the same. The Pharisees are the outstanding examples of people, highly religious people at that, who thought they were O.K. — and they were not. Pontius Pilate seeems to have been a fairly sincere governor of a difficult province, Judea: he may well have believed it would be in the general interest for Jesus to be liquidated — but he was wrong. Saul of Tarsus believed he could put himself in the right with God by meticulously keeping the Law and zealously persecuting the heretics — but he came to realise that his sincere attempt was a hopeless failure. Saul, the fanatical, self-righteous persecutor, who became Paul, the dedicated, loving apostle, is a splendid example of the fact that sincerity is not enough. It matters what you believe.

JESUS TEACHES US THAT SINCERITY IS NOT ENOUGH

It would be difficult to find anyone more sincere than the rich young ruler: but we read that he went away sorrowful, because he did not believe enough in Jesus to give him priority over his money.

Nobody could have been more sincere than the Pharisees. They were meticulous in their worship, fastidious in keeping clear of any defilement, and dedicated to keeping the Law of God. They were sincere — but wrong. It was these very Pharisees whom Jesus had to describe as a viper's brood: it was they who, he observed, 'would not come to me so as to receive life' (John 5: 40). Sincere in their practice, they were mistaken in their belief, and Jesus was more stringent in his condemnation of those dedicated, sincere men than of the quislings and the prostitutes whom they despised. It does matter what you believe. So much so that when the Jews, anxious to please God by *doing* something, came and asked Jesus 'What shall we do so that we may do what pleases God?', he replied, 'This is what pleases God — to *believe* in him whom he has sent' (John 6: 28f).

SINCERITY AND BELIEF

Nowhere in the Gospels does Jesus stress more powerfully the supreme importance of belief than in the best known verse of the whole Bible. 'God so loved the world that he gave his only Son, that whosoever believes in him should not perish but have eternal life' (John 3: 16). The passage continues, 'The man who believes in him is not condemned: he who does not believe is condemned already, because he has not believed in the name of the only Son of God. And this is the condemnation, that light has come into the world, and men loved darkness rather than light because their deeds were evil.' God, you see, not sincerity, is the supreme reality. And God saw that man was perishing, on the way to final ruin, because it is all too easy to be sincere, and wrong. So God did something about it. He sent Jesus who was one with himself and yet distinct from himself — Son is maybe the best human analogy. Jesus lived and died for the express purpose of rescuing us, and enabling us to enjoy a new quality of life, eternal life.

There is just one condition. We are called to believe! Jesus goes on to make it plain that we will not be ruined by our evil ways, which, to some extent, we cannot help. We will be ruined by failing to trust the one who has brought the remedy for our sick condition. The Light has come into the world. The Bridge back to God has been established. It is up to us to believe or reject: we have the choice, and we shall be held responsible for our decision. 'The man who believes in him is not condemned': no, for Another has borne his condemnation. 'But he who does not believe is condemned already', not because he is a sinner (which he is) but because he has been fool enough to reject the remedy. Do not, I beg you, commit this ultimate folly under the claim of tolerance. If there happens to be only one antitoxin for a disease, it is not charity but folly to say, 'It doesn't matter whether you take it or not, so long as you are sincere.' And we all have the disease. It has affected our past. It dogs our present. It threatens our future.

THE LIMITATIONS OF SINCERITY

Can sincerity alter the past? I think of a gangster who found Christ in prison — and I can see him now, out of prison, reconciled with his wife, accepted and loved in a Christian community. He has been released from his past. Sincerity could never produce a change like that. Only Jesus can. Belief in Jesus puts you in touch with the one who died to clean up your past. 'There is no condemnation to the man who is in Christ Jesus' (Romans 8: 1).

Can sincerity alter a man's life in the present? I think of an obsessive gambler who had tried everything to break the habit, and had failed. He discovered that sincerity is not enough. And then he came to Christ. The Spirit of Jesus came into his life, and at once the old slavery to gambling was broken. Not so surprising after all, is it? You'd expect Jesus to make a difference, and he does. I think of a couple whose marriage was breaking up, though they had sincerely tried to make a go of it. But once they both came to terms with Christ, and welcomed his Spirit into their lives, they found each other afresh and are now living a happy and useful Christian life.

Or think of the future. Can sincerity set our minds at rest about death and what follows death? Anyone who has attended the dying knows that it cannot. But the one who rose from the dead, the one who 'holds the keys of death and the after-life', he can take away the dread of death and hell. I think of an old friend of mine, a bishop in China and for years director of one of the biggest missionary agencies in the world. When his time came to die, he asked for the Hallelulia Chorus from the Messiah to be played, murmured 'Wonderful!' and passed joyfully into his Master's presence. Like Handel, like Christians all down the ages, he pinned his faith for the future not in sincerity or tolerance, but in the Risen One.

Do you now see why belief is so important? The Lord offers us so much; the cross to lift the burden of the past; the Spirit to change the selfishness of our lives; the resurrection to assure us of a future with him. Three firm, objective realities — no mere sincerity. No wonder the reformers in the sixteenth century used to rejoice in three great mottoes:

> *Sola gratia*   — by God's free goodness alone
> *Sola fide*   — through faith alone
> *Soli Deo gloria* — and to God alone be the glory!

Incidentally, aren't you glad that we are not judged by our sincerity? What a burden that would impose on every minute of the day; on the motivation of every action; on the expression of every word. The word 'sincere' comes from the Latin *sine cera*, 'without wax'. It is a metaphor derived from bee-keeping. Quality honey has to be wax free, and the Greek word for 'sincere', literally 'judged in the light of the sun' shows how you decided the matter. Why, if I were judged in the blazing sunlight of God's holiness, and every word and deed and motive was scrutinised for sincerity, I wouldn't have a hope. Would you? I'm all too aware of insincerity in myself and others to relish a test like that. 'How nice to see you,' we say, when inwardly furious at the interruption. 'I haven't the time', we say, when faced with something we don't want to do. 'What about those who have never heard the gospel?' we ask, when the wonder and challenge of what Christ has done drives us into a corner. Shallow insincerities, all of them! Even the glib claim that sincerity is all we need itself reeks of insincerity. We do not apply it to any other area of life: it is just an excuse, to evade facing up to the light.

When I am confronted by the God who is too holy to tolerate evil in those he loves, the God whose eyes are like flaming fire — then I am thankful that I shall have something more substantial than sincerity to rely on. I shall be resting my weight on the Jesus in whom I have believed. How about you?

Four questions, as I close this chapter.

WHY IS BELIEVING SO IMPORTANT?

For two good reasons. Partly, because belief is the basis for action. It is foolish to concentrate on sincerity of action if you are casual about the nature of your beliefs. What you believe leads inevitably to what you do and what you are.

But there is an even more important answer to this question. Believing is so important because it is the only conceivable response to love. When God's love is brought to me in Christ, I merely insult him if I say, 'Right, that's very nice of you. Now how about a bit of churchgoing, a bit of sincerity and turning over a new leaf so as to earn your love?' The only proper response to such a generous and undeserved gift is to stretch out the hand of faith and say 'Thank you'.

WHAT DOES BELIEVING ACHIEVE?

Once again the answer can be roughly summarised in two parts. First, it clears up the past, or rather, claims the clearing up that Christ achieved on the cross. 'Being acquitted by faith we have peace with God', was St. Paul's triumphant discovery (Romans 5: 1). It's as if I were in prison and all unknown to me a Royal Pardon was being drawn up for me. I would stay in prison along with my accusing record, until I accepted that Royal Pardon, and stepped out of prison, a free man with nothing against my name.

Second, believing brings a man into God's family. 'To as many as received him, or believed on his name, he gave the right to become the children of God', says St. John (John 1: 12). 'We have received the Spirit who adopts us into the family,' says St. Paul (Romans 8: 15). It is as though we were juvenile delinquents, and the judge not only settled our fine himself, but adopted us into his very family alongside his own son. There is nothing we could do to earn it. We would just trustingly accept the new relationship, say 'Thank you', and try to live lives worthy of it.

WHAT WILL BELIEVING INVOLVE?

It is certainly no cheap option, no easy alternative to costly action. But neither does believing mean that we are committed to endless dreary and legalistic observances. Look at it like this. What will believing in his coach mean to the athlete? What will believing in his teacher mean to the pupil? What will believing in his doctor mean for the patient? What will belief in the parent mean for the child, or the husband for the wife? Certainly discipline and obedience will be part of the total package; but somehow it will not be irksome, because of the relationship. That is what it is like to believe in Jesus. It is a lifelong commitment, a dependence on and an ever-growing obedience to the one who has shown himself to be utterly reliable. Because he came to this world in order to seek me; because he died for me and rose for me; because he offers to share my very life and enter the inmost recesses of my being, I know I can trust him to the full. And what is belief if not trust?

HOW DO I ACTUALLY BELIEVE?

Once again, there are two parts to it. Having got past the stage of thinking that faith is believing what you know is not true, or that it consists in reciting the creeds parrot fashion, it resolves itself into a matter for the head and a matter for the will.

Let's look at the intellectual side first. Belief is no surrender of the intellect. It is no blind acceptance of everything in the Bible, or every dogma of the Christian church. No. Belief is concerned with Jesus Christ. If you like, Jesus is God's right hand of fellowship stretched out to us. Belief is our hand of response, stretched out to him. The two need to meet. I ask you, then, do you believe that Jesus Christ is the Son of God? Do you believe he died for you? Do you believe he is the risen Lord, willing and able to change your life? That is the hard core of Christian belief. The early Christians summarised it in the famous fish symbol — for the five letters which go to make up the Greek word for fish could be seen as the first letters of the following claims about Jesus: 'Jesus Christ, Son of God, Saviour'. Those claims take you to the nerve centre of Christian belief.

But it is all too easy to believe things in your head without getting personally involved with them, or acting on them. That is why it is vital to realise that belief is a matter not only of the mind but of the will. This delightful story about Blondin, the celebrated tightrope-walker of a hundred years ago, makes the point with humour and clarity. He specialised in crossing the Niagara Falls on a tightrope. Variations included crossing blindfold, swathed in a sack, at night, on stilts, and with his feet tied up in blankets. In 1860 he performed before the then Prince of Wales who was visiting Niagara as part of a tour. Blondin offered to carry him over on his back. The Prince declined, but with royal graciousness suggested that the Duke of Newcastle, who was in attendance, might like to accept. Unfortunately the Duke of Newcastle, too, refused!

Now those two men believed, in the intellectual sense, that Blondin could do it, but this was not faith in the full-blooded New Testament sense of the word. There was no act of will, no personal commitment. By way of contrast, Blondin's mother watched him wheel a sack of potatoes over the Falls, and then, at his suggestion, climbed into the wheelbarrow herself and entrusted herself to his skill and balance. She was not disappointed. That is a good example of authentic faith.

How about you and Jesus Christ? Do you believe in him with your head? Then put yourself at his disposal. Climb into the wheelbarrow, so to speak, and tell him that you realise sincerity is not enough, that you entrust your life to him, and that you don't mind who knows it.

A genuine act of self-surrender like that will give birth to a growing conviction that Christ, not merely sincerity, is what you need in this life and the next. For the act of commitment leads on to a life of companionship with him who makes all things new — even for you.

7

'I do my best. No man can do more'

CHRISTIANITY is a rescue religion. That is why it is so unpopular. It goes to the heart of human nature and makes a radical difference. But when men pause from the rat race for a moment to take a long cool look at themselves in the light of their own standards, they tend to come up with two main attitudes. One takes a rosy view of human nature, and says in effect, 'I do my best. That ought to be good enough for whatever God there may be. I'll be O.K.' The other is much more pessimistic and says, 'I've made a mess of things. Nothing can alter the past.' We'll look at them in turn: the optimist in this chapter, and the pessimist in the next. They are closely connected, in actual fact. They are two opposite reactions to the problem of guilt.

THE PROBLEM OF GUILT

However hard boiled you are, there are times when you feel dirty, rotten, guilty. It may nag away at you for years, as it did in one of the Great Train Robbers, Buster Edwards, who found he could not live with it and eventually gave himself up. It may just hit you once in a while, as it comes through in Roger McGough's poem, *Come Close and Sleep Now*.

> It is afterwards
> and you talk on tiptoe
> happy to be part
> of the darkness,
> lips becoming limp,
> a prelude to tiredness.
> Come close and sleep now,
> for in the morning
> when a policeman
> disguised as the sun
> creeps into the room:
> and your mother
> disguised as the birds
> calls from the trees,
> you will put on a dress of guilt
> and shoes with broken high ideals
> and refusing coffee
> run all the way home.

That puts it very clearly and movingly. 'Shoes with broken high ideals'. We all wear them. What are we to do about it?

Well, the obvious thing is to forget about it. Just too bad it happened, but no point in making yourself miserable over spilt milk. Forget it. Ah, but that is not so easy. Something over half of the hospital beds in Britain are taken up with people suffering from some form of anxiety. Over 3,000 million pills are issued annually by our doctors in order to counter depression and anxiety. People have pushed unwelcome aspects of their characters down into the subconscious, and those aspects have refused to go away; they continue to trouble us. I have been engaged recently in some group counselling in which primal repressions of terrifying power have been brought back from that area of the subconscious, and once they were dealt with, dramatic bodily healings have taken place. We human beings are complicated creatures, and to repress our sense of guilt about the past solves nothing: it merely builds up trouble for the future.

And even if it didn't, we should still be in queer street. Suppose a man commits murder, and doesn't get caught; suppose he tries to forget about it, and determines to never do such a thing again — what would happen if the evidence should come to light thirty years later, as it has with some of the Nazi war criminals? The answer is simple: the man is guilty however much he has tried to forget it, however long ago he did it, however hard he has tried to go straight in the meantime. Forgetting it does no good, even in the realm of human justice.

Then what is God to do about human failures? Is he to say, 'Well, let's forget it'? Not the God I read of in the Bible! In a way, I wish he would: it would make it so much easier for me, and, I suspect, for you. But on second thoughts I am glad God is not like that — soft, spineless, devoid of justice, pretending that black is white and white is black when we all know perfectly well that such is not the case. Yes, I'm glad God is holy and opposed to human wickedness. Heaven would be hell otherwise.

Not that it matters very much what I hope God may be like. I couldn't possibly know, unless he has revealed himself. And that he has done. He did it in personal terms, in Jesus Christ — no less, as we saw in chapter 5. And Jesus taught more severely about the judgment of God than any of the Old Testament prophets ever did. Remember, it was Jesus who taught about the two ways a man could go: one led to God and the other to destruction. There were two groups a man could belong to: wheat, destined for the barn, or weeds, destined for the fire. There were two destinies that awaited men: inside the joyous feast, or outside where there was weeping and gnashing of teeth. The teaching of Jesus flies straight in the face of our easy-going optimism that God is a good fellow and won't be too fussy about our achievements. He is good, and therefore he will be extremely fussy. He is the ethically upright God that our conscience uncomfortably suggests he is. He is deeply concerned at the fundamental difference between right and wrong, and will not pretend that the distinction is unreal. He will by no means clear the guilty. The Almighty does not owe us forgiveness, any more than the world owes us a living. Forgiveness is never cheap.

WORKING OUR PASSAGE

All down the ages men have had an inkling of this fact. Forgiveness is never cheap: it is costly, and therefore they must do something to pay for it, to earn it. In a very real sense all religions have their root and their unity in this fact. Man must do something, must achieve something, in order to atone for his failures, to make the Almighty gracious to him. All over the world, all down the ages, man has been trying to earn his passage to heaven. He has been saying, in effect, 'I'm a good fellow. I do my best. Surely that is enough?' It may be through mechanical ways like the Tibetan prayer wheel, animistic ways like worship of the spirits of the ancestors, Communist ways like adoration at the tomb of Lenin, Islamic ways like making the pilgrimage to Mecca. It may be through Eastern ways like the Eightfold Path, or mortification of the body in order to gain a better reincarnation. It may be through Western ways like trying harder, seeking to be decent, never doing anyone any harm, doing our best (and who can do more than that?).

This attempt to establish ourselves is exceptionally common in church circles. 'I've been baptised, and confirmed and married in church — and I'm having the kids sent to Sunday school. I go myself at Christmas — I mean, Christmas wouldn't be the same without going to church and singing those carols, would it?' In ways like this we pay our tiny premium for what we hope, when we stop to think about it, will be a whacking great heavenly insurance policy.

But despite its popularity, despite its prevalence all over the world, in every religious system and the irreligious ones as well, this road is a dead end. It is utterly misguided. And I will show you why.

IT IS SHALLOW

It allows us to rely on deeds, not attitude. It is depressingly superficial and external. Would it satisfy any loving parent if his offspring kept the bedroom tidy and cleaned his shoes but never gave him a kiss, never spent time with him? Of course not. But are we to suppose that the Heavenly Father will be overjoyed to welcome us when we haven't said so much as 'Hello' to him from one year's end to another, but smugly claim, 'I've done lots of good things. I do my best. No man can do more.'?

Listen to Jesus' analysis of the human condition. There is nothing external, superficial or shallow about it. He says that 'from within, out of the heart of man, come evil thoughts, acts of ruthless greed, murder, theft, pride and folly' (Mark 7: 21, 22). Of course we know how to do good things. But that does not change the fundamental twist in our natures: 'you, being evil, know how to give good gifts to your children . . .' (Luke 11: 13) observed the master Physician. You cannot get rid of a cancerous growth by using lots of make-up and running round helping everyone else in the house. It needs drastic surgery. Doing good deeds may well merely drive the dirt under the carpet. It is a very shallow remedy for the human situation. 'It is essential not to have faith in human nature,' wrote Professor

Butterfield, the famous historian: 'Such a belief is very recent and very disastrous.' To reject the doctrine of human wickedness means that you will always be perplexed when you hear the perversity of man on the news each evening; you will always be puzzled by the prevalence of racism, by the exploitation of the helpless, by the oppression of the weak by the strong, and by the quirks in your own behaviour. One celebrated atheist, turned Christian, put it like this. 'To reject the doctrine of human sinfulness, as so many left-wing rationalists do, was to fall victim to the shallow optimism which led men to believe that the millennium was just round the corner, waiting to be introduced by a society of adequately psychoanalysed, prosperous Socialists. It is because we rejected the doctrine of sin that we on the Left were always being disappointed.' So wrote Professor C. E. M. Joad after a lifetime of persuading himself that he was a good chap at heart, and that provided he did his best he'd be all right.

The truth is that our deeds cannot make up for ourselves. That is why Jesus hammered those good-living, religious Pharisees. It is all too possible to have a façade of goodness and religious observance, but all the time to ignore the disease beneath. Jesus Christ demands a more radical solution.

IT IS IMPOSSIBLE

You and I can't get to heaven on our own good deeds, for the simple reason that they are not good enough for God.

'What?' you say. 'I'm a good-living chap. I've kept the Ten Commandments.' Have you? I wonder. Have you kept the first commandment of all, to give God number one place in your life? I haven't. Jesus said it meant loving the Lord our God with all our heart and mind and soul and strength. I simply haven't begun to keep that first and greatest commandment. I break it every day. And that is not a very encouraging start as I set out to establish myself before God as the fine fellow who does his best and can't be expected to do more.

I glanced down the other commandments. I must not make

my own image of God? Well, I don't make graven images, of course. But I do tend to say 'I can't believe in a God who . . .' or 'The God I believe in is like this . . .' I make him in my image, rather than stopping to find out what he has revealed himself to be in the Bible.

I must not take the name of God in vain? I do it every day without thinking. Keeping the Sabbath day holy, one day in seven separate for God and family and rest? Don't make me laugh. Honour father and mother? Not likely. When I'm young I rebel against them as hard as I can. When I'm married I neglect them. When they are old I stuff them in an old people's home. Honour them indeed!

I feel a bit better seeing the command not to kill. I have never done that. But hang on a minute: didn't Jesus say something about the man who hates being just as repulsive to God as the man who gives vent to his hatred in murder?

It's the same with that command about adultery. I may not have gone in for the wife-swapping parties that some of my friends indulge in. But how about that dance when I went a lot further than I intended? How about the lustful thoughts that jostle through my mind whenever I see a shapely woman? Yes, Jesus was right when he put those thoughts down to just the same weakness in human nature as produces adultery.

'Thou shalt not steal.' But I'm afraid I do. Steal goods from the shops, when nobody is looking; steal a free ride from the bus, when the conductor doesn't notice; steal from the tax man by getting paid in cash not by cheque; yes, it happens. And as for not bearing false witness against my neighbour, why, that's what sells the Sunday papers. A little bit of scandal, a bit of exaggeration, of character assassination, of making myself look big in comparison with him. That final command against coveting, against unrestrained desire for what is not mine — man, the whole of our society is built on covetousness! You covet the next man's car and his wife and his washing machine and his freezer and his colour T.V. and . . . Don't be stupid; life is built on coveting. O.K. then, but don't turn round and tell me that you have kept the Ten Commandments and are therefore a splendid chap whom God ought to be proud to know. You have broken the lot. And so have I.

'Well, at any rate I live by the Sermon on the Mount.' It is amazing how many people think they do. I always feel they must be joking. The standards of the Sermon on the Mount make the Ten Commandments look like kid's stuff. Do you hunger and thirst after what is right? Are you among the pure in heart who will see God? Are you a peacemaker at home and in industry? Do you allow yourself to be wronged, persecuted even, for the sake of what is right? Do you go and get reconciled with the chap whose guts you hate before presenting yourself in church with your offering? Are you perfect in undiscriminating concern for the good of all you meet, as your Heavenly Father is, who makes his rain to fall equally on the just and the unjust? 'Don't be anxious about tomorrow: trust your Father, who looks after flowers and birds,' says the Sermon. Do you live like that? 'Don't say, "what shall we eat, or drink, or wear?" But seek first God's kingly rule and his righteousness, and all these things will be added to you,' says the Sermon. Do you live like that? No, of course you don't, and neither do I. Then we ought to be very careful of boasting that we live by the Sermon on the Mount. For that Sermon concludes with the solemn assurance that if we do not follow the teaching of Jesus in this Sermon we face ruin. 'Every man who hears these words of mine and does them,' says Jesus, 'shall be like a wise man who built his house upon the rock. And the rain fell and the floods came and the winds blew and beat upon that house, but it did not fall because it was founded upon the rock. And every one who hears these words of mine and does not do them will be like a foolish man who built his house upon the sand. And the rain fell and the floods came and the winds blew and beat against that house, and it fell. And great was the fall of it' (Matthew 7: 24ff).

On that day it will not do to say, 'Lord, I did my best and even went to church from time to time.' The Sermon tells us he will reply, 'Not every one who says to me "Lord, Lord" shall enter the Kingdom of Heaven, but he who does the will of my

Father who is in heaven. On that day many will say to me "Lord, Lord, did we not prophesy in your name, and cast out demons in your name, and do many mighty works in your name?" And then I will declare to them, "I never knew you. Depart from me, you evildoers" ' (Matthew 7: 21ff).

There sounds the death knell for all man's attempts to justify himself before God. It cannot be done. 'Whoever shall keep the whole law and yet offend in one point, is guilty of all,' says the Epistle of James (2: 10), perceptively. After all, if I am had up for speeding, it won't help me to say that I have never robbed a bank and never mugged an old woman. I am guilty of speeding. I am in trouble. With God I have broken his law daily, hourly. I am in deep trouble. And it will be a very thin excuse to say 'I've done my best.' For one thing, to be honest, I haven't. And for another, my best is not good enough for a holy God. I need something a lot better than my best if I'm going to get right with him. I find that the Bible is very unflattering about my attempts to doll myself up in the sight of God. It tells me that all my righteousnesses (my righteousnesses, mark you!) are like filthy rags, let alone the things I know are not much good. It implies that I have been looking in one of those distorting mirrors and hold too high a view of my own achievements and too low a view of God's nature and demands. 'The heart is deceitful above all things and desperately corrupt; who can understand it? I, the Lord, search the mind and try the heart, and give to every man according to his ways, according to the fruit of his doings' (Jeremiah 17: 9). No, if that is the standard, if those are the stakes, then I can't compete. I begin to see that it is impossible that my best should be good enough for God.

IT IS INTOLERABLE

If heaven were the reward of merit, it would be ghastly. If I got there because I did my best, pushed my way in, and established my own claims no matter who got hurt in the process, it would be intolerable. If heaven were peopled by self-made men waving their own beastly goodness around under every one

else's nose, it would be hell. Ascot is bad enough, with everyone
showing off their clothes for all they are worth. Is heaven to be
one long Ascot? Perish the thought!

I found a gravestone once, in an ancient church. It enshrined
superbly this idea that I do my best and God ought to be very
pleased with it, and it shows how repulsive that idea really is. It
comes from King Ethelred the Unready, and it runs like this:

> I, Ethelred, king of Albion, in order that on the awful
> day of judgment I may, by the intercession of the saints, be
> deemed worthy to be admitted to the heavenly kingdom, do
> give Almighty God the possession of three lands [i.e. farms]
> to be held for ever for the monastery of the aforesaid martyr.

That shows up the proud attitude of 'I do my best. What
man can do more?' in its true colours. It is disgusting. God will
not have his heaven cluttered up with the smug and the self-
satisfied. The very idea is obscene.

Paul put it like this. Writing to some very self-satisfied Galatians he said, in effect, 'If you rely on trying your best in order
to get to God, you have had it. You fall under the curse which
the Law of God imposes on all who break it. Does not the Old
Testament say, "Cursed be every one who does not abide by *all*
things written in the book of the law, and do them"? You cannot
claim obedience like that, can you? Very well, you fall under
the judgment of God.' In other words, it is impossible to get
through to God on the basis of my own good works. But Paul
does not leave it there. He goes on in the very next verse to
show that even if it were possible, it would be intolerable. It
would mean that a man could put a pistol at God's head, so to
speak, and say, 'I've done all these good things. You must make
room for me in your heaven even though I have never given you
a thought and don't love you the least bit.' So Paul maintains,
'It is quite obvious that nobody gets in touch with God just by
doing good things. That would leave the whole principle of
trust out of account. And the Old Testament makes it quite
clear that it is the man who is made right with God by trusting

him, who enjoys life with him for ever. But doing your best has nothing to do with this attitude of trust: it is simply a matter of cold achievement.' That is a rough paraphrase of Galatians 3: 10–12. And it seems to me to be unanswerable. If I rely on doing my best to put me in the clear with God, I shall find not only that it is impossible, because I fail again and again and again; but that the whole idea is intolerable because it leaves me untouched in my pride and self-esteem and takes no account of the loving trust I should have with my heavenly Father.

In a word, all attempts to establish myself before God are bound to fail. He is holy and I am not. My good deeds cannot make up for my crooked heart and my rebellious attitude towards the God I have wronged and from whose gaze I am only too anxious to escape. It is hard and humiliating to have to admit this. That is why so many people prefer to shelter under the bogus refuge of 'I do my best. No man can do more.' But unless I have a better shelter than that, it will let the wind and the rain and the hail in at the Day of Judgment. I need to come to the position of one rich, able, intelligent young pleasure-seeker, sixteen centuries ago, who was man enough to face up to the unpalatable truth and get right with God on God's terms, not his own. He wrote, 'You took me, God, from behind my own back where I had put myself all the time I preferred not to see myself. And you set me before my face, that I might see how vile I was. I saw myself, and was horrified.' That was Augustine, who later became the famous Christian leader. I fancy we all need to tread that humbling path, if God is to be able to do anything with us. He has no room for big-heads in his family. There is one condition for entry; one only. It is to change our attitude, to come down from our high horse, and be willing to trust him and his way of pardon. What that is we shall see in the next chapter.

8

'Nothing can alter the past'

THIS CHAPTER IS a companion piece to the previous one. Both of them deal with the reactions of human beings to guilt. In the last chapter we were looking at the man who hoped the past would go away, so long as he did his best. In this chapter we are concerned with the person who knows all too well that the past will not go away. It is permanent. Nothing can change it. Its stain us indelible. Often one hears a person bewail some awful incident in their past, and say, 'I can never forgive myself.'

Like Lady Macbeth after the murder, they continue, as it were, for ever going through the motions of washing their hands, but are all too well aware that all the perfumes of Arabia cannot remove the smell of blood from it. Nothing can undo the past.

Their problem, then, is precisely the opposite of the one we looked at in the previous chapter. There the self-made man was confident that he would be all right: he did his best, and what more could be required of him? Here, nothing avails to put the past right. But paradoxical as it may seem, both diseases have the same remedy. It is to be found on a green hill far away, outside a city wall.

THAT MAN ON HIS CROSS

Come with me in imagination to that famous scene. It is a bank holiday. A rough, laughing crowd jostles through the narrow streets of Jerusalem. At last the Roman governor has ratified the decision of the Jewish Council, and given sentence against Jesus of Nazareth. He is to die in the approved fashion for criminals of the lower classes in occupied countries, by crucifixion. The knot of soldiers in charge of the execution push through the crowd. Of the three men they are guarding carefully, one stumbles. He has been kept awake all night, without food or drink, and has had a succession of trials. He is exhausted. He collapses under the weight of the heavy cross beam of his cross which he has to carry. The lack of sleep, food and the loss of blood from his back, lacerated as it was with the Roman cat-o'-nine-tails, prove too much for him. He stumbles to his knees, and the soldiers grab a black man who happens to be passing by. 'You'll do: carry his cross, and look sharp about it.' Soon the execution party comes to a spot outside the city wall, while the crowd watches the spectacle of three public deaths with mingled emotions. The soldiers dig pits for the crosses to go into. The crosses are laid on the ground, and the three men are made to lie on them. Long iron spikes are then nailed through their ankles and their wrists. A few years ago the bones of a crucified man were unearthed in Israel. None had ever been discovered before. The spikes had pierced through the two bones at the wrist and had gone through the ankle. Think of the agony it must have been. No doubt the two criminals executed with Jesus cursed and swore and struggled. Jesus breathed a prayer instead: 'Father, forgive them. They do not know what they are doing.'

The grisly job is done at length. The soldiers lift the crosses one by one and slot them into the ground. The men are now exposed to the gaze of the crowd, suspended between earth and sky, with every nerve in agony, fighting for breath. No quick death awaits them, as they hang in terrible anguish, parched by the heat, distraught by the flies.

A GOD-FORSAKEN PLACE

What accounts for the fascination that central figure on the cross has exercised over nineteen centuries of men? It could not be merely his physical suffering, ghastly as that was. Other men have died in as great pain, perhaps greater. The two brigands executed with him had just as terrible an end. No, his physical sufferings do not get us to the heart of what was achieved on that cross. Interestingly enough, the Gospel writers hardly pause on them at all. 'There they crucified him,' is all they say, sparing us the harrowing detail. Nor can his mental suffering exhaust the mystery. How galling to have priests mocking him: 'He saved others, himself he cannot save. Let Christ the King of Israel come down now from the cross, so that we may see and believe.' How heartbreaking to find all his disciples running for cover. How humiliating to be exposed as a failure, his life's work in ruins. How crushing to be rejected and crucified by God's own people whom he had come to teach and to rescue. His mental sufferings must have broken his heart: but they do not penetrate the mystery of that cross.

Darkness falls, a premature darkness, a darkness which could be felt. Curiously enough a pagan historian, Thallus, records it, so it is no mere colourful exaggeration from the Gospels. But none the less it is highly symbolic of the darkness which engulfed Jesus at that supreme moment of his life. Darkness pierced with his cry of agony, culled from Psalm 22, 'My God, my God, why have you forsaken me?' Darkness matched only by that in the Garden of Gethsemane the night before, when he had faced up to his death and what it would entail, and had sweated blood at the prospect. Why indeed was this best of men allowed to feel bereft, God-forsaken in this his finest hour?

The answer which all different strands of the New Testament give is this. He *felt* cut off from his Heavenly Father for the simple reason that he *was* cut off. Paul, as we saw in the last chapter, was clear that no man could approach God dressed in the clothes of his own good deeds. Because all have broken the law of God, all rest under its curse, its judgment. But if you were to ask Paul what lay at the heart of the cross of Jesus, he would tell you, 'Christ rescued us from the curse of the broken law, *becoming a curse for us*.' Unthinkable — that the holy one, the perfect man, the innocent Son of God should end up in the place of judgment, of cursing. But so it was. As a Jew Paul would have known his Old Testament. He knew very well that passage in Deuteronomy which said that anyone exposed on a cross must be seen as resting under the curse of God. He had felt, in his pre-Christian days, that here was an excellent reason why Jesus could not possibly be the longed-for Messiah of his people; he had ended up not merely in the place of failure, but of cursing. On the road to Damascus he had met the risen Lord Jesus. He had had his previous view shattered. He came to see that Jesus had indeed come to meet his death in the place of cursing, but *the curse was ours* which he gladly bore for us. No wonder he gives up his life in glad service for 'the Son of God who loved me and gave himself for me'. As he reflects on the fantastic exchange of positions which Jesus undertook for us, he can do no other. 'For our sake, God made Jesus who knew no sin *to be sin* for us, Jesus who knew no sin, so that we might become the very goodness of God in him' (2 Corinthians 5: 21). No wonder Jesus felt cut off from God: he was cut off . . . and it was in order to enable us to come near.

WHAT DOES IT MEAN?

The New Testament writers struggle to express this un-dreamed of good news in a variety of metaphors. Fantastic that God should underwrite our debts, and lift our burdens and endure our curse, and carry our guilt. Fantastic, indeed; but it takes us to the very heart of Calvary. That is why Jesus steadfastly set his face to go to Jerusalem — when he might so easily have left for somewhere else. He had an appointment with death. He knew that he was going to endure the destiny of the Suffering Servant, sketched out so graphically in the Old Testament prophecies. He knew that the Lord was going to lay on him the iniquities of us all. He knew that he was going to bear our offences. He knew that the lashes which meant our peace would lacerate him. He knew that his death would be a sacrifice for sin such as no sacrificial system in the world could match — the Lord, offering his life for sinners. He knew that the Son of Man, as he called himself, would give his life as ransom for many, on that cross. He knew that he would see the fruit of his labours after it was all over and be satisfied — feel it was worth it. For he was about to forge a new agreement be-tween God and man, a new covenant. All other covenants in the history of religions had two sides to them, man's side and God's side. That was just the trouble about them — man kept break-ing his side of the bargain! But this covenant would bring for-giveness of sins. It would undertake not only God's side but man's side. On that cross he would be perfect man, offering up his life for others: he would also be perfect God, for 'God was in Christ, reconciling the world to himself, not reckoning their sins up against them.' Such was the divine plan, hidden from all eternity in the purposes of God, but revealed in its horror and its glory on the first Good Friday.

Perhaps we could do worse than look at it from the per-spective of three people present that day. It will give us three pictures, three metaphors of what Jesus achieved for us on that cross; three ways of enabling us to see that even if we can't forgive ourselves for some terrible thing we have done in the past, God can and will forgive, and do so with perfect justice and with boundless love.

THE FREEDOM FIGHTER'S VIEW

There was one man on that first Good Friday who vividly came to understand what the cross of Jesus meant. He was a freedom fighter, caught in the act of armed insurrection and murder. Imprisoned with his mates, he awaited the day of execution, glad that he had knocked off a few Romans, sad that he had not managed to deliver his country from the clutches of Rome. Imagine him waiting as the last morning of his life dawned. The steps along the corridor. The key in the lock. And the hairs on his neck stood up. Then to his amazement, the centurion knocked the chains off his hands and feet and said, 'You're a free man, Barabbas.' Incredulously, Barabbas looked at him, and concluded it was a sick joke. But it was no joke. He heard of Pilate's strange offer to release to the people at that Feast of Passover either himself or another revolutionary leader of a very different kind, another 'Barabbas', which means 'son of the Father'. Dazed, he would have hardly been able to drag himself away from the place of execution where his friends were dying for the crimes they had committed on behalf of their country, and where this strange Son of the Father was dying on Barabbas' very own cross, in Barabbas' very own place. History does not relate what became of him. But he could scarcely have missed the point that Jesus was taking his place. Jesus' death was settling his account so that his crimes would never be brought up against him again. He could scarcely have avoided reflecting that he should by rights have been on that central cross. 'He did it for me,' I can imagine him saying: 'He did it for me.'

That strange exchange made its impression on the Christian community. St. Peter was almost certainly an eyewitness of that scene, skulking at the edge of the crowd where he would not attract unwanted attention. He tells us in his First Letter that he was a 'witness of the sufferings of Christ'. After seeing

Jesus carrying that cross up to the place of execution, stumbling
under its weight, nailed to its unwelcome embrace, he wrote to
his Christian readers words which are surely to be interpreted
in the light of what he saw and felt that day. 'Christ suffered for
you,' he writes. 'When he was reviled he did not revile in
return; when he suffered, he did not threaten; but he trusted to
him who judges justly. He himself bore our sins in his own
body up to the tree . . . By his wounds you have been healed' (1
Peter 2: 21). Images of the Suffering Servant of Isaiah, of
Jesus staggering up to Golgotha bearing the load of Peter's sins,
of the innocent Jesus in the place of us guilty Barabbases, may
all have struggled through his mind as he wrote. He put it with
great clarity in the next chapter (1 Peter 3: 18). 'For Christ
also suffered for sins, once for all, the righteous for the unrighteous, that he might bring us to God.' That was why he
died: the righteous in the place of the unrighteous. Peter had
understood what the cross was all about.

So had Paul. In a remarkable passage in his letter to the
Colossians, he tells us that God has forgiven us all our sins,
having cancelled the list of failures which stood against our
names, with its legal demands: he swept it aside, nailing it to
his cross. What a sublime understanding of Calvary! There was
a long list of crimes against Barabbas, but Jesus met them all
when he died in Barabbas' place on that central cross. There
was a long list of much more refined sins against Paul's name;
but Jesus met them all when he died in Paul's place, on that
central cross. The condemned criminal usually had a charge
sheet with his crime written on it hung round his neck as he
went out to execution; this was nailed on to his cross. And Paul
sees Jesus going out to die with — not his jeering accusation
'King of the Jews' round his neck, but with Paul's sins, your
sins and my sins, hung round his neck. That is why he died. To
square our account. To clear our debt to the God we have
wronged. He swept aside all the accusing failures which I have
written against myself through my wilful sins: and he nailed
them to Christ's cross. They will never be raised again with me,
any more than they will with Paul, with Peter, with Barabbas.

For Christ has once suffered for sins, the righteous for the unrighteous, that he might bring us to God. That is one aspect of the meaning of the cross. It settles our debts. It sweeps them aside. It means they will never be raised against us again. For God in Christ has paid the account to the uttermost farthing; even though it took him to that bitter cross in order to do so. Nothing we can do can alter our guilty past. But this act of supreme generosity on his past has altered everything.

THE EXECUTIONER'S VIEW

There was another most interesting character at that cross. We do not know his name, but he made his own impression on the Christian community, for the story is told in no less than three of the Gospels. He was the centurion in charge of the execution squad. He had the closest view of anyone on that grim occasion. He watched Jesus suffer with dignity. He noticed that Jesus was concerned entirely for others, the soldiers who had nailed him there, the mother who had borne him, and the criminals executed with him. He had heard the priests mocking Jesus; he had seen the crowd jeering. He had felt the uncanny darkness: he had heard the great cry as Jesus died. And he burst out with a confession of faith in this man he had just executed. 'Truly this man was the Son of God,' is the bit Matthew and Mark record. Luke's account is more politically slanted: 'Certainly this man was innocent.' Maybe he said both, convinced not only of the innocence of Jesus but of his superhuman quality. Quite what a Roman centurion would have meant by 'Son of God' we cannot be sure. It was one of the titles by which the Emperor liked to be known: so on any showing it was a fantastic confession of loyalty to a crucified member of a subject race. But we can hardly doubt that the evangelists meant us to see far more in that cry. It was the primitive Christian creedal confession: Jesus Christ is Son of God and Saviour. Here was the man who killed Jesus recognising in him the way back to God!

I think we can be pretty sure that this interpretation is cor-

rect. In the verses immediately preceding, the evangelists do a
curious but deliberate thing. First, they record the death of
Jesus: 'Jesus breathed his last.' They then seem to ruin this
climax in their story by a ludicrous bit of irrelevant information: 'And the curtain of the temple was ripped in half from
the top to the bottom.' They then come back to Calvary and tell
us of the centurion's confession of faith. What are they trying to
convey?

It is not difficult to discover, once we recall what the curtain
in the temple was for. It was intended to guard the holiest part
of the temple from intruders. Nobody was to go into that 'Holy
of Holies' except the high priest, once a year, on the Day of
Atonement. He then made sacrifice for his own sins and for the
sins of the people by shedding the blood of an animal and offering it on the altar. The curtain meant exclusion: it meant that
God was holy, and man was not. It was a vast visual aid to get
one simple message across, that God is too holy for sinful folk
like you and me to approach. It spelt 'Keep out'.

When Jesus died on that cross the temple curtain was split: it
was an act of God, and was probably due to an earthquake that
the Jewish historian Josephus says took place about that time
and shook the lintels of the temple. But however it happened,
its message was loud and clear to those Christian evangelists. It
spelt 'Come in'. It meant that Jesus, the supreme high priest,
had made the ultimate sacrifice not for his own sins (he had
none to atone for) but for those of a whole world gone astray. It
meant that those who trusted him could now draw near to God
without fear that they would be excluded. And listen to the way
that confident access resounds through the New Testament.
'Now through Jesus Christ you who once were afar off have
been brought near in the blood of Christ,' says the Letter to the
Ephesians (2: 13), and 'Through him we both [Jews and Gentiles alike] have access in one Spirit to the Father' (2: 18). In
his letter to the Romans Paul thrills to the wonder of our ac-
quittal through what Jesus did on that cross. 'We have peace
with God through our Lord Jesus Christ,' he cries: 'through
him we have obtained access' (5: 1). And the writer to the

Hebrews puts it a bit more allegorically but very powerfully, when he writes: 'Brothers, we have confidence to enter the Holy of Holies through the blood of Jesus, the new and living way which has opened for us through the curtain, that is his flesh . . .' (10: 19). His flesh offered for us on that cross made the way into God's holy presence possible; it split the curtain, so to speak, which kept God so distant and unreal. And instead of one man going in once a year after due sacrifice — repeated annually — we can all go in at any time. There is unrestricted access into the holy presence of God for all who trust the one whose death made it all possible. That death meant access. And we find the centurion making no delay to take that access — achieved through the death of Jesus for which he had been responsible. We are meant to see ourselves in that centurion, just as we are in Barabbas. The death of Jesus settles our account, and means we can go straight into the presence of God unafraid, knowing that the barriers have been broken down, the guilt has been expiated, the dirt washed away by the death of Jesus, the Saviour. And that is good news for troubled consciences which no psychiatry can match.

THE DYING ROBBER'S VIEW

The third figure at the cross of Jesus who catches our attention is the robber who hangs beside him. As they suffer there together, this man makes the most remarkable statement in the whole astounding narrative. He says, 'Jesus, remember me when you come in your kingly power.' The other criminal executed alongside them had been cursing at the silent sufferer. 'Messiah, are you? O.K. then, save yourself — and us!' But the man we have come to know as the penitent thief rebuked him. 'Do you not fear God? You are going to meet him soon enough! And neither you nor I can complain: we are getting what we deserve. But this man has done nothing wrong.' It was then that he turned to Jesus with his fascinating request, 'Jesus, remember me when you come in your kingly power.' What a fantastic example of faith that was. To believe that the man executed alongside you had a future, and would be able to remember you. To believe that he had a kingdom and would come in his kingly rule. To turn to a bloodied, suffering man in his death throes and ask for favourable memory in the life to come — I find it simply staggering. But that is what he did. And Jesus replied with one of the greatest of all his sayings: 'Today you will be with me in Paradise.' Marvellous to know that he would die today — often men lingered on for a day or two after crucifixion. Marvellous to know that he would be with Jesus. Marvellous to have that future described in a lovely old Persian word for a park or garden, the garden of God. But most marvellous of all is the implication which, though unspoken, comes through like a trumpet blast. This man's accusing past will be silenced: his guilt will be expiated; his sins will be forgotten. He will be with Jesus in God's garden. He had done nothing to deserve it: how could he do a thing to earn his forgiveness when he was hanging there on a cross, dying? Not a thing could he contribute to his own salvation — except the sin from which he needed to be saved. But that, St. Luke would seem to teach us, is precisely the condition of being forgiven. 'Nothing in my hand I bring: simply to-thy cross I cling.' It is not the churchmen with lots of religious observances to their name; it is not the Romans with all their political power and influence; but a simple, guilty, condemned criminal who finds pardon with Jesus.

Do ... or done?

That is why the New Testament writers make such a point of telling us that we are not put right with God by anything that we do; rather by something done for us. The worldly man's religion has two letters in it: 'do'. The forgiven sinner's has four: 'done'. And in that 'done' countless people of every age and culture have found peace. 'There is no condemnation to the man who is in Christ Jesus,' writes Paul. 'For what our attempts to keep the law could never do God himself has done through the person and the death of Jesus.' Done! It reminds me of the little girl who was so thrilled when she came to understand the meaning of the cross. 'I'm trusting in the justice of God, Mummy,' she cried. 'You mean in the love of God, dear?' corrected her mother. 'Oh no,' said the little girl. 'Jesus has died and paid all my debts. And God won't charge me for them again. I'm trusting in the justice of God.' How right she was.

I met this summer a remarkable man, quiet, confident. He had been a dance-band leader. And on his way home in the car one night he had been listening to a snatch of a religious radio programme. The preacher asked, 'If you were to die tonight, what possible reason is there why God should allow you into his heaven?' That seemed to James Kennedy a good question. So he did not rest until he discovered the answer. He knew that if his acceptance depended on his own good deeds he would have every reason to feel despondent. But he came to see that it didn't depend on anything of the sort. His acceptance, his pardon, his future with God depended simply and solely on what God had done to make him acceptable: it rested on the cross of Jesus Christ. That discovery revolutionised his life. He trained for ordination and is now exercising a remarkable ministry in the U.S.A. in which this question, that changed his life, features largely. Hundreds if not thousands of people each year come to God through the outreach of that church, as its members go round visiting and asking folk, 'If you died tonight, what good reason is there why God should accept you into his heaven?'

What would you say to that question? If you are just a churchman, if you are an 'I do my best' type, you would be bound to hesitate before answering. You would be suitably modest and non-committal. But the believer can say with joy and confidence, 'I know I would be accepted if I died tonight. Indeed, I am accepted now, and I have many promises of the New Testament to assure me of it. You see, I am trusting not in anything that I do for acceptance with God, but on what he has done. That is why I can be sure about it. My future is guaranteed by Calvary.'

QUESTIONS

It is at this point that questions flood in. Is the cross all that necessary, you ask? Listen. I had meningitis last year: it is a killer disease. Of course, I did not know I was so ill. I just felt a splitting headache. But when the top physician in Durban came to see me in the middle of a Sunday afternoon and rushed me into hospital, you did not need to persuade me I was ill! If that man had to be called in, I must have been in a serious condition. And if nothing less would suffice than the coming to earth and the death on the cross of Jesus, the Great Physician, then we must have been in a bad way. Do you not think that if there had been any other possible way of rescuing us God would have taken it?

But perhaps you feel that the cross of Christ is unfair. Does it almost seem that God is punishing Jesus instead of us? It is not like that. Actually, the New Testament never speaks of God punishing Jesus on the cross. It does speak of his bearing our sins there. It does speak of his doing so in our place and for our sake. But we must not think of three parties, as it were: God sitting comfortably up in heaven; Jesus in agony on the cross; and you and me going scot free as a result. No. The Bible says that *God* was very much involved in what happened on that cross: God was in Christ, reconciling the world to himself. He was coming in person to deal with the mess we had got ourselves into. It also tells us that *we* were very much involved with what happened there. Jesus was our representative: he was man bearing the consequences of man's rebellion. And just as he died and rose again, so those who come to him have a standing call to share in his death (i.e. allow him to nail our old, sinful nature to the cross, so to speak) and in his resurrection (i.e. allow the power of his risen life to set us free from the ruts of bad habit). Yes, God the Father and we ourselves are very much involved in the cross of Jesus Christ. It would be most misleading and crude to suggest that God 'took it out on' Jesus for us. Rather, he was in Christ on the cross, allowing our rebellion to crush him. Such was his love.

Very well then, what happens to those who have never had a chance to hear the gospel? The New Testament makes it plain that Jesus died not for our sins only but for the sins of the whole world. That death availed for believers who died in ignorance of the cross in the centuries that went before. It availed for the great men of faith in the Old Testament days, men like Abraham and David. They could sing, 'Happy is the man whose iniquity is pardoned and whose sin is covered' because they trusted that God would find a way to do just that. They did not understand how he could, but they trusted in him and not in their own fancied goodness. No doubt it is the same for men after the coming of Jesus who have never heard the gospel — if they genuinely trust in God and not in their own good deeds to save them. The cross was for them, too. And when they hear of it, as they sometimes do through a Bible or a missionary, they rejoice and thank the great God who had found such a marvellous way to settle their debts, grant them pardon and secure their access to him. But that does not let us off the hook, does it? We have heard the message of his love, and what he did for us on the cross. The only proper question is, What are we going to do about it?

'But surely, I don't need to do anything about it?' you may be asking. 'Doesn't the whole thrust of your argument mean that I am automatically forgiven, through what has been done for me on the cross?' Not so. Forgiveness is costly. It always involves two parties. To continue the three analogies we have used about the cross: debts remain unless you cash the cheque you have been given to pay them with. Access may be available, but unless you take it, you remain out of touch with your benefactor. Pardon may be offered: but it has to be accepted. A Royal Pardon offered to some prisoner is quite void until it is accepted. I should be a fool if I ignored it. I should be stupid to take it for granted and assume that naturally I would be entitled to a pardon. I should be mad to say, 'What a beautiful document: I will frame it and use it to decorate the wall of my cell.' I would be out of my mind to tear it up. Obviously, I need to accept it with gratitude and humility. That is just what you need to do with the pardon which God holds out to you in the cross of Jesus Christ. It will do you no good if you take it for granted, or if you say in admiration, 'How wonderful.' It will do you no good if you ignore it all your life. It will do you no good if you tear it up and throw it in the face of the donor. One dying thief was forgiven so that nobody need despair, however bad his past has been, however short his grasp on life. But only one was forgiven, as if to remind us that nobody can dare to presume on the pardon of God, without accepting it personally. The cross of Jesus stands between those two thieves. One was saved, and the other lost. The cross of Jesus is equally divisive in today's world. Some know they are guilty, but know equally that because of what he did on that cross they are forgiven. Others try to pretend that they are all right, and that they do not need pardon, do not need to look to Jesus to change the past. The cross divides those two groups of mankind. Which group do you belong to? Don't rest until you get the matter clear. Mercifully it is possible to move from one group to the other. If a dying thief can discover pardon at the cross, so can you. Don't miss it, for this is the only medicine in the world that can change your guilty past.

9
'When you're dead, you're dead!'

'WHEN I DIE, I rot,' said Bertrand Russell. And you can't argue with that. It is obviously true. But is it the whole truth? Does the real 'me' disappear?

AN INTRIGUING QUESTION

Every few years one of the major daily or Sunday papers takes the matter up. They run a series on 'The great mystery of life after death' or some such title. The insurance companies take it up, with all their loaded advertising about Refuge for Life. The question of life after the grave has intrigued men since the earliest dawn of the human race. I remember seeing some of the oldest tombs in existence at Byblos in the Lebanon. The skeletons were buried in a highly suggestive position. Their knees were tucked up under their chins, and they were encased in an earthenware egg. In other words, the men of that far off day cherished the hope that new life would break out of that egg of death. They hoped that when you were dead you might somehow live again.

I remember being fascinated on a visit to Italy by the preoccupation with this subject among the Romans. There are many mosaics dealing with death and the after-life at Pompeii, the Italian city overwhelmed and buried by the terrible eruption of Vesuvius in A.D. 79. There are pictures of skeletons with jugs in their hands, pictures of death in various guises, and one memorable one of the phoenix, a mythical bird which was supposed to come to life again after it had been burnt on the funeral pyre. Underneath the picture the artist had written, 'Phoenix, how lucky you are!'

To be sure, when you're dead, you're dead. It is very final. There is no return to life. But is it the end of you? Or is there a life beyond? It is a fascinating question.

But there's another side to it.

A THREATENING QUESTION

If there is a life after death, what will it be like? It is bad enough if death is the end, but far worse if it is not. Epicurus, the Greek pleasure-loving philosopher, said long ago, 'What men fear is not that death is annihilation, but that it is not.' And Yeats, in his poem *Death*, catches the feeling precisely:

> Nor dread nor hope attend
> A dying animal.
> A man awaits his end,
> Dreading and hoping all.

What if we shall be called to account for the lives we have lived? What if, as the New Testament puts it, 'it is appointed for all men, once to die, and after that the judgment'; Perish the thought: it would be too awful! But it would be fair, would it not? It would match our freedom. We know all too well that freedom and accountability are the two sides of the same coin. A student has almost unlimited freedom: but the day comes when he has to give an account of it in the final examinations. An architect has enormous freedom in designing and building a house. But at the end of the day he is accountable to his employer. What if life is like that? What if it should be true that 'every one of us shall give an account of himself to God'?

What if Jesus was right in his story of the rich fool? The man lived as though this life was all there is; he made success and money and property his gods, and left God out. And then, one night he died. God said to him, 'You fool, tonight your life will be required of you. And then who will come in for all that property you will have to leave behind?' A devastating story, very apt for our materialistic age. Could Jesus be right? If so, it would not be much fun to have God saying 'You fool' to you. I saw an advertisement for life assurance not long ago, advising me to invest in the company, and ending with this sardonic note: 'Let those who think they are going to live for ever make their own arrangements.' What if we do live on — and have not made any arrangements?

What if Jesus is right in his story of the rich man and Lazarus? What if there is a life after the grave and we are accountable for the way we have lived in this one? For our selfishness, our callous disregard of the needs of the Lazaruses on our doorstep, not to mention the half of the world's population who live on the bread line because of economic policies pursued by the greedy West? What if we shall be judged in that day by the way we have treated the coloured bus driver, the dustman, or the old person in the senile ward of the local hospital? Of course, prejudice, including racism, is two-way. One black Christian leader challenged his fellow blacks recently like this. 'At the judgment day, the Lord will say to us, "Why didn't you preach the gospel to all those poor whites lost in affluence and ambition?" ' What if such an unpalatable possibility turned out to be true after all?

'Ah,' you say, 'it is all sheer speculation. How can you possibly know?'

A QUESTION THAT CAN BE ANSWERED

One could only know if there is a life beyond the grave if someone came back with reliable information. And that is, by definition, impossible. Dead men don't rise. When you're dead, you're dead. But this brings us to the very heart of the Christian claim. Alone among the religions of the world it dares to maintain that we can know about life after death, we can know how to get there, we can know something of what awaits us, for one simple and sufficient reason, that Jesus Christ, crucified on the cross, rose again from the grave.

Now this is a preposterous claim. It cannot be true. Or can it? There is, of course, only one way of finding out whether there is a life beyond the grave or not. And that would be for someone to die and come back to tell us what it is like. I suppose it's a bit like space exploration. The moon has fascinated mankind from time immemorial. Was there, or was there not life on this mysterious world of the moon? What were conditions like on the side of the moon we cannot see? Nobody could tell, though that did not stop lots of guessing. Nobody could tell until Neil Armstrong, the first man to land on the moon, came back to tell us what it is like. Not only that, but he paved the way for later space travellers to follow.

THE CHRISTIAN CLAIM

Now that is precisely how the Christian claim about life after death can be assessed. We believe that one man, Jesus of Nazareth, came back from beyond the grave to show us that he has overcome the last enemy and to enable us to follow in his footsteps. Of course we know that dead men are not in the habit of

rising from their tombs. We know that there is no scientifically
established category of dead men who come back to life again.
We are not naïve: we know that this claim makes the imagination boggle. But we believe it all the same, and on good
evidence. I will give you some of that evidence in a moment.
But just now let's be clear abut one thing. We are not making
this claim for any old Tom, Dick or Harry. We are maintaining
that in one man, one very special man, one who was more than
man, the forces of death met their match. We saw in chapter 5
strong reasons for supposing that Jesus was no less God than
man. How can we be dogmatic that he could not rise from the
grave in that case? We saw that he lived an absolutely un-
spoiled and perfect life. How can we be so sure that a life which
has given no foothold to sin could not master death? We have
no other to compare it with. Jesus made his whole credibility
rest upon the assertion that he would 'do a Jonah' on his contemporaries, and just as Jonah came back from his three day
'death' inside the great fish, so he himself would rise from the
jaws of death (Matthew 12: 39–41). So let us lay aside blind
prejudice that says 'It couldn't happen', and see whether, according to all the evidence, it *did* happen in this one solitary
case of Jesus. If he was perfect man, if he was more than man,
we cannot rule it out of court.

I have tried to look at the evidence in some detail in a little
book *Man Alive*. You might care to follow the matter up there.
But here are five points to consider, as you reflect on the events
of that first Good Friday.

1. THE MAN WAS DEAD

Very dead. Roman executions were grimly thorough. As a
matter of fact, the officer in charge of the execution was himself
liable to the death penalty if his job was not done efficiently. In
the case of Jesus, the execution squad saw that he was dead
already, and so did not bother to break his legs (a barbaric way
of ensuring the crucified wretches did not continue to raise
themselves on their crosses and gulp in breath). But just to

make doubly sure, they pierced his side with a spear, and out came 'blood and water' as an eyewitness put it (John 19: 34f). This is a fascinating detail, all the more remarkable because the writer could have no idea of its medical significance. But any doctor now will tell you that the separation of the blood into clot and serum is one of the surest indications of death. That is what St. John records, even though he could only marvel at it, not understand it. But it gives proof positive that Jesus was dead. If we wanted more, we could have it: not only did the centurion report to the governor that the job was done (and he knew a dead man when he saw one — he had despatched enough of them), but Pilate himself allowed Joseph of Arimathea to take the body away (John 19: 38). It is another fascinating touch to discover that the word here used for 'body' of Jesus is, in the original Greek 'corpse': the word is never used of a live man, always of a dead one.

Yes, Jesus was dead all right. So any variety of the 'swoon theory' that suggests Jesus recovered from his terrible ordeal in the cool of the tomb, and crept out, is utterly discredited. It simply couldn't have happened. But so keen have unbelievers been to reject the plain teaching of the New Testament writers (based though it is on eyewitness testimony), that they have had recourse to theories which maintain that Jesus was not really dead. You find it as long ago as Celsus in the second century. He was a strong anti-Christian who explained the resurrection by supposing that Jesus was nursed back to health again by Mary Magdalene: forty days later his wounds got the better of him, and he died and was buried secretly, but not before he had assembled his friends and walked off into a cloud on a mountain top! Such poverty stricken explanations are still put forward from time to time, recently in Hugh Schonfield's *The Passover Plot*. They are wrecked on the massive evidence that Jesus was indeed dead. They are also psychologically inprobable in the extreme. Would disciples who knew that Jesus was not risen from the tomb but he had died ignominiously from his wounds, have gone all over the world proclaiming his risen presence with such joy that men felt they might be drunk, and with such persistence that prison, torture and death could not stop them? You don't let yourself be bumped off for a fraud ...

2. THE TOMB WAS EMPTY

Very empty, on that first Easter morning. And nobody has ever been able to suggest a really plausible explanation, apart from the united testimony of every strand in the New Testament that the tomb was empty because Jesus had conquered death and was alive again.

Of course, people have had a go at explaining it away. One distinguished professor suggested that in the mist of early dawn Mary and her friends found the wrong tomb! Did she not do better later, we might ask? Was Joseph of Arimathea equally clueless on the location of his own personal tomb which he had given over to Jesus? Another crude suggestion, made as early as the end of the second century, has at least a touch of humour about it. It suggests that the gardner was responsible for all the talk about the resurrection of Jesus. He was so fed up at sight-seers stumping around the tomb, treading all over the seedlings he had planted out, that he removed the body and buried it elsewhere! Another rationalisation of the empty tomb appears in the New Testament itself. The soldiers, set to guard the tomb were bribed by the embarrassed Jews to explain the absence of the body of Jesus by asserting that they fell asleep, and then the disciples of Jesus came and stole his body (Matthew 28: 11–15).

But all these attempts to explain away the empty tomb on the assumption that someone stole the body come unstuck very fast, on this simple point. There were only two lots of people interested in what became of the body of this executed teacher: his friends and his enemies. The records all show us that his friends had no idea that he might rise; they were not expecting anything of the sort. Rather, they scattered sadly like any other band whose hopes had been dashed by the death of their leader. There was no expectation in Judaism that any prophet or teacher might personally come back from the grave, though there was the hope of a general resurrection at the Last Day. His disciples were not expecting his resurrection. What's more, if they had been able to spirit the body away (despite the strict guard kept on the tomb), they would scarcely have been prepared to die for their fraud: nor would people all over the world and in all generations from then till now be so confident that Jesus lives.

But if it was not the disciples who stole the body, how could it have been the opposition? They had been working for his execution for ages. And now it had come about. The last thing they would have done is to give colour to any talk about resurrection by moving his body surreptitiously. They had got him where they wanted, dead and buried. We may be sure they spared no effort to keep him there — hence the seal and the guard on the tomb. To suggest that either the Jews or the Romans moved his body is a beggar's refuge from having to admit the truth of the resurrection. Had they been so incredibly foolish, they would only have had to produce the body of Jesus when the disciples claimed his resurrection, in order to squash the new movement at a single stroke. And this is what nobody was able to do. They just got very cross with the apostles, tried to silence them, put them in prison, tortured and killed them. But they could not discredit their story, that the tomb was empty because Jesus was risen.

Did you ever notice the fascinating bit of corroborative detail in St. John's account of the resurrection? He tells with artless simplicity of Peter and the beloved disciple racing to the sepulchre to see for themselves after Mary had brought them the incredible news that Jesus was alive. When they got to the tomb, they stooped down, looked in, and saw the linen bandages that had been wound round Jesus' body, intertwined with spices (the Eastern way of burial) lying wrapped up ... but with nobody inside. They saw the turban which had been wound round his head 'not lying with the linen clothes, but wrapped together in a place by itself' (John 20: 7). At that point, we read, they saw and believed. Why? Because it was apparent to them that the body of Jesus had emerged from those graveclothes, just as a butterfly emerges from its chrysalis: and the turban lay apart, just like the cap of a chrysalis case when the butterfly has come out. Incidentally, this has something to say about the modern suggestion that the resurrection of Jesus was somehow real but not physical. That seems to me rather like trying to have your cake and eat it. To be sure, Christians have never held that the resurrection of Jesus was the mere resuscitation of a corpse. The New Testament proclaims that he was raised to a life of a new quality. Just like the butterfly, in fact. It does not emerge unchanged from when it went into that chrysalis. No, it is transformed to a new dimension of living. No longer is it a caterpillar which crawls slowly and painfully wherever it wants to go. Now it can sail through the air with delicacy and poise. It is freed into another element in its new life. But it is unquestionably the same insect, despite the change brought about by its hibernation in the chrysalis. So it was with Jesus. His tomb was not empty in order to let him out; but to let men in to see that he had indeed risen. The empty tomb and the empty graveclothes are symbols, pointers, to the fact that Jesus, the man, has become Christ, the risen Lord. 'He holds the keys of death and of the after life,' sang the prophet who wrote the Book of Revelation (1: 17). The man was indeed dead. But the tomb was found empty because death could not hold him. And that, as Peter said on the first Day of Pentecost, was a remarkable fulfilment of a prophecy made a thousand years beforehand:

David says, concerning Jesus, 'Thou wilt not abandon my soul to Hades, nor let thy Holy One see corruption. Thou has made known to me the ways of life . . .' Brethren, I may say to you confidently of the patriarch David that he both died and was buried, and his tomb is with us to this day . . . But being a prophet he foresaw the resurrection of Christ, that he was not abandoned to Hades, nor did his flesh see corruption. This Jesus God raised up, and of that we are all witnesses (Acts 2: 25–32).

3. THE CHURCH WAS BORN

In a fascinating and most penetrating study, *The Phenomenon of the New Testament*, Professor C. F. D. Moule, points out a very remarkable thing about Christianity. It had absolutely nothing to add to Judaism, nothing whatsoever — except this conviction that the Rabbi Jesus had been raised from the dead! All the earliest Christians were loyal Jews, of course. They all went to the synagogue to worship. They read and believed the Jewish Scriptures. Their ethics were based on the Old Testament. Only one thing caused this new religion (as it became) to erupt. It was the conviction that Jesus must be the long awaited Deliverer from God, foretold in those Scriptures of the Old Testament, hinted at in all the sacrificial ceremonial of the Jewish people. He must be the Coming One; his resurrection from the dead proved it (Romans 1: 4). Nobody else had done that. Jesus was unique. No wonder they could do no less than give him the title 'Lord', the name usually applied to Almighty God in the Old Testament Scriptures.

That church, armed with such an improbable claim, swept across the whole Roman Empire inside three hundred years. It is a perfectly amazing story of peaceful revolution, without parallel in the history of the world. It came about because Christians were able to say to unbelievers, 'Jesus did not only die for you, but is alive. You can meet him, and discover for yourself the reality we are talking about.' People did discover for themselves. And the church, born out of the Easter grave, spread.

That church had three special characteristics. You found them everywhere it went. The Christians had a special day, Sunday; a special rite of initiation, baptism; and a special meal, the Holy Communion. Now the interesting thing about that fact is this. Every one of the three is rooted in the resurrection of Jesus. Sunday, called 'the Lord's Day' in Revelation 1: 10, was given this remarkable name because it was the day, the first day of the week, on which the Lord Jesus rose from the tomb. The Jews had, from time immemorial, kept the

seventh day of the week sacred. It recalled the completion of
God's work of creation. Indeed, its observance was laid down in
the Ten Commandments, and remains one of the most dis-
tinguishing features of the Jewish nation. Yet these Jews who
knew that Jesus was risen reckoned, reasonably enough, that
God's new creation in the resurrection of Christ was even more
memorable and significant than his act of creating the world
in the first instance. It is quite something to change the day of
rest after several thousand years. It needed nothing less than
the resurrection to trigger it off.

Then there was Christian baptism. You went down into a
river, repenting of your sins, and professing your faith in Jesus
as Saviour and Lord. You were immersed. You climbed out the
other side. What did it mean? Simply this. That you, as a
disciple, were linked to your Lord who went down into the dark
river of death *and came up the other side.* It was an initiation
ceremony which would have been unthinkable apart from the
resurrection of Jesus.

It was just the same with the Lord's Supper, as they called it.
This simple meal of bread and wine was shared by the Christians in memory of Jesus' body broken (like the loaf) for them,
and his blood poured out (like the wine) for them. Understandable enough. But when the New Testament writers talk
about this meal as an opportunity for exultant gladness, we can
see that it is more than a memorial meal for a departed hero.
They believed that the Lord who had died was alive and present in their midst. Death itself was conquered, and the
Conqueror was with them in all his risen power.

Baptism, Communion, Sunday, all point to that resurrection
of Jesus from the grave which acted as a launching pad — the
only launching pad — for the whole Christian rocket which
burst upon the ancient world.

4. THE LORD APPEARED

Quite unmistakably. To lots of people. St. Paul gives a list of
some of them in 1 Corinthians 15, a letter he wrote about

twenty years after the event, when plenty of eyewitnesses were still alive. Curiously enough he does not mention the appearance of Jesus to Mary of Magdala, though all the Gospels are clear that she was the first witness of the resurrection. Perhaps this was because no woman was considered a proper witness in either Jewish or Gentile law in ancient society. Incidentally, if Christians had dreamed up the story of the empty tomb, would they have been stupid enough to attribute the discovery of that tomb and the first sight of the risen Jesus to a woman, whose testimony was legally worthless? That fact alone speaks volumes for the truth of the resurrection story. Although there were plenty of men who saw him later, it was to a despised woman that Jesus first appeared. Somehow it seems typical of him.

Let's glance at this list of witnesses which Paul brings us in 1 Corinthians 15. 'I deliver to you as of first importance what I also received,' he says to the men of Corinth — incidentally using the words 'delivered' and 'received' in their technical sense of passing on duly authorised facts. What did he pass on? 'Christ died for our sins according to the Scriptures. He was buried. He was raised on the third day according to the Scriptures, and he appeared . . .' To whom? First in the list he mentions Peter, the Peter who had denied him. Then 'the twelve', presumably excluding Judas (dead) and Thomas (absent). Then he appeared to more than five hundred Christians at once, probably in Galilee where the majority of his followers lived. 'Most of them are still alive,' adds Paul: as if to say, you can go and check up on the resurrection with them if you like. Jesus then appeared to James, his brother. He appeared to 'all the apostles', presumably including Thomas this time. He appeared also to Paul. Now put together that lot: women, fishermen, a sceptical brother, a fanatical Pharisee opponent, and five hundred ordinary folk. Can any theory of hallucination cover those appearances? Hallucinations tend to happen to particular types of people — no one type here. Hallucinations tend to be allied with wish fulfilment — none of that here. Hallucinations tend to recur. These appearances ended after forty days and never came again. Hallucinations belong to the sick world — and it is hard to maintain that there was anything sick about these early missionaries as they preached the full health and salvation that their risen Messiah brought them. No, these appearances of the risen Christ are without parallel in the religious history of mankind. Nowhere else do you find anybody, still less so great a diversity of people claiming to have had intimate personal contact (even to go as far as eating fish and honeycomb) with a much loved leader recently killed. And it will not do to suppose that these were mere subjective visions. At least one of the apostles, Paul, was accustomed to having visions, was proud of them, and was very sure that this appearance of the Risen One was no vision (1 Corinthians 9: 1, 2 Corinthians 12: 1ff.) It was real.

5. THEIR LIVES WERE CHANGED ...

This has always been one of the strongest proofs of the truth of the resurrection. Those who claim to have come in touch with the risen Christ have had their lives transformed. Think of that list we looked at just now. Peter was changed from a coward who denied and forsook his Master when the crunch came, into a man of rock whom the Establishment could not cow by dint of threats, imprisonment or death sentence. Think of the twelve, who were transformed from defeatists into a task force by the resurrection: theirs is one of the greatest 'come-back' stories in the world. The five hundred were changed from a rabble into a church. All the apostles, including Thomas, came from unbelief to ardent faith. James, Jesus' sceptical brother, becomes suddenly changed into a believer, and more, the leader of the Jerusalem church: a fantastic turn-up for the book. What accounts for it? Simple: 'he appeared to James'. And perhaps most amazing of all is that volte-face of Saul of Tarsus, the violent, bigoted persecutor of the Christians, into the greatest follower Jesus ever had. The reason? 'Last of all, he appeared to me.'

... AND STILL ARE

But that first century stuff is only half the story, remarkable
though it is. It is not quite the same since those days, because
nobody has seen the risen Lord with his own eyes. I imagine
that Jesus displayed himself openly to his followers, allowed
them to feel the holes in his hands and feet, even ate meals
with them, in order to persuade them that he was still the Jesus
they had known. Yet he passed through doors, disappeared
while they were talking with him, and eventually parted from
them for the last time on the Mount of Olives in order to persuade them that he had risen not just to a further span of life,
but to a new quality of life. From then on he would not
appear to their physical eyes. But by his Spirit, no longer restricted to the confines of a physical body, he would indwell the
very lives of his people, not just be alongside them, as he had
during his time on earth. And that is what he has been doing
ever since. So although we cannot say, like the first witnesses, 'I
have seen the Lord,' every genuine Christian can say 'I know
him. He has come into my life. He has made such radical
changes that I cannot believe I am kidding myself.' Every believer is, in this sense, a witness of the resurrection.

This, to me, was the most impressive demonstration of the
truth that Jesus is alive. I watched the lives of Christians for
the best part of a year, and I discovered them to be
different — different from my own, and different from what
they had been. The other day I was having a discussion with a
number of post-graduate scientists, and you can imagine the
number of objections to Christianity which were coming forward. And then one of the agnostics said simply, 'I know there
must be something in it because of the difference it has made to
my friends.'

The life-changing work of the risen Jesus goes on today, and
it is a powerful testimony to the truth that he is indeed alive
and well. I have been a Christian long enough now to be sure
that I am not kidding myself. I have seen Christ's transforming
touch change obviously needy characters, like long-term pris-

oners, compulsive gamblers and alcoholics, drug addicts and prostitutes. I am just as moved by the way he changes attitudes and character in more ordinary people. I think of a brilliant athlete I have known for only six weeks. He also has a brilliant political career ahead of him. He was intensely ambitious. But now he is quite clear that his games are to be used as a talent from God, and that his political career is in the Master's hands and is to be used for His glory, not for the satisfaction of his own ambition. The peace, the relaxation that has come to him through allowing the Risen One to take over, is remarkable. His friends are noticing it.

Or I think of an Oxford student I have known for a similar time. I met her first in church, when she was wrestling against the Christ she had become convinced was real. It was a long and tearful fight. Eventually she gave in. Now she is not only a very different character, more gracious, more outgoing, more thoughtful of others, but she is going to give up two weeks of her vacation in going on a mission to share with others the discovery she has herself made. No matter whether it is in a spectacular conversion, or far more gentle ways, the risen Christ shines through his present day witnesses. It reminds me a bit of the ending of *Godspell*. In this musical the joy of the resurrection is shown through dance. And members of the audience are invited to come up on to the stage and dance with the cast. They do not thereby become the cast, but they share the same experience. Now the cast, so to speak, is the first generation of disciples: Peter, James and John and others who saw the risen Christ. We cannot join that cast of eyewitnesses. But we can join them in the dance of Christian experience, if we have come to know the living Lord.

THE IMPLICATIONS

Those, then, are five pieces of evidence. Together they point to one conclusion, that Jesus of Nazareth did not only die but rose to a new life, an endless life, which enables him to meet and transform character today — your character, even — just as he did in the first century. We can be confident that Jesus pioneered the way through death, just as those first astronauts pioneered the way to the moon. And just as they brought back evidence about what lay on the hidden side of the moon, so he has shown what lies on the hidden side of death. Death is not the end. It is, or it can be, the gateway into a new quality of life, 'butterfly life' instead of 'caterpillar life'.

If this is the case, we would be wise to listen very carefully to what this pioneer, Jesus, has to say about the hidden side of death. He ought to know. He has been there. He is very explicit. 'Let not your hearts be troubled,' he says to his disciples, grief-stricken at the prospect of his death, 'believe in God, believe also in me. In my Father's house there are many rooms. If it were not so I would have told you. I go to prepare a place for you' (John 14: 1ff). Those are words we can trust. They come from the one person who has broken the death barrier, the one person equipped to take other colonists with him to that un-charted land.

But there is another side of the coin. It is true that the Christian can be confident that God will not scrap him at death. It is true he can rest with assurance on this promise of Jesus. He can look forward to death not as the end, but as the end of the caterpillar stage. But what of the man who is not linked to the Risen One? How can he hope to fare? Not very well, obviously. I should not fare very well if I tried to get to the moon under my own steam, however much hardware and rocketry was put at my disposal. I should need the skilled direction of an astron-aut who had done it before. Without that, I should not stand a chance. That is why Jesus said to people who turned their backs on him, 'I go away, and you will seek me and die in your sin. Where I am going you cannot come' (John 8: 21). Does that sound hard? Not really. You cannot get to the moon unless you commit yourself to the astronaut. It is very sad, though. Jesus grieved over people who turned down his offer of life abundant, life for ever. 'You refuse to come to me that you may have life' (John 5: 40). Curiously enough, the practical answer to the riddle of whether or not there is a life beyond the grave lies with us. We may choose whether when we die we rot; or whether death becomes for us the chrysalis case to usher in a new quality of life with the Risen One.

'You can't change human nature'

BY AND LARGE, you can't change human nature. That is why the early years are so important. The influence of home and school, of first years in the job or time at university, tend to form our main characteristics. They will change to some extent with fresh opportunities, new pressures, responsibility (or the lack of it), and age. But once the direction of a man's life and character are set, you do not find that rapid changes of character and attitude occur very often. You have only to think of the married couple whose years of living with one another enable them to predict with painful accuracy how the partner will react, even what he will say, in a given situation. Or think of the man who comes out of prison only to return there again for a similar offence. Only this morning I heard on the radio of a man convicted of selling goods supposedly made by and for the benefit of the blind: he was now out of prison, and was a direc- tor of a firm selling goods supposedly made by and for the benefit of old age pensioners! The leopard does not very often change his spots. You can indeed train up a young tree, or a young dog for that matter, in the direction that you want. But try bending a mature tree; try training a five-year-old dog, and you will be in for disappointment.

Solzhenitsyn put the problem with his customary clarity, 'Human nature changes not much faster than the geological face of the earth.' Indeed, the irony and the tragedy of modern life lies in this: we have become masters of our environment to a very large degree, but cannot produce any comparable control over ourselves. We can alter environment but not people. Of course, we have had a good try.

POSSIBLE REMEDIES?

Political and social liberation has been one greatly favoured avenue of change. Throw out the colonial regime and all will be well. It can scarcely be argued that the result has lived up to the expectation. As I write India is being subjected to curtailment of liberty greater than anything faced in Imperial days. Nigeria seemed to be the ideal of a country peacefully passing from colonial rule to independence — but since then has suffered a disastrous civil war on tribal and financial issues, has refused to return from military to civilian rule, and has thrown out its head of state, while corruption continues unhindered. Do you feel, 'We don't do things that way in the West.' No? But think of the promises offered by political parties at elections, and how ragged and moth-eaten those high hopes seem a year or so later. Political liberation does not change human nature. Neither does the permissiveness of social liberation. Bertrand Russell, one of the foremost advocates of permissiveness in his generation, said with feeling about his own children at the end of his life, 'To let children go free was to establish a reign of terror.' And that is just what is happening in many schools today.

It would be tiresome to multiply examples. Patent remedies for ailing humanity have included education, the Welfare State and psychological medicine. None of these have had more than a marginal effect on the basic problem of changing human nature. Education is more and more non-directional these days, and the same is true of counselling. This is good in so far as it allows a man to find his own resources in himself; but it doesn't help when that same man finds himself to be his prison. Psychological medicine can no more infuse any new element into human nature than education can. And yet human nature cries out for change. Many millions of pounds a year are spent in Britain on pills, sleeping tablets and the like to relieve tension, depression and insomnia. Hundreds of thousands in Britain die every year as a result of the two most common analgesic drugs, tobacco and alcohol. The Welfare State cannot eradicate these human problems. Indeed, in some ways it encourages them to fester. I know unemployed people who will not work because it pays them better to be on unemployment pay and social security. I know students who regard it as their right to fritter away their time at university, rather than treating it responsibly as a privilege for which other people are paying. And there have been more than enough examples of fraud, corruption, avarice, deceit and cruelty under Socialist and Communist administrations to convince most of us that however many benefits we owe to a socialist Welfare State, there is one thing it cannot do: change human nature.

The problem is indeed intractable. Look at unhappiness in the work forces of the world, due to rival policies of greed and lack of job satisfaction. Look at unhappiness in so many homes, due to various brands of selfishness. Look at the tense relationships between many nations, due to rival policies of threat and hate. Look at the ecological situation, with its ruthless pursuance of short-term goals and neglect of future generations. Wherever you look, you see the ravages of the 'human disease'. We all have been infected by it. We do not have to learn to go wrong, though we do have to learn, painfully and slowly, to go right. To steal and lie, to clamour for our own way, to hate and lust, to be greedy and selfish are not imported products. They grow here, in you and me. And they grow with the perverse fecundity of weeds in our gardens: they need no planting, no watering, no care — whereas the flowers have to be cosseted and looked after with tender loving care if they are to survive, let alone bloom. The human disease is like that very troublesome weed, ground elder. The more you pull it up, the more it seems to grow. Leave one particle of root in the soil, and it produces a fertile crop of the weed in next to no time. Nothing seems able to eradicate it. And so it is with the human disease. Nothing seems able to eradicate it, and so we give up trying, and say, 'You can't change human nature.'

DISASTROUS REMEDIES?

Of course, some things *can* change it. Brain operations can do this, and alter the personality of the patient beyond recognition. Brainwashing can, so much so that the captive can be trained actually to think like the captor. And perhaps disaster can. There are instances where the death of a close relative or the collapse of a love affair has changed a person's personality and whole outlook on life enormously. But all three of these possibilities, disaster, brainwashing and brain surgery we instinctively class as bad things. The cure is worse than the disease. If human nature can only be changed at the dictates of brain surgeons with their scalpels, brainwashers with their instruments of refined torture, and personal disasters, it is a pretty grim lookout. For all practical purposes we can say again, 'You can't change human nature.'

There is nothing new about this conclusion. Thinkers and poets all down the ages have recognised it. Herodotus, the father of history, commented on it. Plato, the greatest philosopher there has ever been, discovered the hard truth of it when he tried to educate the tyrant of Syracuse. For all his educative theory and unsurpassed skill as a teacher, he failed miserably, and was ejected for his pains by that unpleasant youth. Ovid, the poet, banished by the Emperor Augustus for his eroticism, combined realism and humour as he wrote, 'I see the better course, and I approve of it: but I follow the worse.' Those words were echoed by his contemporary, St. Paul. He spoke of the miserable human condition which he shared. 'I don't understand myself at all, for I really want to do what is right, but I can't. I do what I don't want to — what I hate. I . . . know I am rotten through and through so far as my old sinful nature is concerned. No matter which way I turn I can't make myself do right. I want to but I can't. I want to do good, but when I try not to do wrong, I do it anyway . . .'

Doesn't that first century rabbi speak to your condition? Isn't it just like that with you? It is with me. Very well then, might it not be worth listening to his momentous claim, since his analysis of our human disease is so convincing? His claim is simply this: that there is a cure. That he had found it and applied it, and discovered that it did change his human nature, but in a way far different from the grim effects of the brain surgery, the brainwashing, and the disasters we have considered. As you would expect with this redoubtable opponent of the Man of Nazareth who became his foremost apostle and preacher, this cure all centres round Jesus. May I recap a little at this stage in the book?

EFFECTIVE REMEDY?

We have seen that the really conclusive answer to whether there is a God or not is Jesus Christ. He is the embodiment of that invisible divinity in terms we could understand, human terms. He brings us all of God we could take in. He was not just a good man, he was God himself joining his nature to ours, and coming on to the floor of our factory, so to speak. All religions

point to a dimension higher than our own. All have within them
some search for the truth. All possess some elements of the light
which has taken full and final form in the Light of the World,
Jesus Christ himself. So God himself has met one of our basic
needs, to know about himself. He has come to show us.

We have another basic need, to get right with this God who
has shown his loveliness of character, his goodness and fierce
hatred of evil, in Jesus. If God is Christlike, it is very plain that
I am not. And there lies a problem. We considered it in chapter
7. No good deeds from me, no payment, no religious activities
could span the yawning gulf between the Lord's goodness and
my — let's be frank about it — my badness. This problem was
so acute that it led to the cross. It directed Jesus inexorably to
the place where he laid down his life for ours, where he took
responsibility for all man's evil in the sight of God. Such was
God's generosity that Jesus did not merely come to show us
what he was like, but he died that most agonising death to
reconcile us, and enable anyone who was prepared to say 'God
be merciful to me, a sinner' to enjoy his company here on earth,
and also (this is one of the important sides to the resurrection
which we considered in chapter 9) hereafter.

All these things St. Paul writes about in his letters which are
preserved in our New Testament. He rejoices in them; he is
thrilled by them. He is completely taken up in loving adoration
and service of the God who makes them available. But there is
one other side in this all-embracing rescue which God has done
for us, that thrills Paul almost more than any of the others. It is
this. God has found a way to change human nature.

THE SPIRIT OF JESUS

Briefly, what it amounts to is this. He is willing not just to
reveal himself to us, not merely to die for us. He is actually
prepared to come and live in us. Now if that sounds stupid,
wait a moment. We get somewhere near it when in ordinary
speech we say, 'Stalin had the spirit of Hitler in him,' or that
'Jimmy is a proper Don Juan.' We mean that the sort of qual-

ities found in Hitler or Don Juan are reproduced in Stalin or Jimmy. Well, that includes what a Christian means when he speaks of Christ's Spirit coming to live in him. We mean that the same characteristics that were seen in Jesus begin to make their appearance in the lives of his followers. Paul put it like this. He said, 'When the Holy Spirit controls our lives he will produce this kind of fruit in us: love, joy, peace, patience, kindness, goodness, faithfulness, gentleness and self-control' (Galatians 5: 22). But Christians mean a lot more than this. We mean that this Jesus who died and rose is not a spent force. He is alive and well. When he was here in Palestine he was limited in what he could do and where he could be. If he was talking to me here, he could not be talking to you there. Such are the limitations of the human body. But shortly before his death Jesus told his followers that it would be a good thing for them if he went away; if he did not, the Spirit would not become available for them. If he did go, however, he would send the Spirit in his place to make his presence real to them. And that was precisely what they experienced.

It all began on the Day of Pentecost, just fifty days after the crucifixion of Jesus Christ at Passover time. To their amazement they had, many of them, seen the risen Jesus during those intervening weeks. They had become convinced that he was vibrantly alive. The Risen One told them that these appearances of his were only temporary, and that as a permanent gift his Spirit would come and indwell their very personalities. They did not understand what he meant, despite Old Testament Scriptures which spoke of God putting his Spirit within his followers, and enabling them each to know him and to walk in his ways. But after their experience on the Day of Pentecost, they knew for sure. They had a living experience of the Spirit of Jesus not merely influencing them from outside, but coming to grow the lovely flowers of his character in the barren soil of their own lives. They were, quite literally, born into a new dimension of experience, as a foetus is when it struggles through the birth canal and draws its first breath, or as a woman does the day she gets married, or a larva the day it turns into a dragon fly. The natural world does prepare us, just a little, for the truth that human nature can be changed by the renewing power of the Holy Spirit of God, once he is accepted into our lives. And this realisation gives the Christian something to sing about. After that heartrending cry of defeat from Paul the un-aided human being, which we saw above, Paul the Christian can proclaim triumphantly, 'There is now no condemnation await-ing those who belong to Christ Jesus. For the power of the lifegiving Spirit — and this power is mine through Jesus Christ — has freed me from the vicious circle of sin and death ... So now we can obey God's laws if we are led by the Holy Spirit and no longer obey the old evil nature within us' (Romans 8:1ff).

In the remainder of this chapter I propose to glance at ten practical examples, taken from the pages of the New Testament or from contemporary experience, of what the Holy Spirit can do in a man, once he is given control.

1. CHANGED ATTITUDES

First, the Spirit of Jesus can change your inner attitudes. I can't combat my own deep-seated prejudices. But the Spirit of the God who made me and died to reconcile me, can do just that. I remember a saintly missionary, Bishop Don Jacobs, tell-ing of a dream he had shortly after beinning work as a white man in a black African area. He still retained some illusions about white superiority, and his work was, not unnaturally, hampered by this. In the dream he saw himself on a hot day standing by a river in which many native people were washing themselves. 'Go and bathe, Don,' the Lord's Spirit seemed to be saying to him. 'Not beneath all those folk, Lord,' was his instinctive response: 'I'll swim upstream of them.' And then he saw in his dream that the river welled out from the cross of Calvary. There was no room for pride of place there. So he gladly immersed himself in that river, downstream of his Afri-can brethren, and on that day the Spirit of God dealt with his inbred arrogance. Thereafter for many years of loving ministry among African peoples there was no hint of pride in his dealings with them. He was a new man: his very attitudes had been changed.

2. LIFESTYLE ALTERED

Second, the Spirit of Jesus can change your whole way of life. It may or may not have been socially acceptable previously; but it needed attention. I think of two eminently respectable people, a mother of four, and a leading civic official. The mother's sharpness with the children, impatience with the chores, and less than kind gossip has changed radically: people wonder what has happened to her. The official's attitude to his subordinates, once overbearing, is now gracious; his love of money has been taken away, and he now sees his possessions as a trust to use for God. But I think also of one not so respectable — a hospital porter who came to Christ at much the same time as these two. He had committed a long list of crimes which had never been detected. What did the Spirit of God prompt him to do? Something that he would never have dreamed of doing of his own accord: to go and confess his crimes to the police. This he did — and they were very surprised! In both 'respectable' and 'unacceptable' the Spirit of Christ was altering lifestyle.

The delightful thing about this transformation is that it is basically the same wherever men and women come to Christ. The Spirit of the risen Lord begins to change their lives for the better, and gradually make them more like Christ. It was so in the first days of the church. Think of those disciples who wanted to burn down a Samaritan village just because they got a cold welcome there in the days that Jesus was with them. A few years later, after they had received his Spirit into their lives, they were spreading the gospel of love and forgiveness to those same Samaritans. Some of the earliest converts, the Thessalonians, who turned from idols to the true God, showed it in the way they lived: Paul can commend them on their increase in faith and love, the holiness that was replacing lust, the hu-

mility that replaced their traditional Macedonian arrogance,
and their patience in suffering and persecution. Last year I met
a man from an animist background like theirs. He was a head-
man among the Naga tribesmen who live in the mountains of
India. Large-scale conversions to Christ have been taking place
there recently. His aim used previously to be to gain his
enemy's scalp. Now it is to present to that same enemy the love
of the Spirit of Jesus which has taken over his own personality
with such evident radiance.

3. HABITS BROKEN

Third, the Spirit of Jesus can break long standing habits. Of
course he can: Jesus was never bound by habits he could not
control, and 'where the Spirit of the Lord is, there is liberty'. A
friend of mine has been inside many of the borstals and prisons
in England, for stealing cars. He found Christ while serving a
sentence in one of those prisons, and has never been back. His
philosophy of 'Get from no matter whom' has changed to 'Give
to no matter whom', and he is now in the ordained ministry of
the Church of England. He does not have much money now,
but he is content. Like St Paul of old, he has found that the life-
giving power of the Spirit of Jesus has set him free from the
vicious circle of the old ways.

This sort of thing is not the exception once the Spirit of
Christ gets inside a man; it becomes the rule. I think of an
obsessive gambler set free from his craze to gamble. I think of
chain smokers, knowing their habit to be harmful but unable to
break it, who welcomed the Spirit of Christ into their lives, and
discovered the reality of his power to snap the habit. I think of
folk who could scarcely utter a sentence without an oath, whose
long standing habit was broken by the Spirit of Jesus. It is not
only with the famous people and the great sins that the Spirit of
Jesus can help. The Spirit, endued with all the power of the
risen Lord Jesus, is meant for *you.*

4. LOVE FOR HATE

Fourth, the Spirit of Jesus can replace hate by love. Hate is one of the two most powerful human emotions, and love is the other. Although in some ways they are very near to one another, so that a lover, once jilted, can passionately hate the person he once loved, you don't very often find it happening the other way round. But the Spirit of Jesus makes a habit of it. I have seen the faces of black South Africans filled with joy and love for white brother Christians who belong to the race of those who have oppressed them. I have seen the love of Biafran Christians towards Nigerian Christians during and after the war. I have seen the absence of resentment and sheer caring generosity shine out from the Kenyan Christians tortured by their fellow Kenyans in the Mau Mau risings. I think of the love of those missionaries who in the late 1950s went to try to evangelise the savage stone-age tribe of the Aucas in South America, and got speared to death for their pains. Their wives and sisters devoted themselves to the same task, and saw such fruit from their work that the majority of this small tribe turned to Jesus Christ. One of them, who had himself killed one of the original missionaries, toured England a few years ago with the wife of the man he had killed: both of them not only taught, but demonstrated that the Spirit of Jesus had replaced hatred by love. Love is the greatest thing in the world. We need it badly these days; and the Spirit of Jesus can supply it in unlimited measure. 'God has given us the Holy Spirit to fill our hearts with his love' (Romans 5: 5).

5. A MIND ENLIGHTENED

Fifth, the Spirit of Jesus can renew your mind. My job for the last fifteen years has lain in theological education. I have seen folk who have failed every exam, and been thrown out of school at fifteen, not only equip themselves for the intellectually demanding work of the ordained ministry, but in many cases get a degree as well. If this had occurred once or twice it would have been remarkable. But it happened every year. Once the Spirit of Christ takes over the personality, he opens up all sorts of doors: the mental door is one of them. I believe that the Spirit enlivens our intellectual faculties, enabling us to see truth in a way we had been blind to before. And by this I do not mean merely spiritual truth, as though such a thing existed. All truth is God's truth, and once the Spirit of Truth enters a man's soul, we ought not to be surprised if his capacity for truth and knowledge grows. I think of a colleague of mine on the college staff whom I had taught in earlier days. He had left school at fifteen, entirely unqualified. He found Christ shortly afterwards, and thereafter the growth of his personality, not least on the intellectual side, began. He taught himself up to 'O' and 'A' level standard, gained entry to college, got a good degree, followed it with a M.Th. and a Ph.D., and is now an author, a university teacher, and a minister in the heart of a great university city. That is perhaps the most outstanding example I know of what the Spirit of God is constantly doing: opening blind eyes to the truth. The Spirit of life invariably enlivens our perceptions. St. Augustine found that. He held out long enough against the Spirit of God, but eventually he gave in, and his mind as well as his heart was captivated and renewed by the Spirit of the Lord. It can happen with you. You will not necessarily become an Augustine, but you will find your insight deepened, and your capacity to read, understand, and learn enhanced.

6. A BODY RENEWED

Sixth, the Spirit of Jesus can change your bodily health. I wish to be careful here, because many false claims are made on this score. Instant healing is as suspect as most other 'instant' products of our impatient world. Moreover, it is clear that the Spirit of Jesus does not always heal a man physically. Even in the days of Jesus and the apostles not everyone who came to them with illnesses was healed. In some cases, we are told it was because of their unbelief. Paul himself was not cured of an affliction he called his 'thorn in the flesh', and we read of him leaving Trophimus at Miletus sick, and Timothy with an un-healed stomach complaint. Nevertheless he had the power to heal, and the pages of the Acts, as well as the Epistles, are full of examples of the healing work of the Spirit of God once he is allowed into a man's life. And isn't this just what you would expect? God is the author of all healing, whether 'miraculous' or through normal medical means. Would it be all that sur-prising if he undertook major repairs in the body he was be-ginning to inhabit? After all, the New Testament makes it very plain that church buildings are not where we are to find the Holy Spirit, but people themselves: 'Your bodies are the temples of the Holy Spirit.' All over the world Christians are waking up to this long-neglected truth, that the Spirit of God can and does heal, not only non-organic diseases, but organic ones like cancer and blindness. I have been slow to admit this, and have even written cautiously against it in a previous book, but have now met so many people who have been healed once they opened their lives to the Spirit that I can only bewail my previous unbelief, and rejoice in the healing work which the Spirit of God does do in some cases reckoned incurable by the medical profession.

7. THE CONSCIENCE CLEANSED

Seventh, the Spirit of Jesus can cleanse the conscience. There is a lovely passage in the Letter to the Hebrews which explains that the blood of Christ, that is to say his atoning death on the cross, when applied to the individual by the Holy Spirit, can cleanse the conscience. Now that is a marvellous thing. One eminent psychiatrist said that if his mental patients could have their accusing consciences stilled and be assured of forgiveness, half of his hospital beds would become empty at once. I think of a woman I know whose conscience deeply accused her for sleeping with a married man. She cared a lot about him, and could not break it; but she knew it was wrong. Then she heard the good news of Jesus, his love, his pardon, and his ability to change people's lives. She surrendered her life to him. She poured out her heart in confession. She was absolutely sure of his pardon, for 'if we confess our sins, He is faithful and just to forgive us our sins and to cleanse us from all unrighteousness'. The Spirit of God not only broke the power of that habit in her at one fell swoop, but gave her deep assurance in her inner being that Christ has dealt with her sin, and that her conscience could no longer condemn her. That woman came with me some weeks later on a ward round, talking to patients about Jesus. Her joy, her confidence, and the manifest change in her life were wonderful to see. The Spirit of God assures us we belong; he gives an inner witness that God has accepted us into his family (Romans 8: 16). And that is treasure indeed.

8. SEX LIFE TRANSFORMED

Eighth, the Spirit of Jesus can change your sexual life. This is an area that requires spring-cleaning in most of us. It did in the earliest Christians too. Paul is explicit on the point. 'Do not be deceived,' he says. 'Neither fornicators nor adulterers nor homosexuals . . . nor drunkards shall enter the kingdom of God. And such were some of you. But you are washed. You are acquitted. You are set apart for the Lord, through the person of the Lord Jesus and the Spirit of our God' (1 Corinthians 6: 10, 11). The lives of these immoral folk in Corinth had been transformed by the power of the Spirit entering their lives and setting them free. The same remains true today.

I think of a girl who had turned violently anti-Christian. The reason, I discovered, was because she had been sleeping with her boy friend, and found this incompatible with carrying on a Christian life. She came to rededicate her life, and was willing to sleep with him no more until they got married. She was, however, very frightened of how he would react. But such is the generosity of God that he dealt with her boy friend just as he had with her. That very weekend forty miles away — and quite unaware of what had happened to her — he allowed the Spirit of Christ to take control of his sex life: but he wondered what his girl friend would say! You can imagine the joy with which they met, and the new level at which their relationship continued. I still possess a delightful letter from them telling me of the tremendous joy it brought them to surrender their relationship to the Lordship of the Spirit and discover the moral power and the joy in self-discipline which he brought them.

Again, I think of several occasions when a marriage has been on the point of breaking up; and then the Spirit of Christ has been welcomed into the hearts of both partners. The result has been staggering. No longer were they jaded with each other, no longer in search of fresh thrills with other partners. They had discovered a new bond of unity, undergirding the physical, legal and mental unity which threatened to be insufficient to hold them together.

I had a letter not long ago from a homosexual. He had heard the Gospel, rejected it, and had gone to live in a homosexual flat. He had not been able to forget what he had heard about Jesus, however, and set himself to read the New Testament. What he found there, and the testimony of another Christian he came across, brought him to Christ. He surrendered his sexual urges to the Lord, and found that he was able thereafter to have a normal heterosexual relationship. He is now happily married. I do not know whether this is possible in all cases of inversion. Very possibly not. But the Spirit of God which can enable a heterosexually-inclined person to live a pure single life, can also enable a homosexually-inclined person not to indulge his appetites. Of that I am very sure. And the single life is no dead end. It enables you to do many things that a married person cannot do. See what Paul had to say about its advantages in 1 Corinthians 7. And remember that Jesus, the most balanced man who ever lived, remained single — *and fulfilled*! Do not believe the modern myth that nobody can be normal and fulfilled without overt sexual activity. That is a lie. If the Spirit of God calls you to a single life, he will so fulfil and satisfy you that you are thrilled with your lot, and would not choose anything different if you could have your time all over again. Yes, the Spirit can and does make an enormous difference where our sexual drives are concerned.

9. RESCUE FROM DESPAIR

Ninth, the Spirit of Jesus can change your despair. Maybe you haven't got any, but lots of people have these days. Not just despair at the political, industrial and moral chaos of our times, but the much deeper despair of living in a universe which seems to them to be random and purposeless. Jacques Monod put it well in his *Chance and Necessity* when he wrote, 'Our number came up in the Monte Carlo game. Is it surprising that the person who has just made a million at the casino should feel strange and empty?' Or, as Camus put it in his *Caligula*, 'What is intolerable is to see one's life drained of meaning, to be told there is no reason for existing. A man can't live without some reason for living.' The Holy Spirit gives just that reason for living, just that sense of purpose which many of the most perceptive modern men are painfully aware that they lack. The New Testament writers spoke of 'joy in the Holy Spirit', and they showed it in the quality of their lives. They certainly had something to exult about, and so have we. If your Creator sets such value on you that he died to reconcile you to himself and then comes to indwell your very life, that gives fantastic sense of worth and purpose to your very existence. I remember being struck by this a few years ago when reading of the joy of some prisoners in Penang jail who had been brought to faith in Christ by a prison visitor before their execution, and who wrote a letter so remarkable that although I quoted it in *Man Alive* I think it bears repetition. It shows with great clarity the sense of wellbeing, of purpose, of joy which the Spirit of Jesus brings into a life, even if that life faces almost immediate extinction on the human plane.

Our dear Rev. Khoo,

We do thank you from the bottom of our hearts . . . for all you have done for us. You were everything in our hour of need. You were the beacon that guided us to the haven of Jesus Christ. You taught us to have unquestioning faith in God's Word, to pray to him, and to ask for his forgiveness.

During these long agonising months of mental torture ... till now we stand at the very brink of death, at the very edge of eternity, you have given us so much of yourself in selfless devotion. It is through you that we now look death in the face with courage and calmness, for we doubt not God's promise of forgiveness by the simple act of belief and acceptance. We know that in three and one half hour's time when we pass from off this earth, our Lord and Saviour Jesus Christ will be waiting with open arms to lead us to our new home in the house of the Father ... With our dying breath we once again affirm to you our undying gratitude — gratitude that will transcend even death itself.

I think of a man I met today. He is a black Rhodesian, a leading member of the Africa National Congress. He had been operating with the freedom fighters in the north of Rhodesia, filled with hate towards the whites, filled with despair about his country's prospects under continued domination of the six million blacks by a quarter of a million whites. But his life had been transformed by the power of Jesus Christ, replacing hatred by love and violence by non-violent (but equally passionate) opposition to oppression. No longer does he think in terms of colour and revenge. He has close friends among the whites who also share his loyalty to Christ. The man is a new creature in the same old skin. He is liberated. He has no trace of a chip on the shoulder, despite having been five times imprisoned and beaten by the Security Forces. He has a clear vision of how his life is to be deployed: in building a new society in Rhodesia, black and white together, in the liberating power of Christ who rescues men from despair.

10. CHARACTER REFINED

Tenth, the Spirit of Jesus can make a new man of you. The pages of the New Testament are full of examples of the transformation the Spirit of Jesus makes to the most unlikely characters once he is invited in. Think of the change in a top ranking Roman governor like Sergius Paulus. Think of a vacillating cowardly braggart like Simon Peter in the Gospels, who became the rock man of the early church, fearless in the face of opposition, sleeping peacefully the night before his execution: that change was due to the Spirit. Think of a rabid opponent of Jesus like Saul of Tarsus, converted and changed beyond all recognition by the Spirit of the one he had once persecuted and then come to love. Perhaps, though, there is no more remarkable example of the way God's Spirit makes new men of people than the tiny one-page letter of Paul to Philemon. Philemon was a rich landowner, converted to Christ through St. Paul's ministry. He had a slave, Onesimus, who took his opportunity one day, and ran off with a fair whack of Philemon's cash. By one of the humorous coincidences that God seems to delight in, Onesimus landed up in the same prison as Paul! You can guess what happened next. Paul led the man to Christ, and at once Onesimus' conscience started to work. Ought he not to go back to the master he had robbed? Yes, but Philemon would surely kill him, as owners were in a habit of doing to runaway slaves. So Paul wrote this little gem of a letter to the Christian landowner about his runaway and now Christian slave. He commends Onesimus not only to Philemon's forgiveness, but also to his respect as a fellow man and to his love as a fellow Christian. Now think of the revolution in those two characters, Philemon and Onesimus. It so happens that we have a papyrus fragment from roughly this time, coming from a slave owner whose slave had run away. The writer encourages the recipient to hunt down the man and kill him. And Philemon forgives his slave, respects his slave, and loves his slave like a brother! As for Onesimus, the last thing in the world he would normally do would be to go back to the landowner from whom he had escaped. Now that he had come to Christ, and was beginning to be changed by his Spirit, his conscience awoke, and he was prepared to go back, risk death, offer reparations for what he had stolen, and live on as a slave in Philemon's employment. As a matter of fact, reading between the lines of Paul's letter to Philemon, we find a strong hint that Philemon should release the man and give him his freedom. I guess he did. And it may be mere coincidence, but we do find that the Christian bishop in that part of the world twenty years later was a man called Onesimus . . .

That runaway slave reminds me of a modern half-parallel. I know a man who went into the ordained ministry, but who did not know the life-changing power of the Spirit of Jesus. He laboured away for five years without any results, threw in his hand, and resigned from the ministry. He dropped out of 'straight' society. He became an unemployed thug, slave to women, to drink, and to smoking. He was one of life's casualties. I had the joy of introducing that man to Christ. There was a group who loved and cared for him and sustained him in the early days. He came to train afresh in Britain before going back overseas to the ministry from which he had withdrawn. And God has given him particular gifts as an evangelist among the tough down-and-outs, the drug-takers, the drunks and prostitutes whose scene he knows so well. Needless to say the slavery to drink and tobacco has been snapped, and his whole character gradually transformed.

We may not be slaves and thieves like Onesimus. We may not be in bondage to alcoholism and promiscuity like my friend. But in a sense we are all Onesimuses. We all have habits to which we are enslaved. We have learnt to live with those habits, to be comfortable with them, to excuse them with the refrain, 'Well, you can't change human nature'. To that the Spirit of Jesus replies, 'You must be joking. Changing human nature is my business.'

II

...To the Reader

IF YOU HAVE been with me thus far, where does this land us? I
began, you will recall, with a plea for honesty; to have done
with parrot cries that come so unthinkingly to our lips as we
evade the issue of God. We then looked at a series of these
common responses about religion. It was clear that we cannot
with integrity claim that we are not the religious sort, as if that
got us out of looking at the evidence. We went on to examine
some of that evidence which made it much harder not to believe
in God than to believe in him, whilst recognising that you
cannot actually prove personal existence of any kind, your own

or God's. It became clear that although there are many true sayings preserved in many religions and many impressive lives lived by their practitioners, it is neither logical nor possible to suppose that all religions lead to God. Indeed, there is more than a streak in human nature which does not want to know too much about God and is very keen to profess agnosticism about his existence, or at least to keep him at a distance: his closer presence would be altogether too demanding and uncomfortable. But his closer presence is just what we seem to have to face. Jesus confronts us with it. And it simply will not do to class Jesus Christ among the great prophets or the good men of the world. The old dilemma remains: he is either God or he is not good. No 'good man' made the claims he did. No 'good man' rose from the dead.

If, in Jesus, God himself has come to look for us, it clearly will not do to imagine that so long as we are sincere, it does not matter what we believe. Nor will doing our best solve our problems. Our best is manifestly not good enough for ourselves, let alone God. Even if we could keep the Ten Commandments and the Sermon on the Mount for the rest of our days, that would not alter the past, or erase its ugly blots. The more I know people, the more certain I am of the truth of the Bible's diagnosis: 'The heart of a man is deceitful above all things, and desperately wicked.' Everybody has a past which contains things of which he has good reason to be ashamed. And nothing can alter the past: nothing, that is, if we leave out of account the death of Jesus to put sinful people like us in the clear with God. Had there been any other way, we can be sure God would have taken it, rather than allow Jesus to go to that grim cross. The cross, then, is very much the heart of Christianity; ours is a faith which has a gallows as its badge. On that gallows the most important battle of history was fought and won: Christ there suffered for sins, the righteous one for the unrighteous, to bring us to God.

Nor was that all. Christians do not remember with gratitude a dead Christ. They rejoice in the companionship of a living Lord who rose from the grave and lives today. This resurrection is as crucial to Christianity as is the cross. It means that there is a life after death. It means that Jesus can bring us there. It means his atoning death was sufficient to deal with a world's sin. It means his conquering presence is available to battle on against ingrained evil in his people. And this is where the Holy Spirit comes in. For, as we saw in the last chapter, the Spirit can be described as Jesus' 'other self', the one who makes him real to believing people all over the world, and who works out in them the character of Jesus.

Such is God's provision for us, when really we had no claim on him at all. His generosity is breathtaking. What is to be done about it? May I make some simple suggestions?

RESPONSE

Reflect on this amazing fact, that he did this not just for the world or for the next man, but for *you*. He loves you. He made you. He died for you. He waits to come and live in your life. You need his spring-cleaning. You need his pardon, his guidance, his joy, his sticking power, his courage in the face of death. These qualities are available to you, but only in Jesus Christ.

Is this, perhaps, the moment to kneel down and make your personal response to the love of God? 'The gift of God is eternal life,' says the New Testament. What do you do with a gift? You accept it gratefully. It is just the same with Jesus. He is God's great gift to you: all the other gifts are wrapped up in him. Do not duck the issue by waiting till you're good enough: you never will be. Just accept the gift thankfully, perhaps in words like these:

> Lord, I am amazed at your generosity. I don't deserve it. I can hardly believe it. But I do dimly feel you are there, and I realise that you came to this earth for me in Jesus Christ. I do believe he died for my sins and is alive so that he can come by his Spirit into my heart. I realise that he wants to involve me in his ongoing work and among his people, and I

am prepared for that. Lord, here and now I accept in faith the gift of Jesus to me personally. Please never allow me to go back on this decision, and please enable me to live worthy of it in your strength, wherever future circumstances take me.

PROSPECT

Having taken this momentous step, tell someone about it. Write to me if you don't know anyone who would be sympathetic. But better, tell a Christian friend or relative. They will be thrilled and encouraged. Maybe they have been praying for you for some time — someone (a mother, a friend, a colleague) nearly always has when a person makes a definite commitment to Christ. To tell someone else is important for two reasons. One, it puts you into contact with others who can help you on in the early days of your discipleship. Two, it enables you to nail your colours to the mast: and the New Testament is insistent on the need for this. 'If you confess with your mouth the Lord Jesus, and believe in your heart that God raised him from the dead, you will be saved.' Of course, this will involve in due course 'letting your light so shine before men that they may see your good works and glorify your Father who is in heaven'. But it may be as well to start with Christians first, before going to tell the toughest atheist you know that you have surrendered your life to Jesus Christ! At all events, open, unashamed discipleship is called for. Secret disciples never grow.

Next, it would be a good idea to read something on the basic essentials in Christian living, so as to have, as it were, a bird's eye view of what it will involve. If you have almost no time, read J. R. W. Stott's booklet *Being a Christian* (Inter Varsity Press). If you have a bit more time, read David Watson's *Live a New Life* (Inter Varsity Press), or my own recent *New Life New Lifestyle* (Hodder & Stoughton). In this way you will quickly get some ideas about going on in the companionship of the one you have begun to trust.

Third, it is most important to get involved in Christian fellowship. The church, for all its failings, is not a luxury but a necessity. Jesus did not just come to save individuals but to set up on earth a first instalment of the Kingdom of God. And that means a society. You cannot get away from it. From now on your lot is cast with the Christian church. Where it is corrupt, purge it. Where it is slack, enliven it. Where it is right, follow it. But join it you must. So if you are not baptised, it is high time to seek out a minister in some lively church who will prepare you for baptism. If your denomination baptises infants, you may well already be baptised. In that case, you will want to get confirmed, or the equivalent way of entry into full membership, so that you can pull your weight in the local congregation, take part in the Holy Communion, and give public testimony to your allegiance to Christ.

Next, may I pass on a piece of advice which I found invaluable in the early days of following Christ? Is there some Christian friend whom you know well? If so, he will be able to help you a great deal if you meet him regularly, not only socially but in order to read a bit of the Bible together, to talk over any difficulties as they occur, and to learn from him how to engage in real prayer (as opposed to the bedside noises you may have uttered for a long time without developing them at all). I had, for some months, a weekly session with such a friend, and it made all the difference.

Finally, get involved in some piece of Christian service. It does not much matter what it is so long as you do it for Jesus' sake and to help other people. Pray to be guided to the contribution you could best make. But get stuck in. Don't be a drone in the Christian hive, sucking up the honey and doing none of the work. Christian service is one of the great ways of growing to maturity in the Christian life.

Well, there it is. That would be the author's hope for his readers. I am sure that if you commit yourself realistically and wholeheartedly to God in this way you will cease to produce the parrot cries that may have satisfied you up till now ('All religions lead to God', 'It doesn't matter what you believe so long as you are sincere' and the rest). Instead you will begin to produce the cries of the newly born child of God as the Spirit gets to work within you, enabling you to cry, 'Abba, dear Father'.

Further Reading

for those who wish to examine some issues in greater depth.

ABOUT GOD

Knowing God, James Packer (Hodder & Stoughton)
The Living God, Dick France (I.V.P.)
The God Who is There, Francis Schaeffer (Hodder & Stoughton)
Does God exist? A. E. Taylor (Fontana)

ABOUT ALTERNATIVES TO CHRISTIAN BELIEF

The Dust of Death, Os Guinness (I.V.P.)
Christian Faith and Other Faiths, Stephen Neill (O.U.P.)
The Finality of Christ, Lesslie Newbiggin (S.C.M.)
Christianity and Comparative Religion, J. N. D. Anderson (I.V.P.)

ABOUT SUFFERING

The Problem of Pain, C. S. Lewis (Fontana)
A Grief Observed, C. S. Lewis (Fontana)
Why do Men Suffer? L. Weatherhead (S.C.M.)
Taught by Pain, ed. Mary Endersbee (Falcon)

ABOUT MAN'S NATURE

I Believe in Man, George Carey (Hodder & Stoughton, publishing 1977)
What is Human? T. M. Kitwood (I.V.P.)

ABOUT SCIENCE

Beyond Science, Denis Alexander (Lion)
World without End, Roger Pilkington (Macmillan)
Adam and the Ape, R. J. Berry (Falcon)
Science and Christian Belief, C. A. Coulson (S.C.M.)
The Clockwork Image, D. M. Mackay (I.V.P.)

ABOUT PHILOSOPHY

Faith Facing Facts, R. N. Williams (Coverdale)
Teach Yourself Philosophy of Religion, H. D. Lewis
    (Hodder & Stoughton)
Philosophy and the Christian Faith, Colin Brown (Tyndale)

ABOUT CHRISTIAN EVIDENCES

Runaway World, Michael Green (I.V.P.)
Mere Christianity, C. S. Lewis (Fontana)
My God is Real, D. C. K. Watson (Falcon)
Christianity on Trial, Colin Chapman (Lion)

ABOUT JESUS

The Gospels — in a modern translation
The Founder of Christianity, C. H. Dodd (Fontana)
Meet Jesus, Geoff Treasure (Falcon)

ABOUT THE RESURRECTION

I Believe in the Resurrection of Jesus, George Ladd (Hodder
    & Stoughton)
First Easter, Paul Maier (Mowbrays)
Man Alive, Michael Green (I.V.P.)

ABOUT THE CROSS

Why the Cross? H. E. Guillebaud (I.V.P.)
The Cross in the New Testament, L. Morris (Paternoster)
The Death of Christ, James Denney (Tyndale)

ABOUT THE HOLY SPIRIT

Reflected Glory, Thomas Smail (Hodder & Stoughton)
I Believe in the Holy Spirit, Michael Green (Hodder & Stoughton)
The Go Between God, J. V. Taylor (S.C.M.)

BIBLE READING AIDS

The Scripture Union Notes,
The Soldier's Armoury (Hodder & Stoughton)
Every day with Jesus (Christian Literature Crusade)
The Bible Reading Fellowship

PRAYER

The Prayers of the New Testament, Donald Coggan (Hodder & Stoughton)
Prayers of Life, Michel Quoist (Gill)
How to Talk with God, Stephen Winward (Hodder & Stoughton)
Our Understanding of Prayer, I. T. Ramsey (S.P.C.K.)
Prayer, O. Hallesby (I.V.P.)
The Use of Praying, J. Neville Ward (Epwarth)

NEW LIFE,
NEW LIFESTYLE

I am grateful to the Rt Rev. Hugh Montefiore for permission to quote his version of the Ten Commandments, and the Rt Rev. Trevor Huddleston for permission to quote from a BBC broadcast. 'The Act of Love' by Roger McGough is reprinted from LOVE, LOVE, LOVE, edited by Peter Roche, published by Corgi Books Ltd.

FOR PEG BYARS

who is distinguished in commerce
and distinguished in nourishing
new life into new lifestyle among
the many she brings to faith

Preface

Currently I live and work in western Canada, where the Christian gospel is not in good shape. The Church is weak, disunited, and has departed widely from its New Testament heritage of faith. There is still a lot of belief in God, there is still substantial nominal attachment to the Church, but in practice people live for money and success. The climate of the day is pluralist: the philosophy of the day is hedonist.

And yet the gospel of Jesus Christ still has its ancient power. It is not as if it has been tried and found wanting. It has simply not been tried.

This very morning in our congregation, which did not even exist four years ago, one person who had only been a Christian for a year or so introduced a friend to me – a friend who had been brought to faith by one of my books which I wrote some time ago. This happens regularly at speaking engagements, I find. People will come up afterwards and thank me for introducing them to Christ, who has become the greatest influence in their lives. I will look at them in amazement, never having seen them before, until I realise that they are referring to a book I have written which, in the mercy of God, has been of special value to them.

That is why I am glad to revise and reissue this book, written originally twenty years ago. It is not out of date, though some of the illustrations and language were – hence the revision. And it remains relevant precisely because the situation it addresses is every bit as pressing today as it was then. It is all about how to grow and develop in the Christian life after taking those first tentative steps of faith to Jesus Christ. I do not *think* this is a continuing problem. *I know it is!* Wherever I go, I find Christians who lack assurance that they are really in God's family, Christians who are hopelessly defeated, Christians who have no devotional life, Christians who are painfully ignorant even of the basics of discipleship. And so whether it is in post-Christian Canada, or among the surging tides of new believers in Tanzania, there is a continuing need for a book which explains in a simple, readable way, how to go on with Christ once you have begun with him.

This is such a book. It is not comprehensive, or even adequate. It is not scholarly or hard to follow. It is a book about the basics of Christian living, where I have tried to paint on a broad canvas the main features of the landscape that unfolds before the new believer — or the long-time churchman who suddenly stumbles into the recognition of what it is all about. It is meant to help such people to 'grow in grace and in the knowledge of our Lord and Saviour, Jesus Christ'.

I am grateful for the permissions granted me to quote copyright material. I have also found it helpful to quote, anonymously, from my correspondence, much of it from new Christians. Thanks are due to Carolyn Armitage and James Catford, both editors at Hodder's, for giving a great deal of help in the revision of this book. I am grateful to Edward England, Pat Dearnley and Roy Catchpole for assistance earlier along the line.

Michael Green
Regent College, Vancouver

Contents

1

Twice is the Only Way to Live!

The fourth dimension

He was a young man in his twenties, hooked on drink
and drugs. One night, when he was stoned with liquor
and high on LSD, he heard about Jesus, the real living
Jesus who could take him and change him. He
surrendered his life to Christ, and the change began
to take place. I met him ten months after this new
beginning. He was radiantly happy, self-possessed and
integrated. I asked him how long he had been a
Christian. He told me, 'Ten months'. I asked him if
he had introduced any others to Christ in this time,
and he laughed – so did the others who were standing
round in the room in Toronto where this conversation
was taking place. 'More than I can remember,' was his
memorable reply.

I think of an occasion when I was teaching in a
theological college. One of our students came to tell
me that the previous weekend he had been revisiting
a country church where a team from the college had
recently conducted a mission. One of his many
encouragements was to sit at the back of a room where
about thirty villagers of different ages, backgrounds
and outlooks were engaged in a Bible Study – led by

11

a man and his wife who had found faith in Christ during the mission a couple of months earlier. It reminded me, as he spoke, of an RAF officer who had become a believer in Christ through reading a book I had written. He gave copies to five couples among his Service friends, and then invited them to meet my wife and myself in his home one evening. He sat us down, put us at our ease, and then explained why he had invited everyone round. He had only been a believer a few weeks himself, and had certainly never heard anyone speak about Jesus Christ to a group of friends in a home. He told us that he would not have believed it if anyone had informed him two months ago that he would be sitting at a group like that, discussing Jesus: if they had gone on to suggest that *he* might be organising the group, he would have thought them mad! But he had found Jesus Christ in the meantime – the living Jesus who had begun to make a new man of him. So naturally he wanted to share the news with his friends. You can imagine how well that evening went. His friends had expected me to talk about Christ – after all, I was a minister, and was paid to do that sort of thing. But they hadn't expected anything so definite, so full of a sense of discovery, from *him*. He was like the man in Jesus' parable, who had been ploughing a dull and dusty furrow in a field, and then suddenly struck a box; on examination, it turned out to be full of treasure. That's what it is like, according to Jesus, when someone discovers the Kingdom of God. It's like finding treasure, when you weren't expecting anything of the sort. Well, my friend had found treasure: and it made a great impression on his circle.

These people I have mentioned (and the list could

be extended indefinitely) have one thing in common. They have found a new world of experience, a new dimension to living. It's as if they have been living in a pond all their lives up till now, like the tadpole. And now they have turned into frogs, and have emerged from the pond to start a fresh existence on dry land. Of course, like the frog, they are thoroughly at home in the pool still; they retain all the experiences they had before. But they have this new world opening up to them. It is almost as if they had been born all over again: that was, in fact, how Jesus described it to a learned theologian, who knew all about God and the Scriptures, but had never found the treasure of this new life for himself.

New life

I am writing this book for people who have begun to emerge from the pool; for those who are making their first cries as babes in the family of God; for those whose eyes have been opened to a new world round about them, after Jesus has laid his hand upon them. I hope I am writing for you. I trust that you know what this new life in Christ means. If you do, you can skip the rest of this chapter. But if you don't, the next bit is rather crucial. Without it the rest of the book won't make any kind of sense. Lots of books on Christian behaviour make the cardinal error of assuming you can lay down a code of conduct to be followed, and call it 'Christian ethics' *without changing human nature*. I tell you it can't be done.

Incidentally, this is why we all feel that talk about morality is so dull and unattractive. It sets before us a standard which we can't keep; and that is

13

depressing. It presents us with a set of rules; and that makes our hackles rise. We say, 'Why should I bother with that one? Why should I keep this?' I have only to see a notice – 'Keep off the grass' – and I immediately want to trample all over it. Don't you? Very well, we understand each other, you and I. We know that dead orthodoxy, codes of rules, moral behaviour patterns leave us cold. To commend Christian ethics to people who have no Christian faith is simply asking for failure if they try to keep the standards, and for hypocrisy if they don't. It is as ludicrous as going round tying apples on to a dead apple tree. The only way you will get any satisfaction with apples is to pick them off a live tree. You need to have Christ's new life coursing through your personality before you can produce the fruit of a Christ-like character. Obvious enough, when you come to think of it. You can't have the new lifestyle without the new life.

Dead and alive

Fair enough. But how do you get the new life? The answer is not difficult. But it is costly. Costly to God, and costly to us. It is like this. God made men and women as the crown of his creation. We share in and transcend the different levels of life displayed in the rest of creation. A stone has life of a sort: it exists. A flower has a more developed life, with its ability to breathe and to feed, to bud, to blossom and to die away . . . before the cycle begins again. Animals have a higher form of life, equipped as they are in varying degrees with mobility, intelligence, adaptability and strength. Some of the monkey family are almost human in their abilities. But there are very distinct differences between us and the animals from which we may long ago have been developed by the Creator. We can think. We can pray. We can communicate logically. We can make ourselves the object of our own reflection. We have a sense of beauty, of truth, of goodness. We have a conscience. In all these ways, and others, we transcend the animal creation. Our life is fuller than theirs. We rejoice in our physical, mental and aesthetic vitality. Especially if all of these are in good health, it is just wonderful to be alive.

But the Bible teaches, and experience confirms, that in a very real sense we are dead while we live. Dr Herbert Kohn once wrote in a Sunday newspaper: 'The biggest single problem facing us is no meaning and purpose. Why do we stay alive? What are we here for? My grandfather walked with God, and knew why – but we don't.' That puts the human situation in a nutshell. In the graphic picture given us in the Book of Genesis, man was made to enjoy God's company – no less. Our human race was meant to 'walk with him in the garden in the cool of the day'. We were meant to enjoy this supreme dimension of life – sharing the very company of God who gave us life. Notice the accent is on sharing. But what did we do? We decided to go it alone. We ate the fruit of the one tree that God had forbidden. And disobedience broke the relationship. We ceased to walk with God. God was no longer a companion to be enjoyed, but a sinister figure to be dreaded. He might enquire, 'Why are you hiding?' Feeling guilty, we preferred to keep out of God's way. Reluctantly God endorsed our choice. We human beings were expelled from his garden, cut off from what is picturesquely and significantly described as the Tree of Life.[1]

It makes little difference whether you take that story literally, or whether you regard it as a timelessly acute description of Everyman, a sort of Aesop's Fable, whose truth is not dependent on its mere historicity. On either showing, that is the human situation: we are aliens from our homeland. It has been well said, 'Modern man is no longer merely an exile. He has forgotten his home and has no hope of a promised land.' We have rejected this highest range of life, sharing in the fellowship of our Creator. Spiritually speaking, we are already dead. So dead that we are for the most part unaware of God's existence. So dead that we will not listen to his claims upon our lives. So dead that any talk about God seems utterly foreign to us, almost as if it were spoken in another language. Jean-Paul Sartre went so far as to claim, 'God is dead, even in the hearts of believers.' Indeed, many sensitive folk feel themselves to be 'dead'. Fellini, the film producer, and director of *La Dolce Vita*, wrote, 'Like many people I have no religion and I am just sitting in a small boat, drifting with the tide. I just go on working, shooting, cutting, editing, looking at life and trying to make others see. Today we stand naked, defenceless and more alone than at any time in history. We are waiting for something – perhaps another miracle, perhaps the Martians – who knows?'

True enough! We are indeed waiting for someone to restore meaning and purpose to life. But the man of tomorrow came yesterday. Jesus was his name. That word 'Jesus' means, quite literally, 'God to the rescue'. Christians believe that Jesus was – and is – just that. I don't propose to argue the case for that stupendous

claim. I have had a go at it in *World on the Run* and
You Must Be Joking! But I believe it with all my heart.
I have scrutinised the evidence, and I am satisfied. So
confident that I am prepared to gamble my future and
my life on its truth. And I believe that the whole
objective in God becoming one of us for thirty years
or so in the first century was to enable us to recover
this 'high octane' life, this possibility of life shared with
him, which was lost by human disobedience in the
mists of long ago, and which people continue to
jettison daily as carelessly as they throw away a plastic
cup.

Life through death

How was the situation of broken relationships to be
restored, so that once again we could enjoy his life?
Well, the essence of the operation was this. Jesus came,
not primarily to teach us how to live, nor to heal the
sick, nor to be an anti-establishment leader, but to
bring new life to the spiritually dead. 'My purpose is
to give life in all its fullness,'[2] said Jesus. St Paul,
reflecting on Christ's achievement, has this to say,
'Time was when you were dead in your sins. In our
natural condition we, along with all the rest, lay under
the dreadful judgment of God. But God, rich in mercy,
for the great love he bore us, brought us to life with
Christ, even when we were dead in our sins.'[3] The
whole New Testament bears witness to the fact that
it was through the cross and resurrection of Jesus that
this new life has become available. We *can* live twice!

It is very difficult to understand how Jesus' death
so long ago can be of any use to us today, and how
it can make any difference to our relationship with

17

God. There are various pictures sketched by the New Testament writers to help us understand. Sometimes they talk as if we were all captives in a foreign land to a hostile power, and the death of Jesus was the price paid to repatriate us and deliver us from this enemy power. But pursue that analogy too far and you get into trouble. You start asking to whom was the ransom paid, and at once you are in difficulties. So the wise thing to do is to look at another word picture and regain perspective. Sometimes St Paul speaks of Jesus dying on the cross as the means of reconciling two estranged parties, us and God. Sometimes he speaks of Jesus as the mediator in a broken relationship (we have plenty of this sort of thing in industrial relations) and he only succeeded in restoring good relations at the cost of his own life. Sometimes New Testament writers see his innocent suffering as the ultimate way in which evil is conquered: once you retaliate you only double the evil. Jesus not only taught but demonstrated the tremendous moral power of the innocent, willingly and lovingly accepting cruelty and brutality at the hands of the guilty in order to absorb and neutralise the wickedness, and bring men to their senses.

The meaning of the cross

All of these insights given us by the Bible writers shed some light upon his death. But perhaps the simplest and at the same time the most profound way of looking at it is this. *Our life was forfeit: he forfeited his life for us.* That needs spelling out a bit. Our rebellion against God had cut us off from enjoying his company; we were 'aliens, without God in the world'.[4] Jesus, on the other hand, himself both God and man, himself tempted more strongly than any of us, nevertheless lived a life of perfect obedience. There was no rebellion against God in that life: rather, he could say with integrity, 'I always do those things which please him.'[5] He had no need to die, physically or spiritually. But die he did, by his own free and deliberate choice. He died physically in great agony on the cross, and spiritually in greater agony as he willingly made himself responsible for all the horrors, all the filth and guilt of the world's rebellion, including yours and mine. He took your death, so that you could have his life. He died in the place where the rebel should have ended up, so that the rebel could be adopted into the family from which he had played truant. He died that we might live, forgiven, accepted, in touch with God. Listen to the thrill of it coming over in Paul's writings. He never got over the wonder of it. 'The Son of God loved me, and gave himself for me.'[6] Or again, 'We beg you, as though Christ himself were here pleading with you, receive the love he offers you – be reconciled to God. For God took the sinless Christ and poured into him our sins. Then, in exchange, he poured God's goodness into us.'[7]

That idea of the exchange, his life willingly given for our lives that were forfeit, gripped the early Christians and made them deeply indebted to the love of the Lord. I think it explains why they gave so much notice to Barabbas in the story of the crucifixion. The cross on which Jesus died was meant for Barabbas. He deserved it, if anyone did. He was a robber, an insurgent and a murderer. Yes, he deserved to die. His life was justly forfeit. But Jesus took his place. He died on Barabbas' cross, though he didn't deserve to. And

Barabbas went free because Jesus died on his cross, though he didn't deserve to, either. That exchange seemed to get to the heart of the meaning of the cross for the first disciples. Our life through his death.

Just after the New Testament period an unknown Christian wrote in these terms about what the cross meant to him: 'He himself took on him the burden of our iniquities, the holy one for sinners, the immortal for mortals. For what else could cover our sins but his righteousness? O sweet exchange! O work of God beyond all searching out! That the wickedness of many should be hidden by a single righteous one, and that the righteousness of one should put many transgressors right with God.'[8]

Any questions?

A few quick questions come to mind at this point. 'Surely it is not fair of God to punish Christ for our misdeeds?' That is not what the New Testament says. It is not as though God was determined to take it out on somebody for the broken relationship, and if we were to get off scot-free, then he would make Christ pay. That is a travesty of the truth. No, we read, 'God was in Christ, reconciling the world to himself.'[9] No third party was involved. God, in Christ, personally undertook to restore human relations with himself, though it involved nothing short of death and hell for him.

But again, people often ask me, 'How can the death of Christ so long ago possibly be effective for sins that hadn't even been committed then – mine for instance?' Part of the answer to this is to realise that the cross gives us a window into God's unchanging attitude towards human rebellion. He always has to judge it, and he always determines to taste its ashes himself so as to deliver us from the results of our wilfulness and folly (if we will allow him to). And part of the answer lies in the fact that Christ laid down his infinite life on that cross for the finite number of people in the world: and the finite, large though it be, is always outweighed by the infinite. On the cross we see God dealing in person, dealing at unspeakable cost, with the problem of human rebellion at its very root. Because he was going to do so, he could gladly accept anyone who lived BC. Because he has done so, he can gladly accept anyone who lives AD. The cross lies at the mid-point of time, and can avail for all.

'But does that mean that this new life you talk of is free, and that I have nothing to pay?' people ask. That is precisely what it does mean. Suppose you are in debt to the tune of thousands of pounds and are absolutely broke; and suppose your creditor says, 'Right, you can go free: the debt is cancelled, and here's £50,000 to start you off in a new life' – what can you do but take it in wonder and gratitude, and say a heartfelt 'Thank you'? To attempt to pay for it would be as impossible as it would be impertinent. That, said Jesus, is the position we must take up before God's offer of a new life. We are his debtors, and he declares our debts discharged. We were doomed to death under his laws, and he tells us, 'Your doom is remitted: you are free to live a new life.' You can't pay for something like that. You can only take a Royal Pardon *as* a pardon; take it and be profoundly grateful.

But we have still only been considering half of the story. If the cross means that Jesus forfeited his life for ours which lay forfeit, the resurrection means that his

21

new life can surge into our dead spirits. This is just what the early Christians found. To their amazement they discovered that Jesus was not dead and gone. He rose from the grave that third day; the tomb was empty, the last enemy defeated. Jesus had tried conclusions with death, man's greatest foe, and he had overcome. 'It was not possible for him to be held down by it,' they concluded.[10] The only person who had lived a life of perfect obedience, Jesus was the only person on whom death, the fruit of human rebellion against God, could maintain no grip. He rose, and he is alive today, thank God. When someone becomes a Christian, it means that this person allows the risen Christ to come into his or her spirit and take up residence. And the Christian life is no less than Christ's own life struggling to show itself from inside us.

It is as if our life is a garden – derelict, overgrown and devoid of fruit trees. The day we become Christians, the Spirit of the risen Christ is planted in our garden. He has to contend with lots of weeds which always hinder, sometimes threaten to stifle any growth completely. The climate is often cold, and the neglect to which the plant is subjected something awful. But gradually, over the years, the tender sapling grows into a fruitful tree, and people come and refresh themselves with the luscious fruit, even though there are still plenty of nettles round the base. That is how the new life of Christ takes root in our personalities and makes itself known even though every one of us still has a long way to go. St Paul can rightly say, 'The fruit of the Spirit is love, joy, peace, patience, kindness, goodness, faithfulness, gentleness and self-control.'[11] Those lovely, mature fruits of Christian living are only possible when Christian life has begun, when the Spirit of the risen Christ has been welcomed into your life. Remember, it's no good tying apples on to a dead tree. You achieve nothing, and only make yourself look ridiculous. You have to live twice!

From death to life

The issue is now crystal clear. It comes to this. Have you got new life? Has the Holy Spirit been planted in your life? 'If anyone does not have the Spirit,' said Paul, 'he is no Christian.'[12] We may have been born in a Christian country, and have gone to a Christian school at the instigation of fond Christian parents. We may have attended church regularly and be able to say the creed backwards! But if we have not made room for the Holy Spirit to come into our life, whatever else we are, we are not yet a Christian. It sounds hard, but it isn't really. A plant can't bear fruit until it has been planted and taken root. A person can't grow and develop until he has been born. Obvious, isn't it? And yet so many people fail to see it when it comes to spiritual things. You can't live the Christian life until you have been born into the Christian family. You can't produce Christian character until the Holy Spirit of Christ has been planted in your life.

Has he? You know if this has happened or not. You and God. If you know you have not begun, I suggest that before you go any further in this book, you get this matter sorted out once and for all with God. It doesn't matter how you express yourself: it's your attitude of giving in to God that matters. If it helps, you could say something like this:

God, I begin to see why you have seemed so unreal

to me. I have been alive physically and mentally, but spiritually dead all these years, cut off from your life. No wonder I was very doubtful at times whether you even existed. But I do thank you very much for coming to meet me in my confusion. Thank you for Jesus and his amazing love in being willing to go to that cross for me. I don't understand it all, but I believe he did it for me, and that because he died there, I can be forgiven and have the past wiped out. That is a wonderful welcome, God, and I don't deserve it. I can't begin to earn it. So I won't try. I shall simply come to you and say 'Thank you'. And I am putting the rest of my life at your disposal. I want to use it for you now. I want the life of the risen Christ to come in and possess me. I want him to shine out through me. God, you have shown me through the cross of Jesus that you accept me, just as I am. Well, here and now I accept you. You're going to have to look after me, Lord, because I know I can't make it on my own. But then, I don't have to, do I? For you have promised that you will come and share your very own life with me. Please come in, Lord, and do just that.

You know, that old James Bond film was quite right, more right than its producers realised. 'You only live twice . . . and twice is the only way to live.'

NOTES

1 Genesis 3:24
2 John 10:10
3 Ephesians 2:1–2
4 Ephesians 2:12
5 John 8:29
6 Galatians 2:20

7 2 Corinthians 5:20–1 (LB)
8 Epistle to Diognetus, 9
9 2 Corinthians 5:19
10 Acts 2:24
11 Galatians 5:22–3 (RSV)
12 Romans 8:9

2

Getting it Straight

Two types of feelings

Once you put your hand in the hand of Christ, a new life begins. To quote St Paul again, 'When someone becomes a Christian he becomes a brand new person inside. He is not the same any more. A new life has begun!'[1] Sometimes the new life bursts exuberantly on the scene. This, for instance, is how one person wrote to me recently, five days after surrendering her life to Christ. She was a mature person, a mother, a strong character and an experienced hostess. She was certainly not the emotional sort: would you understand what I mean if I tell you she was a brigadier's widow? Well, this is what she wrote:

> I must write and tell you what a tremendous experience this has been for me. No words can explain it. If anyone had told me last week that I should feel like I do this week, I am afraid I would not have believed it. In the past I have not prayed very much, or gone to church very much, and still I seldom read the Bible. I want you to know that it was for this reason that I wavered so long on Saturday morning, taking so much of your time. I

did not think I could be ready to take such a step. But how right you were, and my heart is full of thankfulness: to Graham for bringing me to you, to you for bringing me to Christ, and to Christ, above all, for entering in, for there is absolutely no doubt about it. In fact I still feel rather in the clouds, but I know that there is a lot of work to be done as soon as I return home . . .

Yes, some people feel like that immediately they start the new life. But some people don't. Here is another reaction after almost exactly the same period of a few days.

Really, I scarcely know what has happened to me this week. Perhaps this is the best test of the validity that God really did respond and come into my heart – that there was no spectacular emotional experience, of which I would have been very mistrustful; but somehow there really was something different. I felt as if I was being pushed from one thing to another all through the usual routine, by something inside me. Instead of frantically trying to plan my time to fit everything in, I scarcely had to think about it. I'm still afraid that the assurance will not last. I didn't really believe that I could have a personal relationship like this with God, so I suppose it is natural for me to be surprised and rather unsure of it. It's too soon to say, 'It has made such and such a difference in my life.' At present I just want to get to know him better.

That last sentence could almost be the theme of this book. It is the authentic Christian longing. Having

27

found Christ, we want to explore him more and more, and to give ourselves over to him in every department of our lives. That is the very heart of the Christian life: getting to know him better, and working out the implications of it in our behaviour and attitudes, our career and relationships.

We shall be examining some of these areas in subsequent chapters. But there is a prior issue to sort out. It came up in both of those quotations from my correspondents. It is the problem of what to do with our doubts, and how far we should allow our Christian assurance to be governed by our feelings.

Dealing with Doubts

There are a good many uncertainties and doubts we cannot avoid; and in our own generation these are far more pressing than ever before. Insecurity arising from the threat of unemployment, poverty, political and industrial unrest, broken relationships and the general state of the world today. These are uncertainties we have to live with. However, we can have, and are meant to have, complete confidence that we belong to Christ. Indeed, unless we are sure about this relationship with him, we shall neither be able to develop it nor to introduce others to him. We would be building the house of our lives on sand instead of rock.

But doesn't any suggestion that Christians can be sure where they stand smack of smugness and self-confidence? That is an accusation often made, but it is simply not the case. Of course, there are Christians who are smug, but that is their fault, not the fault of their Christianity. It is possible to be sure without being smug.

Suppose you give your child a bicycle for Christmas. You mean her to know that she has got it, don't you? She can be sure of your gift, but she has nothing to crow about. She didn't earn it: it's a gift.

Now it is like that with God. If we start thinking about what we deserve, then the New Testament tells us straight: 'The wages of sin is death.' We do not and cannot earn new life. 'The *free gift* of God is eternal life through Jesus Christ our Lord.'[2] New life is his gift: I know I've got it; but I also know it is entirely due to his generosity, not to my merits. That is what the famous phrase 'justification by faith' means. We are justified, acquitted, put in the right with God (a status which nothing can destroy) not by our 'works', our efforts at self-justification, but by 'grace', God's undeserved favour to us.[3] And this we receive by 'faith', by trusting him. 'So now, since we have been justified by faith, we can have real peace with God because of what Jesus Christ our Lord has done for us. In response to our faith, he has brought us to this place of highest privilege in which we stand, and we rejoice in the expectation of becoming all that God has in mind for us to be.'[4]

Is it wrong to be sure?

What I want to ask those Christians who believe it is wrong to be sure about their relationship with Christ, is this: 'Do you know what family you belong to? Do you know if you're married?' Of course they know, and would never dream of saying, 'Well, I *think* I am in the Green family and that my name is Michael, but

29

I'm really not sure,' or, 'I think I'm married; I hope I'm married; but it is presumptuous to say that I *am* married.' What nonsense that would be. It is just as nonsensical and much more impertinent to doubt God. He says that we are the bride, and Christ is the bridegroom; we are linked to him for ever in the closest of all possible ties. He says that he adopts us into his family, so that we are sons in the family of God, and fellow heirs with Christ of all his bounty.[5] He says it, he means it and we can take him at his word.

It comes down to this, really: trust. As in all personal relationships, trust is fundamental. How does the wife know her husband won't play her false? How does the patient know the doctor won't poison him? How does the client know the lawyer won't swindle him? How does the child know that his mother loves him? The answer in each case is simply trust. Why should it be different with God?

Look: Christ says he will accept you. 'The one who comes to me I will never, no never, throw out.'[6] And you have come to him, as best you know how? Very well then, he *has* accepted you, for the simple and utterly sufficient reason that he said he would. Your feelings may be up or down: it matters not one whit. Your experience is nil to start with. You have nothing but his naked word to go on. But it is enough. It brought assurance to Dr Livingstone over a century ago as he struggled with doubt and loneliness in the jungles of Central Africa. He recorded in his journal his reflections on the promise of Jesus I have just quoted. And his comment was, 'That is the word of a gentleman of the most strict and sacred honour. He cannot break his word.' A very Victorian way of putting it, but the point is unarguable.

Very well: we have God's word of acceptance. The God you cannot see offers to accept you into his family when there is nothing you can do to deserve it — and a great deal to disqualify you. What are you to do with such an offer? You trust his word, for a start. And then you discover, to your amazement, that God gives you a remarkable adoption certificate — baptism.

The mark of belonging

Baptism is the mark of Christian belonging. Christians in the Baptist tradition believe this should be by total immersion and only after you have put your faith in Christ. Most other Christian churches believe that it is immaterial whether baptism precedes faith or faith precedes baptism, so long as you believe in your heart and have this outward mark of baptism upon you. But both traditions are clear about its importance.

You have only to go to a predominantly Muslim or Buddhist country to discover how baptism sets you apart. You may believe secretly, and nobody worries too much: but as soon as you get baptised, then you have to face the music. I remember several of my Jewish friends of student days being disowned by their parents because they had confessed Christ, not merely in personal faith but in open baptism. Baptism is, therefore, very much the mark of discipleship: the irrevocable pledge that I belong to Christ and am committed to being 'his faithful soldier and servant until my life's end'.

It is important to stress the decisiveness of Christian baptism as the mark to others that I am a follower of Christ. It is even more important to stress the decisiveness of Christian baptism as the mark God

31

gives to me to assure me that I belong. If, in a moment of doubt, a young bride separated from her husband finds herself wondering whether she is really married or whether it is all just a dream – she has only to glance down at her ring. There it is, the mark of belonging, the love gift from her bridegroom to assure her that she does belong to him for keeps. Baptism acts as a physical reassurance of our relationship with Christ. And if a believer's baptism gives the clearest picture of *our* side of the agreement (publicly acknowledging our allegiance to Jesus and burning our boats behind us), infant baptism gives the clearest picture of *his* side in it all. He accepts us, forgives us, adopts us into his family and offers us his Holy Spirit to live in us, not because we have done a thing to deserve it (how can a child a few weeks old possibly earn such wonderful things?) but simply because God is love. In his love he came to this world for us. In his love he died for us. In his love he welcomes us, irrespective of our qualifications. And baptism, not least of infants, graphically declares this.

To assure you

Whether, then, baptism is administered in infancy, or as a believer, the important thing is that all Christians should be baptised. If you have committed your life to Christ and have not yet been baptised, you are clearly bidden by the New Testament to get baptised. Baptism and belief belong together as the visible and the invisible side of the same relationship. If you have already been baptised as an infant, and have subsequently come to faith, there is no indication in the Bible that you should be rebaptised – rather the reverse. Baptism is the sacrament of justification, of the new birth, of becoming a Christian, of receiving the Spirit, of entering God's family.[7] The new beginning only happens once: logically, then, the sacrament of initiation cannot be repeated.

But the point I want to stress is this. Whether baptised as an infant or a grown-up, your baptism is not only the mark of your faith, but of God's gracious acceptance of you. Seen in this light it is a visible, tangible promise. It is as if God says to you by it, 'Yes, I know you have let me down, since you came to faith. I know you are racked with doubts. But I have given you this mark of baptism in your body to assure you that you are accepted, unacceptable as you may be in yourself. You are now in the family, through my dear Son, Jesus Christ.'

As time goes on, you won't be tempted to doubt in the same way as you are tested initially. There's no point. The devil realises it is a dead loss to tempt an old, experienced Christian with doubts about whether he has really begun the Christian life or not. I may have thought it incredible that Rosemary, my wife, should care about me in the earliest days of our love, but now we've been happily married for years and doubts of her love never cross my mind. We have had too much experience of living together to doubt its reality and the strength of our relationship. And it is like that with the Christian. As the months and years go by you will discover that the devil finds plenty of other ways of tripping you up, but leaves this initial gambit pretty much alone. You will also discover that you have become as sure of your relationship with Christ as you are with some friend you know and love well.

A Letter for Doubters

One of the New Testament Letters was written for people who had not so long ago entrusted their lives to Jesus Christ. St John tells us at the end of his gospel that its supreme purpose was to bring people to the conviction that Jesus was God's Son; and further, to that personal encounter with Jesus that would start them off on a new life. He wrote his First Letter, he tells us, to people who already believe in Jesus, so that 'they may know that they have eternal life'[8] – this new quality of existence of which we spoke in Chapter One. Notice that word 'know'. We are meant to be in no doubt about it. And in that Letter John outlines several of the ways in which the new life will make itself felt.

New sense of pardon

There's a new sense of forgiveness. Those who cannot even forgive themselves are assured, as they look at the cross, that they are forgiven by God. 'If you sin, there is someone to plead for you before the Father. His name is Jesus Christ, the one who is all that is good, and who pleases God completely. He is the one who took God's wrath against our sins upon himself, and brought us into fellowship with God: and he is the forgiveness of our sins, and not ours only, but all the world's.'[9]

New desire to please God

Then there's a new desire to go God's way. Previously I did not care too much if I did wrong, so long as I

34

was not found out. But now I do begin to care —
even if nobody is watching. Because I know that
wrongdoing was the thing that took my Lord to the
cross. It hurts him. And I don't want to hurt the one
I have begun to love. 'Someone may say, "I am a
Christian; I am on my way to heaven; I belong to
Christ." But if he doesn't do what Christ tells him to,
he is a liar . . . That is the way to know whether or
not you are a Christian. Anyone who says he is a
Christian should live as Christ did.'[10]

New attitude to others

Here's a third pointer: a new attitude to other people.
'So now we can tell who is a child of God and who
belongs to Satan. Whoever is living a life of sin and
doesn't love his brother shows that he is not in God's
family.'[11] In other words, we see the man next door
not just as a nasty piece of work (which he may very
well be — but then so are we, until Jesus gets to work
on us). We see him as the nasty piece of work for
whom Christ was content to die. And if Jesus did that
for him, well, it rather changes things does it not? We
begin to see others as Christ sees them, and to act
accordingly.

New care for Christians

There's a very special side to this new love which
characterises Christians. It is a love for other believers,
a sense of belonging to them in the same family.
Indeed, so significant is this that John gives it as one
of the ways of deciding whether a man is a Christian
or not. 'If we love other Christians it proves that we

have been delivered from hell and given eternal life . . . We know what real love is from Christ's laying down his life for us. And so we ought to lay down our lives for our Christian brothers.'[12] That is just what the early Christians did, and it so impressed the world that people exclaimed, 'See how these Christians love one another.' Sadly, in many churches today there is little of that infectious gaiety and unselfish love for other Christians; instead, you find rather a carping and critical spirit. But that is not the true family characteristic. I have had the chance in recent years of going into many parts of the world, Africa, black and white, the Far East, Australia and North America, and I have been more than ever struck by this love for fellow Christians which always springs from true conversion. You may never have seen them before; you may never see them again. But even in a short meeting you seem to go right down to bedrock with another member of the Jesus family. You feel that you have known them for years. You sense that you are on the same wavelength, both forgiven sinners, both people with a message and a new purpose in life, both with the same Holy Spirit at work changing you from inside. This love for other Christians, irrespective of colour, background or nationality,[13] is one of the most precious gifts God gives his children – and thereby assures them that they really do belong.

New power over evil

Do you want another sign of the new life surging within? Here it is. 'The person who has been born into God's family does not make a practice of sinning, because God's new life is in him; so he can't keep on sinning, for this new life has been born in him and controls him – he has been born again.'[14] In other words, there is a new power released within the Christian, none other than Christ himself who is now resident inside us. Of course, Christians can and do sin. John knows that perfectly well.[15] What is more, he knows the way of pardon for the guilty Christian conscience – as we come straight back to our heavenly Father, tell him the mess we made and rely on his forgiveness, which is guaranteed to us by the cross of Jesus. But sin should increasingly become the exception, not the rule. The new life in us does not do what is wrong, because it is God's life at work in us. In so far as we allow that new life free play, we shall find that the power of Christ does deliver us daily from the forces of evil that have for so long dragged us down.

It is interesting that the first letter I had from a newly converted Canadian friend, whose life had been in a bad way, made this very point about a new power let loose in him: 'I purposely have not written to you until now, because I wanted to see if what had happened to me would last,' he wrote after a couple of months. 'It has lasted! . . . My craving for alcohol and cigarettes left me immediately, and I have had no desire for either of them since.' How about that? The power of alcoholism, and the power of smoking were snapped overnight, as if the Lord was giving him a foretaste of what he could do. Of course he had a long way to go. There were plenty of battles to come, and he may have had a sense of what was to come when writing what followed: 'My resentments are gone, and my fears, but I find that when I'm not watching they can sometimes creep up on me again.' Don't we all? What

37

is the way to meet them, then? My friend had already discovered it. 'So I have to keep on coming back to God. But the big difference is that now I have him to come back to.' The Christian life begins with Christ and continues with Christ. He is the only one who can change us. And the wonder of it is that he does, if we let him, and just as much as we let him. It is perfectly true that 'every child of God can obey him, defeating sin and evil pleasure by trusting Christ to help him'.[16]

New joy and confidence

There are other things that gradually emerge as we press further and further into the new country of life with Christ. For one thing, there is the joy he gives. St John says that he wrote this Letter 'so that you, too, may be full of joy', a joy that comes from 'our fellowship with the Father and his Son Jesus Christ'.[17] For another thing, there is the still, gentle voice of the Holy Spirit inside us, assuring us that we are in the family. 'The man who believes in the Son has this voice of testimony within him,' says John, 'the voice of the Holy Spirit in our hearts.'[18] It is not easy to describe what this means to anyone who has not experienced it, any more than it is to describe what it means to be loved to someone who has had a loveless life. John does have a go at it in another place in his Letter. 'We know how much God loves us because we have felt his love, and we believe him when he tells us that he loves us dearly. God is love, and anyone who lives in love is living with God and God is living in him. And as we live with Christ, our love grows more perfect and complete; so that we will not be ashamed and embarrassed at the day of judgment, but can face him with confidence and joy, because he loves us and we love him too.'[19] If you've been a Christian even for a short time, you'll understand what John is talking about. That is what is meant by the inner witness of the Holy Spirit.

New experience of prayer

One other thing begins to change: prayer. We shall have more to say about that in the next chapter, but just for the moment notice this. John marvels at the new experience of answered prayer which opens up once we come into the family of God. In the old days, nobody seemed to be there, nobody seemed to listen. Prayer was a hopeless exercise; it did no good; and probably we gave it up entirely, except perhaps as a last resort in some emergency. Look at the change now. 'We are confident of this, that he will listen to us whenever we ask him for anything in line with his will. And if we really know he is listening when we talk to him and make our requests, then we can be sure that he will answer us.'[20] A new world, you see. No longer is God a stranger, but a friend, a father, one who delights to have us talk to him, and open up the whole of our lives to him. And, no less amazing, we begin to want to do it. We actually come to enjoy prayer. Fantastic, but true, as any Christian will tell you. It is one of the signs of new life.

So these are some of the marks of God's new vitality which gradually makes itself felt in different aspects of our life. They take time. But they do come. They justify Paul's tremendous claim with which we began, that, 'When someone becomes a Christian he becomes a brand new person inside. He is not the same any more. A new life has begun!'[21]

NOTES

1 2 Corinthians 5:17 (LB)
2 Romans 6:23
3 Ephesians 2:8–9,
   Romans 3:24–5
4 Romans 5:1–2
5 2 Corinthians 11:2,
   Romans 8:15–17
6 John 6:37
7 Romans 6:3–4,
   Galatians 3:26–7
8 1 John 5:13
9 1 John 2:1–2 (LB)
10 1 John 2:4–6 (LB)
11 1 John 3:10 (LB)
12 1 John 3:14–16
13 Colossians 3:11–12
14 1 John 3:9 (LB)
15 1 John 1:8–9
16 1 John 5:4 (LB)
17 1 John 1:3–4
18 1 John 5:10
19 1 John 4:16–19 (LB)
20 1 John 5:14–15
21 2 Corinthians 5:17 (LB)

3

A Fresh Perspective

He was writing to me to describe the change in attitude that had come about since he became a Christian.

> It is rather like a cyclist who, when he has climbed a long hill, feels he should be able to free-wheel down the other side. It is not until he reaches the top that he sees that his task has only just started, and that the road winds on, with even steeper hills than the one he has just climbed. When people accept Christ, they tend to think it will all be free-wheeling from that point. But then they discover it is only the beginning. At least, that's the case in my experience.

And in mine too. Now why should this be?

It is important to get clear about this right away because it is bound to influence the way we approach the rest of our Christian life. Why is it harder once you have become a Christian than ever it was before?

Going with the crowd

It is harder because in the old days you were largely influenced by what *you* wanted to do, or by the group you went round with, or what happened to be the fashion or the good cause of the moment. On the whole you saw no particular reason to be different, unless it suited you to be. You went with the crowd. It was more convenient that way. Anyhow, what could one individual do, even if you wanted to? So why bother? According to most people, right and wrong are just matters of personal choice or convention. They don't hold good for all people everywhere. So why not take the easy way, the way that pays best? After all, the world isn't going anywhere. There is nothing that ultimately matters. We came from nothing and we go to nothing. So make the best of it. Get as wide a range of experience out of life as you can. That's what it's there for. If you should die young, it would be a pity to have missed any of it. So by all means take crack and sleep with whom you like, provided nobody gets too badly hurt. It will be interesting to find out what each new experience is like. And why not? There is no heaven or hell, no God or devil . . . or *is* there a devil, after all? There's certainly something in all this Satan worship and black magic. But anyhow, there is no God we can be sure about. So nothing is forbidden unless, of course, you personally don't like it. Do your own thing and enjoy it. I'll do mine.

These are among the current attitudes of modern people, especially the young. And they are very reasonable, too: reasonable, that is, if you don't believe in a God of truth. Today a generation has arisen which doesn't so much reject the idea that God exists, but rather is willing uncritically to accept any god, or gods. The current rise of the 'New Age' beliefs is proof of this. They claim that as in the physical world anything is possible, so in the spiritual world anything is acceptable. Do your own thing – everything is permitted.

Let's have a closer look at this notion. What I am saying is this. People today have knocked the Absolute out of their world, and are left with only the relative. There is no absolute standard for human behaviour left – so we can set up our own standards of what is acceptable. There is no absolute standard for truth left, and so even the philosophers have given up trying to discover the nature of truth, justice and goodness which they used to wrestle with: instead, they have taken to analysing words. And in a society increasingly influenced by New Age ideology, rationality is commonly subordinated to feeling. 'Is it true?' gives place to 'Is it relevant?' Much new legislation is no longer based on principle, but on attempting to determine what most people want. In industry, or in personal relationships, the notion of 'I want' is paramount: 'I ought' is at a discount. It is the terrible but logical outworking of pluralism.

Swimming Against the Current

Now do you see why it is harder to be a Christian than it was to stay uncommitted? Then you swam with the current. Now you are up against it in every conceivable way. You have dared to put the Absolute back into the picture. You have recognised God and his truth as the centre of all existence, and you have got in touch with him. You belong to a minority, a guerilla band. You are out on your own.

Others may think life has no real meaning or

purpose. You know it has. Life is meant to be shared with the Source of all being.

Others may think that the world is the result of a fluke or the influence of the stars. You know it is the product of a wise and loving Creator, not some 'god within you' but the God of heaven and earth.

Others may think that the universe is silent and unfeeling. You know it shouts aloud of your loving heavenly Father who made it, and who discloses himself in the colour and scent of every rose or the glory of every sunset.

Others may think that human personality is thrown up by luck in a world that is basically mechanistic. You know that it is the highest gift of a personal God. That's why human beings matter so infinitely. They are made in his likeness.

Others may think that truth and beauty and goodness are merely a matter of taste, or a transcendental experience. To you they are different aspects of the Lord himself, who is the model of goodness, the source of beauty and the essence of truth.

Others may see that love is the one hope for humanity, but have no answer to the problem of why we should bother to love and how we can manage to do it. For you, love is the personal trade mark of the Creator, himself Love, who has shared something of his very nature with us – even with those who don't believe in him. And as a Christian you bother because all people are the object of that love of his; you cannot manage to love others by your own efforts. It didn't take you long to discover that. But once allow the love of God to reach you and it's bound to find a way out through you to others.

Everything, yes everything, is different once God is restored to his rightful place. And you have done that, have you not? He is in the middle of the picture? Then don't be surprised that things are tough. What revolutionary ever had them easy? And Christianity is for revolutionary spirits, not for pale conformists. It is for people who have the guts to be different.

A changed life – God's will

I think the greatest area of difference is going to be our behaviour. And you will have noticed that this is precisely what people expect. No sooner claim to be a Christian at work than they will expect you not to swear and not to tell dirty stories. They will expect you to clock in on time and work hard. No matter what they may say about not wanting Holy Joes about the place, ordinary non-religious people expect a Christian to be different and to have higher standards than themselves. And that, though it is rather embarrassing and challenging, is a healthy instinct. I'll tell you why.

Wherever you look in the religions of the world, you will find few essential links between religion and morality, except in the religion of Israel which flowered in Christianity. You worshipped a god or gods in the pagan religions of the ancient world, so as to have an insurance policy in times of trouble, and in order to fulfil the instinct to worship which is found in every nation under the sun. But your worship did not make many – if any – ethical demands on you, apart, maybe, from a few taboos, such as a ritual bath or abstinence from sexual relations for a few days before worship. Worship and morals were not linked.

But with Israel it was different. It was not a bit of

45

good worshipping the Lord if the worshipper then went out to 'sell the needy for a pair of shoes'. God was not to be kept quiet with a worship service at the weekend while people continued oppressing the poor and swindling their neighbours in the weektime.

The need for righteous living among those who claim to worship a righteous God cannot be over-emphasised. God, the source of all that is good and true and upright, demands these same qualities in his worshippers. Not, mind you, as a condition of accepting them. We have already seen that he accepts us just as we are. But in due course he does expect the family likeness to become visible in members of his family.

He has gone to considerable trouble to make himself plain on that point. He does not leave us with mere generalities, evocative though they may be, such as, 'You must be holy for I am holy, says the Lord.'[1] Throughout the Bible, and particularly in the writings of the Old Testament prophets, God lets us know what this holiness of character is going to mean in ordinary, daily behaviour. But we aren't very good, on the whole, at listening to other people, even if they are prophets, lecturing us about right and wrong! We are much more liable to be moved by a good example. So that is just what God, in his generosity, provided.

A changed life – Jesus' example

Jesus Christ came not only to be our rescuer from the mess we had got ourselves in: but to be our example of the right way to live. He lived the perfect life. Never a foot wrong. Never a word out of place. Never a loving act neglected. Never a need unmet. In Jesus

Christ we see the ideal for human life. Perfection walked this earth in his person. We no longer need to wonder what the good life might involve. We can no longer plead ignorance. It is there before us, plain for all to see. Unlike any other teacher before or since, Jesus actually lived up to his own teaching. He who told men to love their enemies did that very thing. He who told men not to lay up treasure on earth was so poor that he had no home. He who told men not to worry about their food and clothes lived a life of radiant peace despite the lack of what we would consider even the necessities of life.

Examine the moral teaching of Jesus and I think you'll find that he completely lived up to his own standards. His life was a moral miracle. He showed us not just by his unique teaching but by his matchless living what holiness meant, what the character of God was like. And the implication was painfully obvious. 'Christ . . . is your example,' cried Peter (and he should know, having lived three years in Jesus' company, watching his every move). '*Follow in his steps!* He never sinned, never told a lie, never answered back when insulted; when he suffered he did not threaten to get even; he left his case in the hands of God who always judges fairly.'[2]

But does that really help? It is one thing to recognise that the God we worship is holy and expects us to become increasingly like him. It is another to realise that he has given us a personal demonstration in terms of a human life to show us what he means by practical holiness. But my trouble is, how can I begin to match up to a standard like that?

A changed life – the Spirit's power

Well, once again, God has made the necessary provision for us. Paul puts it in a nutshell in his First Letter to the Christians in Thessalonica, fresh converts from paganism in northern Greece. In almost the same breath he sets before them Christian standards, 'God wants you to be holy and pure,' and Christian resources, 'God gives us his Holy Spirit.'[3] The holy God does not lower his standards. He gives us the Holy Spirit to enable us to keep them. God's Holy Spirit is none other than Jesus Christ in spirit form. When we respond to Jesus, we allow his Spirit to enter our lives. And gradually that Spirit will, as we saw in Chapter One, repel the forces of evil habit from our lives. 'So now the fair claims of God's standards can be achieved in us, if we do not live with the self in control but with the Spirit.'[4] Paul knows what a battlefield his life has become since he declared himself a follower of Jesus. 'I love to do God's will so far as my new nature is concerned; but there is something else deep within me, in my lower nature, that is at war with my mind and wins the fight and makes me a slave to the sin that is still within me.'[5] That is the problem. God does not remove the tendency to evil which lies deeply entwined with the very roots of our nature as human beings. But he does give us his Holy Spirit to combat it. Jesus Christ was always victorious in his battle with evil, facing it as he did continuously through his life, and supremely in the crisis of the cross. He was the conqueror, all along the line. And the Holy Spirit is given us in order, among other things, to work out in us Christ's victory over evil. 'Who will deliver me from my slavery to this deadly lower nature?' cries Paul. 'Thank God! It has been done through Jesus Christ our Lord. He has set me free.'[6]

Yes, he has broken the back of evil. He pioneered the way. He sets us free from condemnation, free from despair, to enable us to fight evil. And we fight (if we are wise) not in our own strength, but in his. When tempted, we should look to his Holy Spirit who lives inside us, and say, 'Lord, please give me your self-control, your generosity, your peace of mind (or whatever it is) *now*.' And he will. You will find that, like St Paul, you will be able to say, 'The power of the life-giving Spirit of Christ has set me free from the vicious circle of sin and death.'[7]

Now let us get two things very clear about this life-changing power of the Spirit. In the first place the change doesn't happen automatically. In the second place, it doesn't happen overnight.

Change doesn't happen automatically

The Spirit of Jesus isn't going to force change on you. He didn't force his way into your life, did he? Well, he won't force you to go his way. If you determine to hold on to some evil habit, he will not stop you. It just grieves him very much. He will reluctantly not be able to use you as fully as he wants. But he is love. And love never forces itself on the beloved. I remember asking a wise Christian in the early days of my Christian life why I could not get power over one particular thing in my life, although I had seen Christ clean up a number of other areas. He asked me, 'Did you *want* his power, Michael?' Of course, I had to admit that I did not: I wanted to go my own way.

Sadly, the Lord would not stop me. So be very clear about this. Christ can and will deliver you from any evil habit. He can do it at once. *But you have to be willing to let him!* That's the rub. When you are willing, his power is a reality which nobody can deny.

There is a very interesting example of this in the area of drug addiction. Several years ago, at the Second International Symposium on Drug Abuse, Frank Wilson, one of the six British delegates, listened to the learned papers being read on the virtual impossibility of keeping real hard-liners off drugs once they left hospital. Then he quietly informed them of the sixty per cent success rate sustained over five years in his explicitly Christian rehabilitation unit at Northwick Park. It certainly raised some eyebrows. Much the same reaction followed a few years later when David Wilkerson, of *The Cross and the Switchblade* fame, was able to show a professional body in the USA that by means of full-blooded conversion to Christ and filling with the Holy Spirit he had been able to record a success rate among hardened dope users five times that of any secular agency. The point is inescapable. Christ can transform cases that would otherwise be hopeless. His power can change intractable habits in any one of us.

We all know what the expulsive power of a new affection can do: it can make the teenager forget his motorbike if once the girl of his dreams really crosses his path! Well, once a man has Christ inside him, he can discover a power to set him free from his own worst nature. 'I can do everything God asks me to with the help of Christ who gives me the strength and power,'[8] claimed Paul. And you and I can have the same experience.

Change doesn't happen overnight

Secondly, beware of thinking you will become Christ-like overnight. You won't. Some habits will be very reluctant to give way, just as some ice is so thick that it takes a long time to be thawed out by the warmth of the sun. And even though we may experience immediate deliverance from any particular wrong thing that is getting us down, we will then merely be ready for God to show us something else in our life that needs attention. The process of refining will go on all through our lives. We shall need time if we are to grow like Jesus. It is a slow process, just like growing a good fruit tree.

Have you ever planted a garden? Then you know how impatient you are for the young apple tree and the pear tree you put in to bear fruit? Not a sign of any yet. But there is life, and there is growth, and next year, perhaps . . . So be patient. Keep in close touch with the holy God who has called you. Study the life and teaching, the behaviour and example of Jesus if you want to know how God wishes you to act and react in the pressures of everyday life. And ask the Holy Spirit who lives inside you to take control of your personality and make you progressively more and more like Jesus.

There is a lovely promise in Paul's Second Letter to the Corinthians which speaks of the Holy Spirit changing us from one degree of Christ-reflectingness to another as we live in conscious and constant companionship with him.[9] We shan't notice it, but others will. It was said of the early disciples that men observing them 'were amazed and realized what being with Jesus had done for them'.[10] That is God's strategy. He wants to take men and women who are humble enough to say sorry and come to him in simple trust; he wants to rehabilitate them and demonstrate in their changed character what he can achieve even in spoiled human lives when once he is given a chance. That is the strategy, and that is the perspective from which to plan your Christian life. Nobody will believe you have a new life unless they see a new lifestyle. And when they do see it, they'll be ready to listen about the new life – not before.

NOTES

1 1 Peter 1:16
2 1 Peter 2:21–3
3 1 Thessalonians 4:3, 8
4 Romans 8:4
5 Romans 7:22–3 (LB)
6 Romans 7:25 (LB)
7 Romans 8:2
8 Philippians 4:13
9 2 Corinthians 3:18
10 Acts 4:13 (LB)

4

A Transforming Friendship

1. A Friendship that Lasts

One of the most staggering statements in the Bible is contained in the simple words of Jesus: 'I have not called you servants . . . I have called you friends.'[1] Jesus, who shares God's very nature, Jesus who was God's agent in creation, Jesus at once origin, goal and sustainer of the entire universe – Jesus is prepared to call us friends. Friends, when we have disobeyed him. Friends, when we have not wanted to know him. Friends, when we have been rebels. It is an amazing offer.

Pie in the sky?

When we commit our lives to Christ we begin a life of friendship with him which is meant to go on and get richer and deeper until our dying day. And then we shall see him face to face, and it will be wonderful. The one I now know by faith I shall then see. The one I fitfully love I shall be united to for ever. 'In your presence is fullness of joy, and at your right hand are pleasures for evermore,'[2] sang the psalmist: and I believe it. If the first instalment of life with Christ here

53

on earth brings such joy and fulfilment, there is every
reason to believe him when he promises that the climax
of it all after this life is over will be infinitely satisfying.
This means that I can see my life steadily and see it
whole; as a friendship from now on with Christ who
will stick with me, change me and in the end receive
me into his presence. Now notice two things about this
Christian hope. It is not pie in the sky when you die.
The pie, or a great deal of it, is available as we enjoy
the Lord's company day by day. It would be infinitely
worthwhile even if this life were all there is. But Jesus
has said that this life is not all there is, and he has
backed up his words with the resurrection. I'm
prepared to take it from him. He has penetrated
beyond the bounds of death. He knows.

Rewards and punishments?

No, it is not pie in the sky when you die; nor is it a
refined form of selfishness to look forward to heaven.
I do not love my Lord Jesus because I fear hell (though
I believe that without Christ hell is my portion). I do
not love him because I want to go to heaven (I don't,
if he is not there. Endless existence without him would
be exceedingly tedious and unattractive). I love him
because he went to that cross for me, because he
patiently waited until I was willing to make room in
my crowded life for him. I love him because he is so
patient with me when I am such a poor follower of his.
That is why I love him. The thought of reward does
not play any significant part in my motivation as a
Christian. Nevertheless, I believe him when he says
that, 'There are many homes up there where my
Father lives . . . When everything is ready then I will

come and get you, so that you can always be with me where I am. If this weren't so, I would tell you plainly.'[3] I believe in heaven, in short, because Jesus taught it, and I trust him. If he says our friendship is too precious for him to scrap it at death, that is good enough for me. It is wonderfully generous of him to be willing to go on sharing his new life with us for ever. Yet it's just like him – his name is love.

Growing old with Christ

But this chapter is not about heaven and the ultimate enjoyment of his friendship there, though I think we should lift up our eyes from time to time to the future God has promised us. It is a wonderful thing to recall that life is not slipping away from us as our physical powers decay: we are getting nearer the day when we shall enjoy Christ's loving companionship to the full. And that has an enriching and broadening effect upon the character. One old Christian man, when asked his age, replied with a smile, 'The bright side of seventy.' He knew what he was talking about. That is why for the Christian old age is not an unmitigated menace, nor is death the worst thing that can befall him. As St Paul contemplated the process of ageing and the approach of death, he wrote,

We never give up. Though our bodies are dying, our inner strength in the Lord is growing every day. These troubles and sufferings of ours are, after all, quite small and won't last very long. Yet this short time of distress will result in God's richest blessing upon us for ever and ever . . . How weary we grow

of our present bodies. That is why we look forward
eagerly to the day when we shall have heavenly
bodies which we shall put on like new clothes . . .
We look forward with confidence to our heavenly
bodies, realizing that every moment we spend in
these earthly bodies is time spent away from our
eternal home in heaven with Jesus.[4]

What man could write like that if he did not share the
friendship of Christ now, and expect its consummation
hereafter?

The supreme ambition

Yes, Christ is the friend who will receive us at the end
of our lives, just as Christ was the friend who accepted
us in the first place. The Christian life begins and ends
with him. It is significant that St Paul, who came to
know Christ initially on the Damascus Road, should
disclose, some quarter of a century later, what was his
supreme ambition, in these words, 'My aim is to know
him.'[5] *To know him*: that was the very centre of
Christian living for the great apostle. He knew him
already, of course. He had known him over a quarter
of a century in times of success and loneliness, elation
and depression, in the banqueting hall and in the
dungeon, on dry land and in shipwreck: and yet his
aim was to know him better. Perhaps in that simple
ambition we have plumbed the innermost secret of the
greatness of St Paul. Christ was his friend, and for that
friend he was willing to work and to suffer, come what
may. But most of all, he wanted to know him better.
He would have approved of the famous prayer of
Richard of Chichester:

Thanks be to thee, my Lord Jesus Christ,
For all the benefits thou hast won for me,
For all the pains and insults thou hast borne for me.
O most merciful Redeemer, Friend and Brother,
May I know thee more clearly,
Love thee more dearly,
And follow thee more nearly
For thy name's sake.

2. A Friendship that Develops

The phone and the letter

But how are we to develop that friendship with the
Lord? After all, we can't see him. How *can* you develop
a friendship with someone you can't see?

There are basically two ways. People who love each
other can keep in touch, when separated, by writing
letters and by using the telephone. You should see the
students making a bee-line for the letter rack in the
morning, or queueing up outside the phone kiosk in
the evening. If I were insensitive enough to ask them
why they should think it worthwhile being late for
their breakfast because they were eagerly fingering
through the pile of letters in the hope that she might
have written; or if I were tactless enough to enquire
whether the nightly phone call to some far-away
woman was worth the price of the call – the answer
would be short and utterly sufficient. 'Of course it's
worth it. I love her.'

It's like that with Christ. Before we came to know
him we had no particular desire to get in touch, even
if we believed in his existence. But now that we know

him and love him, it's different. We shall want to use the letter and the phone. It won't be a dreary rule that we have to keep in order to develop a friendship. It will be the most natural thing in the world, for we love him.

The open letter

Our Lord has in fact written an open letter to all members of his family. In it he tells them about himself, about his plans for their good, about successes and failures of past members of the family, about love and self-discipline, about the family characteristics and the resources available to all the members. There are promises to claim, commands to obey, advice to note, prayers to echo, as well as examples to follow and warnings to heed. Best of all, this time of reading the Bible will warm your heart with love for your beloved Friend, and strengthen your determination to please him in the affairs of that day. It will become an important part of your life, this reading of his letter. You will find, I think, that the Scriptures do not exaggerate when they describe their own function as food, without which we shall starve; as a sword, without which we shall be defeated; as a mirror, for lack of which we shall fail to see what we really look like; as a lamp, to shed light on our path; as a fire, to warm our cold hearts when they lose their glow; and as a hammer to break the rock in pieces when we are being wilfully disobedient.[6] This book contains God's message for men and women, brought to us by the human writers, who themselves lived close enough to God to hear, assimilate and interpret his will.[7] If you want to grow in your friendship with your Lord, you simply cannot afford to neglect it.

Does it look as if I am legislating? As if being a Christian involves a series of rules, of which one of the most important is 'Read your Bible daily'? No, that is not the case. There is no rule about it. But it stands to reason that if you love someone you will want to explore them fully: and if you can't see them and can only communicate with them by letter, then you don't find it any hardship to study the letters! Sometimes Christians have made a fetish of Bible reading. They have implied that unless you read it daily, and preferably before breakfast, you are going to make a mess of the day. Indeed, they have implied you are on the road to spoiling your friendship with Jesus.

There is a general reaction in Christian circles these days against such legalism, and rightly so. Jesus is not so mean as to withdraw his friendship if we skip reading the Bible for a day, or two, or three. But if it is true that the Bible is one of the main sources of nourishment for the Christian (and it is) then ask yourself how well you would grow physically if you ate your meals at rare and irregular intervals. And if you react against 'the morning hour' of traditional Christian devotion, ask yourself if it is because you are really at your best for your Friend later in the day, say in the evening – in which case, fine. Have it in the evening. Or is it because you are too idle to get up in the morning? It may be a curious coincidence, but most great men and women of God in the past have found that if they didn't make time for Bible reading at the beginning of the day (for however short a time) they didn't make time at all. The rest of the day somehow seems to slip away. But you may be different. You may be iron-willed. You may be a busy housewife who can get alone for half an hour after your husband and the kids have gone off in the post-breakfast exodus. You may be the type that wakes up at night, and is able to guard the last half hour of the day for being alone with your Friend. Get a time that suits you, and keep that special for him. The important thing is that you should really meet with your Lord, not where or when you do it, or how long you spend at it.

How to begin

Do you wonder 'How am I to set about it?' Perhaps the best advice would be to seek out Christian friends and ask for help in learning how to read a passage devotionally. It would be a good idea to meet them once a week for, say, a couple of months, so that together you can study some chapters of the Bible that bear on the major aspects of Christian living. For instance, Luke 11:1–13 is a splendid passage on prayer, Ephesians 4:17–5:1 on Christian living, Romans 12 on Christian service. In such a regular, relaxed, weekly meeting you can share with your friends the many teething troubles that come up in the early days of every Christian's experience. They have almost certainly had similar problems to face, and are sure to be delighted to give you a hand. I personally found this weekly session with a more experienced Christian friend more help than anything else in developing my friendship with Christ.

But if no such friend is available, don't be discouraged. You have at your side one who will 'never fail you nor forsake you'.[8] 'You need no other teacher,' wrote St John, 'for he teaches you all things, and he is the Truth.'[9] I would advise you to get a good modern translation of the Bible. There are lots of them, though increasingly The New International Version is winning worldwide acclaim for its mixture of accuracy and readability. You would also be wise to get a regular system of reading it, or you may otherwise start at the beginning and get bogged down in the Book of Numbers, or do a circular tour of your favourite passages! *Words of Life* is a very popular method of Bible reading devised by the Salvation Army. The Scripture Union is a worldwide and interdenominational method of reading the Bible in short, manageable portions, with some helpful explanatory comment in the various series of notes that are issued. It would certainly be a help to begin with one of these systems.

But don't be afraid to change it later on if you feel in need of some variety. Perhaps branch out on your own. Sometimes you might read a whole book at a sitting: the Book of Jonah, maybe, if you are feeling rebellious; or Peter's First Letter if you are going through tough times at work. Sometimes you might study a single verse intensively. For instance John 3:16, perhaps the most famous verse in the Bible, tells us of our great need: we are perishing, like someone drowning in a river. It speaks of God's great love: he gave Jesus to meet that need of men. And it speaks of a step of faith whereby everyone who believes may have for himself God's new life. And by the time you have dug into a verse like that, you will find you have learned it by heart, and that may well prove very useful to you later on when you are trying to help other people.

More ways than one

There are lots of other ways of Bible study. You can make a character study, and trace the references in the New Testament to a man like Andrew who is mentioned only three times in the Gospel of John, but on each occasion he is introducing someone else to Jesus. Or take one of the great heroes of faith in the Old Testament such as Abraham, and see how he faced the temptation to take the easy course for fear of looking odd, the temptations to selfishness, to self-pity and to water down God's promises. That man faced the same difficulties that come our way, and more. The way he trusted God long ago can inspire and teach us today.

Alternatively, you may study a theme: what the Bible has to say about money, work, marriage, faith or perhaps what was the message and what were the qualities of the early Christians who had such striking success in the ancient world. As a change, you could take a single chapter, and see what its main teaching is. Romans 8 is a great chapter, with its assurance about a Christian's past, his present and his future with Christ; so is 2 Timothy 2 with its seven distinctive pen pictures of a Christian worker. Or you can trace a single significant word such as 'inheritance', 'faithful' or 'able'. I have discovered a great deal by investigating the Christian inheritance that God has provided, by considering areas where he is calling me to be faithful, and by reflecting on what he has pledged himself able to do in and through me.

These are some of the different ways in which you can study that inexhaustible book, the Bible. But whether you are doing some exploration on your own, or following a system like the Scripture Union, remember that you are coming to read the Bible for a quite specific purpose. For you it is not 'The Bible as Literature' or 'The Bible as History' or 'Biblical Criticism'. It is the Bible as God's love-letter to you. So come to him in prayer before you begin. Ask him to bring it alive for you as you read, and to speak to you through it. And then read it through, and through again, looking for a promise you can claim, a warning you can heed, an example you can follow, a prayer you can use or something you had never spotted before about your Lord and Friend.

Two-way traffic

This Bible-reading is not one-way traffic. You will want to pause to thank God for some new truth that has struck you; to adore him for some fresh insight into what he has done for you; to search your conscience over some requirement of his; to think out the implications of some promise you have read. Bible-reading, in fact, leads naturally into prayer. The reading of his letter drives you to pick up the phone of prayer. I once asked a student who had come to the Christian life only a month earlier, 'What is the greatest difference you have noticed?' Her reply was interesting. 'I have begun to love praying. I sometimes go on for ages, because I am really in touch.' That girl had learnt the meaning of prayer; it is talking with God. Talking with him about anything and everything of concern to us: friends, the job, time off, home relationships, future career, disappointments, joys, everything, including the day's timetable. Prayer is assuredly not a matter of set words (though there is a real place for formal prayers in a church service, so that all present can join in them) nor of fixed times (though without fixed times our praying will become spasmodic and probably chaotic). It is the sharing of our life with our Friend. Why do you think Christ died for us? To show us his love? Yes. To take responsibility for our sins? Yes. But supremely in order to share our life with us. 'He died for us in order that we might *live with him*,'[10] with all the barriers formed by unforgiven sin knocked away, and with nothing between us to spoil the friendship.

The phone of prayer

The following letter came to me from a young woman who had been a dancer, a model, a nanny, and has subsequently married a clergyman! When she wrote it she had only been a Christian for a few months, and this is what prayer was beginning to mean to her.

When I pray, it is to get close to God, to thank him for all he has given me and done for me, and to praise him in his glory. To ask for strength to do his will, so that through my actions people will see him in me. To get so close in the quietness of the mind that God can tell me what he wants me to do for him. To ask for help for myself and all my friends and family and for this world and its sin. To ask for forgiveness and strength not to sin again. To talk quietly with my Friend and my God and tell him all my inner feelings that I could never share with anyone else.

That is the essence of prayer: talking with God. But

it involves listening to him, too. We aren't very good at this – at least I'm not. I tend to talk too much, and it is hard for him to make his will known to me. You may be the same: so busy talking you don't realise that he may well be calling on you to visit that lonely person down the road, to take a bag of fresh fruit to that poor old thing in the mental hospital, or not to be impatient with your children. It may be that there is a gift of money he wants you to part with, or a word that would help the person you work alongside. So long as you will give him the chance by listening to him, it is up to him to get through to you, is it not? I find that comforting. It is his responsibility to show me his will. It is mine to do it.

Finding a structure

If you want a structure to build your prayers round, how about using the Lord's prayer as a pattern? After all, that's what it's meant for.[11]

'Our Father' – come to him with the confidence of children in the family and thank him for accepting you and making you welcome.

'Who art in heaven' – that keeps the perspective straight and stops us getting over-familiar with God. He is great, glorious, heavenly: and I am puny, and should approach him not only with intimacy but with awe and reverence.

'Thy kingdom come' – pray for the extension of God's kingly rule in the lives of those in your circle (and wider) who do not give him their allegiance.

'Thy will be done' – pray for God's will to be done in the lives of those who do know him on earth, just as it is done in heaven. Here is the place to pray over the details of your day's programme, to recall your special weaknesses and to pray for your church and your Christian friends, as well as those who are serving the Lord overseas, or seeking to extend his kingly rule in industry or in government.

'Give us today our daily bread' – here you can include prayer for all your physical needs. God is concerned about them and invites you to make them known to him. The 'daily bread' in the original Aramaic seems to have meant 'the bread of tomorrow'. Give us today a foretaste of the wedding feast in heaven! That takes up our physical needs but transcends them. It asks for all we need in order to spend our day as citizens of the Kingdom.

'Forgive us' – we never get past the need to ask for forgiveness from the daily sins and failures that all of us fall prey to. Call them to mind. Confess them. And receive his pardon. And remember, as Jesus told his followers, that you must be willing to forgive those who wrong you, if you are going to be able to enjoy God's pardon.

'Lead us' – how we need his guidance each day. Commit to him any special problem which is concerning you at present. Particularly anything that is going to 'put you to the test'.

'Deliver us' – from the unwelcome attacks of the evil one today: temper, greed, lack of self-control, or whatever your particular weak points may be.

For I am handing over to you the kingly rule in my life today, Lord. I am looking to you for the power to live as a Christian in today's world. And I promise that I will hand back the credit to you direct, and not take it for myself. 'Thine is the kingdom, and the power, and the glory, for ever. Amen!'

Keeping it natural

This structure may well be a help in the special time you set aside for prayer. But friends do not only talk on fixed occasions! Christ is a friend, so turn to him at odd moments in the day. Is there some specially nice meal you have enjoyed? 'Thank you, Lord,' you say: and there's no need to shut your eyes or to kneel down in order to say it. Or is it some pressing temptation that attacks you? 'Lord, please give me your strength.' Or have you failed him? Don't wait until the evening to get it put right. Tell him at once. 'Lord, I've let you down. I am so sorry. Please forgive me, and help me to learn from my mistake, and to ask you for your help in good time when I am tempted to repeat it.'

One final thing. Friendship is all the more delightful when shared. If you are out for the evening with some other Christians, why not spend a few minutes in prayer to the Lord before you break up? You are sure to feel shy to begin with, because it will seem strange to talk to God out loud in your own words in the company of others. But why not? Break the sound barrier: launch out, however haltingly, and you will not regret it. I think I get to a deeper level of fellowship with other Christians when praying with them in this way, than at any other time.

There it is then. Christ is your Friend. And friendships need to be cultivated. Make sure yours doesn't fall into disrepair through neglect. The letter and the phone are indispensable for absent friends if they are to keep in touch. And though the analogy is not exact (for Christ is not absent: he is wonderfully present with you always) nevertheless the point holds good. You *must* keep in touch with him and he with you, and the Bible and prayer are prime ways to do this.

NOTES

1 John 15:15
2 Psalm 16:11
3 John 14:2 (LB)
4 2 Corinthians 4:16–17,
   5:2, 6 (LB)
5 Philippians 3:10
6 1 Peter 2:2,
   2 Timothy 3:14–17,
   Ephesians 6:17,

2 Corinthians 3:18,
Psalm 119; 105,
Jeremiah 23:29
7 2 Peter 1:21
8 Hebrews 13:5,
9 1 John 2:27
10 1 Thessalonians 5:10
11 Matthew 6:9,
   'Pray *like this* . . .'

5

A New Attitude

1. The Principle – Pleasing Christ

On human bondage

In this age when we are more sensitive about freedom than almost any subject, there are unmistakable signs that people remain in bondage. I received a letter from a man who was a habitual gambler. Even though it was wrecking his family life, even though it was driving him to bankruptcy, he could not stop it. He was enslaved. With you it may be something much less obvious than gambling. Swearing? Smoking? Alcohol? Drugs? Bad temper? Ambition? These things may begin with the thinnest of threads; but progressively they grip us, they inhibit our freedom and mould us into becoming the sort of people we don't want to be. We can't help ourselves. 'The man who does wrong,' said Jesus, 'becomes a slave to wrong.'[1]

Human nature hasn't changed since his day: we still please ourselves. However subtly it is dressed up, however various the guises it takes, self-centredness is the motivating factor in human life. 'Thank you very much,' we say, 'but I'll please myself.'

The Bible writers were well aware of this universal

69

tendency, and very honest about it. 'Once we, too, were foolish and disobedient; we were misled by others and became slaves to many evil pleasures and wicked desires. Our lives were full of resentment and envy. We hated others and they hated us.'[2] That is Paul's summary of the governing factor in human attitudes before Christ comes on the scene. Hear Peter: he is writing about the paradoxical situation whereby the advocates of the permissive society in his day found their freedom shackled by the very things they allowed themselves. 'The very teachers who offer this freedom from restraint are themselves enmeshed by evil habit. For a man is slave to whatever controls him.'[3] Or notice the way James pitches into the rich and selfish monied classes of his day: 'Listen! Hear the cries of the workers in your fields whom you have cheated of their pay. Their cries have reached the ears of the Lord of hosts. You have spent your life here on earth having fun, satisfying your every whim, and now your fat hearts are ready for the slaughter.'[4]

Yes, men and women remain now what they were then, 'lovers of pleasure, not lovers of God'.[5] You, too, used to be like that, did you not?

But now you're a Christian. What is to be your governing attitude? Is it to be determined by endless rules? Ought you to go out and buy a textbook on Christian ethics? Should you be bound by the taboos of the Christian group you have got attached to? What is the right attitude for a Christian facing the practical and perplexing decisions of daily behaviour?

A Christ-centred ethic

Mercifully the basic attitude is very simple indeed.

Simple, but difficult. As ever, you find your example in Jesus. The supreme ambition of his life was to please his heavenly Father. Was it a question of the timing of his programme? He waited till he was sure when the Father's 'hour' had come. Was it the ultimate question of the manner of his death? 'Not my will, but Thine be done.'[6]

'Christ didn't please himself,'[7] said Paul, with masterly understatement. The implication for Christians is so obvious that it scarcely needs drawing. Our aim should be to please not ourselves, but him. He is like the general who has recruited us to his forces. 'As Christ's soldier do not let yourself become distracted by worldly affairs, for then you cannot please the one who has enlisted you,'[8] said Paul. When in doubt about the rightness of some course of action, 'we cannot just go ahead and please ourselves. Let's please the other fellow, not ourselves, and do what is for his good and thus build him up in the Lord.'[9] The subject specifically under discussion by St Paul in that chapter is whether Christians should be vegetarians or not. His principle, however, is a fundamental one: we should please Christ, and act as his responsible agents in society.

And that is really all we need to know about Christian ethics! For we are not shackled to a code of conduct but are responsible to a person, Jesus Christ himself. Our motivation is not the stiff upper lip of duty, but the gratitude of those who have been set free. How does Paul pray for Christians at Colossae, whom he has never seen? I guess he would pray for us in precisely the same terms, and it couldn't be bettered. 'Ever since we first heard about you we have kept on praying and asking God to help you understand what

71

he wants you to do; asking that the way you live will always please the Lord and honour Him, so that you will both be doing good, kind things for other people and at the same time getting to know God better and better.'[10]

There in a nutshell you have the revolution that underlies all truly Christian behaviour. My main ambition is no longer to please myself but to please him. Once pleasure was king. Now Jesus is king.

Just think for a moment what that involves.

The freedom it brings

It gives full play to our freedom. The Church, alas, has not always been noted for its advocacy of freedom. It has been unduly conservative about its traditions, timid in allowing Christian people their heads, and not infrequently committed to policies of reaction rather than reform. But when it has acted in this way it has done so in straight contradiction to the New Testament. There we read such sentiments as these: 'So Christ has made us free! Now make sure you stay free and don't get tied up again in the chains of slavery to laws and ceremonies.'[11] In this age, which is dedicated to the pursuit of freedom, Jesus offers us the key to freedom we could never enjoy without him. A liberty to do what we know we ought: a liberty which is rooted deep within us as 'the Spirit who brings new life in Christ sets us free from the downward pull of sin'.[12]

The flexibility it gives

There's another advantage in this Christ-centred ethic.

It gives great flexibility. It means we are not governed by a set of unfeeling, unbreakable rules which we must keep, but by a living, loving person whom we aim to please. The focus of behaviour is not external to us, a code of conduct we are expected to live up to: it is internal, as the Holy Spirit first helps us to *want* to go Christ's way, and then enables us to work out that allegiance in the complexities of modern life.[13]

The reflection it demands

That leads on to another important point. It means that you and I have got to apply our minds to the question of behaviour. There is no slick answer to what Christian action may be in any given circumstance. We can't even simply look at the New Testament and read the solution off the page. We need to see how the early Christians tried to please Christ in their day and situation, and then translate that attitude into today's terms.

This is even true of the Sermon on the Mount, where, if anywhere, Jesus seems to be laying down a new code of behaviour for the members of the Kingdom of God. Is he not legislating? Not really. To be sure, he tells us that if a man hits us on one side of the face we should turn the other cheek. But are we to carry that out literally, without thinking about the principle behind it? If we actually do get clobbered by a man in a fit of temper, the fastest way to drive him really wild is to do a smart about-turn and offer him the other cheek. Literal obedience to the command could completely destroy the principle behind the command. The principle in this case is one of non-retaliation. Right. We must work out how best to show non-retaliation when we are provoked. But the ways of doing so will be legion, and may not include literally turning the other cheek. Thank God, we are not called to obey a code of rules but to please a person. Fulfilling that aim will amply engage our mind, our will and our attitude to Christ.

The variety it allows

It also means that there will be a number of variations in the way Christians work out their faith in their life. Let nobody persuade you that there is only one Christian attitude to disputed issues. There may well be several. Thank goodness, God is not interested in dull uniformity. Return for a moment to the New Testament Church and see how Paul handled diversity in Christian practice. Some of the Christians at Rome and Corinth would not eat meat that had been offered to idols for fear they should tacitly seem to condone idolatry. Others said, 'It can't do any harm. These idols don't exist. We have one Lord and Master, and he has given us food for our good. I shall eat it and be grateful.' Diversity in Christian practice, then, from people who interpret the will of the Lord differently on this matter. But notice how wisely Paul handles it:

Don't criticise a brother Christian for having different ideas from yours about what is right and wrong. For instance, don't argue with him about whether or not to eat meat that has been offered to idols . . . Those who think it is all right to eat such meat must not look down on those who won't. And if you are one of those who won't, don't find fault with those who do. For God has accepted them to be his children.

They are God's servants, not yours. They are responsible to him, not to you.[14]

In point of fact, he goes on, God is pleased with both attitudes, conscientiously held as they are. 'The man who eats meat eats it as a gift from the Lord, and he thanks God for it. The man who refrains from eating does so out of anxiety to please the Lord, and he too is thankful.'[15]

What a splendid, liberal and responsible approach to ethics! Splendid because it is so humane. Liberal, because it takes full account of the priceless gift of Christian freedom. Responsible because it anchors Christian behaviour in all its variety to pleasing Jesus, the supreme pattern for human beings.

The joy it brings

Mention of Jesus reminds us that there is nothing cramping or burdensome about Christian morality. God does not want to make life dull and dreary for us, but to make it full to the brim, and overflowing to those who do not know him. To please him is not restrictive: on the contrary it is to take our proper place in creation whose very existence is in order to fulfil his will and do his pleasure. The will of God is not arbitrary: it is 'good and acceptable and perfect'.[16] Just because it is perfect, it is acceptable; we need not feel there is anything limiting in seeking to follow that will. It is nothing less than the very best purpose of God for us, the children he has brought into new life.

Such then, is the revolutionary attitude brought about by Jesus. Freedom from evil habit through the indwelling of the Liberator. Freedom from rules and regulations through loyalty to Jesus. Freedom from smugness about our achievements, both because no one can be smug about responding to love, and because there is still so much more to be attempted for him. Freedom from a critical attitude towards the way other Christians work out their obedience; remembering that they may discern the will of the Lord more clearly than ourselves, and that variety can be honouring to God providing it stems from a genuine desire to please Christ. Yes, the Christian ethic is certainly liberating.

That, then, is the proper attitude: to ask, 'What would please Christ? What would he do in my situation? What action on my part is likely to bring credit to him?' Now let's be very practical and apply this principle to a single example, money. We'll look at a broader field in the next chapter.

2. The Application – One Example

The god of wealth

Money is god for a great many people. It is taken for granted that we should get as rich as we can, and that the more we have the happier we shall be. An improved standard of living is the goal of political parties of the Right and of the Left. What difference is being a Christian going to mean in this highly sensitive area of money?

The Jesus we follow was remarkably unconcerned to acquire money. He appears to have been so poor that he had to borrow a coin when asked a question about tribute money: when required to pay it, he was glad to find a coin wedged in a fish's mouth. He was prepared to trust his heavenly Father for his needs. This did not mean that he was not equally prepared to work as a carpenter for his pay, and no doubt, to live off the proceeds of the catch when he went out with his fishermen friends. There was no doctrinaire opposition to money in Jesus of Nazareth; but no slavery to it, either. To be sure, he advised one rich young man to go and get rid of his cash, but he did not ask that of everybody. It is clear that money was standing between that man and discipleship. He was unwilling to let Jesus touch his pocket. And until he was allowed in there, Jesus could do nothing with that rich young ruler. 'No man can serve two masters', as he said on another occasion: 'you cannot serve God and money'.[17]

The love of money

No, there is nothing wrong with money: but there is a great deal wrong with the love of money.[18] Greed, oppression, avarice, dishonesty, fraud, robbery and often murder as well, all spring from this love of money. And there's a curious, two-fold irony about it. First, money does not satisfy. As the Romans recognised long ago, money is like sea-water: the more you have of it, the thirstier you get. And second, money does not last. Jesus spoke of the moth and rust that spoil the possessions of those who go for money on earth: today, income tax, inflation and the vagaries of the stock market replace moth and rust! But even if our fortune survives those hazards, it won't survive death. It is very short-lived. I remember talking to a woman who had nursed a man so rich that the ordinary cups in his house were made of silver. She discovered that it did not make him any the less miserable as he lay dying. The one certainty about our wealth is that we shall leave it all behind.

Don't be a fool, will you? It is not crucial that you make that extra pile, or get that foreign holiday. It doesn't matter that the Joneses have a swimming pool and you haven't. And don't envy your friend's sports car: it is only a status symbol. Surely you aren't in need of any such boost to your ego? You may be poor all your days, but you are *rich*: you're heir to a kingdom.

Money – our security?

Firstly, we shall not trust in our money. This is one of the most insidious dangers in wealth: it tends to make people arrogant, independent and unwilling to rely on God for their needs: they have such a big bank balance they don't feel they need to trust anyone. And you don't have to be rich to trust in money. It's just as big a danger to the poor. They are tempted to feel that if only they had money all would be well, and they would have the security they have always lacked. Poor and rich alike need to remember that the Christian has one security only, God. In poverty or wealth I am his and he is mine, and that is enough. 'Don't always be wishing you had more money,' writes the unknown author of the Letter to Hebrew Christians. 'Be satisfied with what you have. For God has said "I will never, never fail you nor forsake you."'[19] One Christian friend of mine, himself very poor, had his few choice possessions stolen from a friend's locked car. 'No matter,' he wrote. 'They are welcome to my stuff. But praise God, they cannot take Jesus from me.' And he meant it! I believe that if Christians were less attached to their possessions and more ready to trust God over their finances, the effect on society would be tremendous. It would stand out in such striking contrast to the prevailing attitudes on both sides of industry, and also to those of the man or woman in the street.

Money – to get or to give?

Secondly, we shall want to give. This is all part of the inner revolution begun when the Spirit enters our lives. When Jesus was asked into the home of Zacchaeus, the notorious tax gatherer, the effect was electric. Zacchaeus was so magnetised by Christ's generosity that he said, 'Sir, from now on I will give half my wealth to the poor, and if I find I have overcharged anyone on his taxes, I will penalise myself by giving him back four times as much.' Jesus' comment is instructive: 'This shows that salvation has come to this home today.'[20] One of the yardsticks of a man's conversion is the change in his attitude to possessions.

Some years ago I was speaking at a conference in Jerusalem. One of the members had lost her luggage en route. In it she had packed a good deal of Christian literature written in both Hebrew and Arabic for free distribution in Jerusalem. Efforts to trace it failed until the last day, when it turned up damaged but with its contents intact. Indeed, there was one addition – a note from the thief who had stolen it. It read as follows:

I stole this from you because I was a thief, but after reading your cards I decided that your way, the way of the Lord, was the only way. So I am returning this to you and returning to the ways of the Lord. You have saved my soul, and I am now high on his way. Bless you.

I don't know whether that man had a sense of humour, but he added this slight misquotation from the gospels to his letter of restitution:

> Seek and ye shall find.
> Take and ye shall receive.

Well, he had taken unlawfully, and had received far more than he ever imagined. So immediately it affected his attitude to money. No longer was 'findings keepings'. Greed had been deposed by God in his life. The mark of a saved soul was a theft restored. It spoke volumes about the inner change in the man.

That, I suppose, is what Paul had in mind in these very illuminating words of advice to recent converts at Ephesus. 'If any of you have been stealing he must stop it and begin using those hands of his for honest work, so that he can give to others in need.'[21] The one whose philosophy had been all 'get' now begins to give. The man who stole from others because he had been too idle to work, now works in order to be able to give to others. How about that for a new attitude?

Money – our right?

Thirdly, we shall see ourselves as accountable to God for our use of money. Hear Paul on the subject; and he must have been rich at one stage or he could not have been a Roman citizen.

Tell those who are rich not to be proud and not to trust in their money, which will soon be gone, but their pride and trust should be in the living God who always richly gives us all we need for our enjoyment. Tell them to use their money to do good. They should be rich in good works and should give happily to those in need, always being ready to share with others whatever God has given them. By doing this they will be storing up real treasure for themselves in heaven – it is the only safe investment for eternity! And they will be living a fruitful Christian life down here as well.[22]

Whether I have a lot of money or a little is immaterial. As a Christian I ought to give a proportion of my income to God: the Jews used to give ten per cent and I do not see how a Christian can give less (even if he is a pensioner or a student on a grant!). But characteristically, the New Testament does not lay down any amount, or even any proportion. For giving is not so much a duty as a highly personal demonstration of our love to the Lord. Paul could write of the Christians in Macedonia, 'Though they have been going through much trouble and hard times, they have mixed their wonderful joy with their deep poverty, and the result has been an overflow of giving to others. They gave not only what they could afford, but far more; and I can testify that they did it because they wanted to, and not because of nagging on my part.'[23] Naturally enough: 'For you know the love and kindness of our Lord Jesus: though he was rich, yet to help you he became poor, so that you, through his poverty, might be rich.'[24] That was Christ's attitude. Not surprising that it rubbed off on his

81

followers. It still does. I think of a carpenter who had found Christ, and pressed a valuable banknote into my hand at Christmas-time shortly after his conversion. 'Use it for the poor,' he said. I think of an able young architectural student who celebrated his discovery of Christ by giving up his compulsive smoking and sending me a cheque to use in Christian work with the money thereby saved. Giving comes naturally to the heart that has responded to the giving of God. Too often Church financial needs are tackled at the wrong level, it seems to me. 'Give to save our old church' inspires nobody. But 'Give because Christ gave himself for you' is a very different matter.

Money for sharing?

One of the strongest ways of demonstrating the supranational character of the Christian Church is the loving contributions members make for brother Christians in other parts of the world. Whenever there is a disaster, Christians are among the first to supply aid. Guatemala, Haiti, Bangladesh, Ethiopia, Poland, Uganda: in all these places Christians from other lands have put their money where their mouth is. It is impossible to neglect human need if you are a Christian. 'If anyone has this world's goods,' said St John, 'and sees his brother in need, yet closes his heart against him, how does God's love abide in him?'[25] Nor is it necessary to leave Christian relief work to the official agencies like Compassion International, TEAR Fund and Christian Aid. The church I served in Oxford sent three of its members for preaching and teaching in Uganda: and they went with many hundreds of pounds' worth of provisions and other necessities provided by the members of the congregation. On another occasion a single lady on a fixed income was so overwhelmed by the needs in Poland that she mobilised help from all over the city of Oxford, stored the provisions in the church building, and then took a convoy out to Poland herself. Money and possessions are for sharing.

Jesus had a special concern for the poor and needy. He told his followers that when they were meeting the needs of the sick and poor, the outcasts and the prisoners, they were in a very profound sense ministering to him.[26] The disciples took this to heart. The first Jewish Christians in Jerusalem were not too busy preaching Jesus as the Messiah to organise relief for widows and orphans. The first Gentile Christians in Antioch were not too preoccupied with their extensive missionary work to mount a famine relief fund for their stricken brethren hundreds of miles away in Jerusalem.

It is an interesting and significant fact that the New Testament writers use the same word, *koinōnia*, both for 'fellowship' and for 'financial contribution'. The two are not unconnected! One of the most moving examples I have known of Christians giving in order to express fellowship was in West Africa. There was civil war in Nigeria, and the Christians on both sides showed a love which transcended tribal loyalties and the peculiarly bitter feelings generated by civil strife. The moment the war ended Christians led the way in the generous giving and receiving of financial aid. Their nationalism said, 'Hate the other side and show that hate by fighting.' Their Christianity said, 'Love the other side and show that love by giving.' Their Christianity prevailed over their nationalism. Freely they had received from Christ. Freely they gave. That's what Jesus would do, isn't it?

And that's just the start

Let's leave the subject of money there, though the New Testament writers have a lot more to say about it – appropriately enough in view of its importance. They certainly do not share our coyness in talking about the proper use of money. They tell us, for instance, not to judge other people by their money and their clothes, and not to dress extravagantly or eat luxuriously ourselves when others are in need. They tell us that we have a responsibility to be scrupulously fair and generous towards any people we employ, remembering that we have an Employer in heaven. They tell us that we are duty bound to make provision for our family if humanly possible – remember how Jesus provided for his mother even when he was dying on the cross? Paul says bluntly, 'The man who does not make provision for his own family is worse than an unbeliever.'[27] They tell us that we can invest our money in lives, by contributing to the cause of the gospel throughout the world. They remind us that not only the proportion of our income which we give direct to God belongs to him – so does the rest. How about your will, by the way? Are you planning to leave all your money to the family – or to leave some of it to Christian work? We are accountable to him for the way we use our money. It is only lent to us. We act as administrators of Another's possessions.

You see how the Lord refuses to be boxed away in one little corner of our lives, labelled 'religious'? He wants to lay his honest, loving, unselfish hand on the whole thing. Work out the details for yourself – such is your Christian freedom. I have certainly found it a rewarding and somewhat shattering experience to study what guidelines the New Testament has to give on this question of pleasing Christ in our financial affairs. But it is tremendously liberating to realise that all we have and are is his, and to use our resources deliberately and joyfully for him.

Of course there will be differences in the way Christians work out in practice that loyalty to Christ. There are no hard and fast rules. I think of one man who works in the Stock Exchange and yet is utterly surrendered to Christ in his use of money. I think of another who knows that for him financial obedience to Christ means having no assured income and working for a Faith Mission in the Philippines. In both men, despite the enormous differences, there is the same revolutionary principle at work: the principle of give, not get, of pleasing Christ, not self, in this matter of money. And that is what matters.

In this chapter I have taken money as just one example of the new attitude a Christian begins to adopt. But the principle of pleasing Christ applies equally to all the other areas of our life. We shall be looking at three of them in the next chapter.

NOTES

1 John 8:34
2 Titus 3:3 (LB)
3 2 Peter 2:19
4 James 5:4, 5
5 2 Timothy 3:4
6 John 13:1,
   Luke 22:42
7 Romans 15:3
8 2 Timothy 2:4
9 Romans 15:2

10 Colossians 1:9–10
11 Galatians 5:1
12 Romans 8:2
13 Philippians 2:13
14 Romans 14:1–4
15 Romans 14:6
16 Romans 12:2 (RSV)
17 Matthew 6:24
18 1 Timothy 6:10

19 Hebrews 13:5
20 Luke 19:1–9
21 Ephesians 4:28
22 1 Timothy 6:17–19 (LB)
23 2 Corinthians 8:2–3 (LB)
24 2 Corinthians 8:9
25 1 John 3:17 (RSV)
26 Matthew 25:34–40
27 1 Timothy 5:8

6

Silent Revolution

Some years ago I remember being struck by a remarkable film title. It was this: *Start the Revolution Without Me!* It seemed to me that the Christian life was the very opposite of this, and consists of the new believer saying to Christ, *'Start the Revolution Within Me!'* That is certainly what he does. It is a gradual revolution in most cases – no overnight coup. But over the course of a few years there is no doubt about it. We find we have been revolutionised inside.

We examined in the last chapter the basic Christian attitude of pleasing Christ. And we saw one example of the way this works out, in our finances. In this chapter we shall select three other important areas of life to illustrate something more of the change Christ makes.

1. Sex

How free is 'free sex'?

Let's begin with possibly the biggest area where Christian behaviour will run counter to the current of today's society. It is taken for granted by many these days that sexual love is the most important thing in life – perhaps the only thing that gives life meaning – and that we are entitled to pursue it as and where we can.

However even the advocates of free sex are finding that everything in the garden is not so lovely. For one thing, the pleasure doesn't last. The trouble is that the act of sex can become separated from a lasting relationship between the people involved. And that dehumanises sex and demoralises those who do it. Roger McGough has caught this spirit of bitter disillusionment on the morning after, in his poem 'The Act of Love':

> The Act of Love lies somewhere
> Between the belly and the mind
> I lost the love some time ago
> Now I've only the act to grind
>
> Brought her back from a party
> Don't bother swopping names
> Identity's not needed
> When you're only playing games
>
> High on bedroom darkness
> We endure the pantomime
> Ships that go bang in the night
> Run aground on the sands of time
>
> Saved in the nick of dawn
> It's cornflakes and then goodbye
> Another notch on the headboard
> Another day wondering why

> The Act of Love lies somewhere
> Between the belly and the mind
> I lost the love some time ago
> Now I've only the act to grind

Of course, the unsatisfactory nature of mere physical sex is widely admitted by advocates of permissiveness. Robert Chartham, in his sensational sex book *The Sensuous Couple*, begins by maintaining that 'Physical sex should be a visible, tangible expression of the emotional love the partners have for one another,' and, 'If you make love only for the physical experience you are downgrading both yourself and your partner to the behaviour of the barnyard.' He protests that love-making should prevent you from being selfish. But the rest of the book goes on to talk blithely about the variety of partners emancipated lovers will have! What has happened to the unselfishness? The woman is jettisoned and another takes her place. For all his talk of consideration for his partner, Chartham's sophisticated eroticism is just as selfish, just as sub-personal as the quick job in the back of a car which he despises.

Christ's attitude

What would Christ say to all this? We are fortunately left in no doubt. He quotes the Old Testament on the whole purpose of marriage and sexuality. 'It is written that at the beginning God created man and woman, and that man should leave his father and mother and be for ever united to his wife. The two shall become one – no longer two but one!'[1] In other words, marriage is for keeps, and God's intention is that the sexual relationship should be the uniting bond between two partners throughout their married life. Fornication is out. Adultery is out. That is what Jesus stood for. That is what the early Church stood for. Christians are committed to it.

What's wrong with sex outside marriage?

Now why this very tough line? Because love, marriage and sex are meant to go together by the One who invented all three. Sexual intercourse is the closest possible relationship you can have with any other person, and the Maker's intention is that we use it as an outer symbol of the inner love we have for that other person: a love that, like God's own love, is fully personal, does not act selfishly and does not give up. What passes for love in these casual liaisons is often depersonalised, frequently selfish ('how much can I get out of it?') and normally short-lived, leaving behind it disillusionment and loneliness as the erstwhile partner is discarded on the human scrap heap.

What happens when the Maker's instructions are neglected? We have seen plenty of the bitter fruits of free sex in the past decade. It is a plain flouting of the will of God. It carries with it a sense of guilt. It frequently has to be covered up by lies and hypocrisy. It dehumanises sex and makes it into an act in itself, separable both from a relationship and from a person. It causes traumas to the personality of those jettisoned, and a hardening in the attitudes of the 'notch on the headboard' man. It artificially separates sex from love, fidelity, companionship and children. It takes something that can never be returned. It betrays an inability to control our instinctive drives. And it undermines trust. The man who cannot be trusted to master himself before marriage cannot be trusted to do so in marriage. Inevitably the woman he eventually marries (whom, hypocritically, he would like to be a virgin!) will have to live with the gnawing doubt, 'Will he remain faithful when my back is turned?' And what sort of a foundation for marriage is that?

Indeed, there are few things so disruptive of personality, home life and society as unrestrained sensuality. As I write, Madonna is the sex goddess of the moment, and in an interview with *Time* magazine she has this to say: 'I have to humiliate men publicly. I am living out my hatred of my father for leaving me for my stepmother after my mother died. On the one hand you could say I am turning men into swine; on the other hand I am forcing men to behave in ways they are not supposed to in society. If they want to wear a bra, they can wear a bra. If they want to cry, they can cry. If they want to kiss another man, I give them licence to do that. I have these men whom I have emasculated with bras on who are attending to me and offering me sex. But in the end I would rather be alone and masturbate. Until God comes, of course, and frightens me. I think of death a lot, maybe because I don't know about life after death. So I strive as hard as I can to suck every drop out of life.'

It is tragic to see the confusion and forlornness in such an attitude. Not every libertine can express it as well as Madonna. But the experience is universal. Even Masters and Johnson, the celebrated American sexologists, have come to the conclusion, after endorsing the permissive lifestyle for decades, that the only lastingly satisfying sexual relationships are those between one man and one woman for keeps. And they are certainly guided by no Christian persuasion: merely by observing in detail what happens when the Maker's instructions for the use of sex are flouted.

It's not because Christians are against sex that they are hot on chastity before marriage and fidelity in it: on the contrary, it is because they value it so highly. Sex is too good a gift of God to cheapen. It is no mere animal coupling, but the deepest way in which two people can express mutual self-giving. It serves not only to symbolise but to deepen and enrich the unity and love between the partners. It is fun. It is satisfying. It is exhilarating. But take it away from the context of marriage and it becomes dishonest. For it isolates one type of unity, sexual unity, from the other areas of self-commitment that are meant to go with it. It is acting a lie. That is why the New Testament is so strongly against extra-marital sex. It separates what God has joined together — sex on the one hand, and lasting companionship, love and self-giving on the other.

Subsidiary questions

Once take your stand on this, and many of the other sexual questions are not so very difficult to answer. Should any variety of sex play be enjoyed by Christian couples? Why not, within the marriage bond? How can any practice be wrong which deepens the delight of the couple in each other?

Should contraception be practised? Why not, provided it is done within marriage, and in order responsibly to space children, not selfishly to avoid having them? Indeed, the appalling overpopulation of the world makes contraception no longer a questionable matter but a plain duty: we can thank

God that just at the very moment in history when it has become so necessary, technical advance has made it so simple.

How about homosexuality? This is a highly complicated question requiring expert advice, perhaps from an experienced Christian doctor. The Bible is very clear that the practice of homosexuality is wrong, just as the practice of fornication is wrong. You may have a physical and psychological make-up which attracts you to members of your own sex in the same way that most people are attracted to the opposite sex. This problem can often respond to treatment. But it is possible for people with homosexual inclinations to refrain, through the power of Christ, from homosexual intercourse, just as it is possible for unmarried heterosexuals to abstain from heterosexual intercourse. You can't stop birds flying over your head, as the old Chinese proverb has it: but you can stop them nesting in your beard!

How about sexy literature and films? If this stuff arouses you, then you are making things difficult for yourself by indulging in it. Erotic literature may be a legitimate stimulus to love-making for the married but it is a cancerous growth in the mind of the unmarried Christian. If you're one who suffers from vertigo, don't see how close you can get to the edge of the precipice. Steer well clear!

How about masturbation? This used to be the unmentionable sin of Victorian literature, the thing that sent you mad, the thing that could only be overcome by much exercise and cold baths. Now it is commonplace. What is the Christian, with his new attitude of pleasing Christ, to make of this? Well, on the one hand it is selfish, habit-forming and leaves you

93

feeling rather dissatisfied and ashamed. On the other hand it is nowhere expressly forbidden in Scripture, it has no lasting ill effects and is a much less harmful way of dealing with the overweening sexual urges of adolescence than sexual experimentation with others. Can you do it with an uncondemning conscience? That is the question. 'Happy is the man who does not condemn himself for what he allows himself to do.'[2] If not, it must go. And Christ the Liberator can break its grip.

Pornography

There remains that controversial matter of pornography. Controversial because nobody has succeeded in giving a foolproof definition of porn. Controversial because nobody can prove whether people are depraved by pornography, or go for it because they are depraved. Controversial because legislation against it would limit the liberty of the individual (though you have only to apply that argument to race relations to see the fallacy in it!). What is beyond controversy is that to separate sexuality as a sort of cult object, in isolation from lasting relationships and as the supreme goal of human desire, is out for the Christian. Bishop Trevor Huddleston once put the Christian view very succinctly:

The Christian religion takes its stand on the dignity of man, because it proclaims that man is made in the image and likeness of God. It goes even further than that. It proclaims that God himself has become man, and has, therefore, given a dignity to man which is infinite. Pornography is a symptom — it isn't a disease in itself. It is a symptom of a sick society. It's the consequence of society's thinking about the final end of man. It is the substitution of what, in truth, is the final end of man (namely the vision of God and the glory of God) by a limited and totally inadequate conception of what man is made for. Flowing from this real misunderstanding of what man is created to be in this world comes the idea that you can use the human body for a purpose which is wholly trivial. And this is what pornography does. Putting it crudely, you are substituting lust for love.

He continued the broadcast from which this quotation is taken by calling on Christians to be prepared to face the opposition this emphasis on chastity will bring. 'Marvel not if the world hates you. It hated me before it hated you,' was Jesus' comment on the inevitable difficulty of swimming against the current of society which is at odds with God. Huddleston concluded, 'In fact purity of heart, chastity, lies at the very centre of the gospel, and if we preach the whole gospel then we are bound to preach purity of heart.'

2. Suffering and Death

The problem of pain

If sex is the main preoccupation of our thoughts when we are young, pain and death take over the top positions when we grow old. Just as sex is regarded by our society as the best thing in life, death is universally held to be the worst disaster that could overtake us, and suffering the next worst.

One thing we can be sure of. Pain and death will come our way. How does being a Christian alter our attitude to them? You have only to visit in a hospital to hear questions like these: 'Why should this happen to me? What have I done to deserve this? How could God allow it?' We shall be better able to face suffering when it comes if we have done a bit of thinking about it beforehand.

The problem of pain is an intractable one: nobody has got to the bottom of it, and nobody will. We need not, however, be embarrassed by this. The Christian faith enables us to see suffering in a more positive light than any other religion or philosophy in the world.

Why does God allow it?

Let's be clear about this to start with. The Bible makes it very plain that God wants the utmost good for his creatures. Suffering and pain are never the direct will of God for us. He may permit them, but he does not send them. 'He does not willingly afflict the children of men.'[3] There are, however, four limitations on God's designs for our good.

Firstly there is the nature of our planet. It is consistent. It works to regular laws. And that is just as well, or we should never know where we were! But it means that if a knife will cut bread it will also cut my finger. The useful force of gravity, which keeps me on this earth, is not suspended for my benefit when I fall out of the window. So at least the possibility of pain is built into the very structure of our world, where cause and effect prevail. This is inevitable: it is also invaluable.

Pain can be nature's red light of warning. Were it not for the pain given by an inflamed appendix it would burst inside you, and you would die.

Secondly, there is the existence of Satan. The Bible is quite clear about the reality of this anti-God force, the devil, and I would have thought that there was plenty of evidence the world over to show that he is still in business. But the Bible is equally clear that the devil is not an equal and opposite figure to God. There is no dualism here. The devil remains 'God's devil', as Luther called him: he is on a chain, albeit a long one. His eventual destiny is destruction, but in the meantime he is out to spoil God's world in every way possible. He spoils personal life by sin, family life by discord, social life by greed, national life by war – and physical life by disease. Although making it clear that individual illness is not the result of individual sin, Jesus left us in no doubt that the devil has a hand in disease. When he healed one woman on the Sabbath day, he referred to 'the bondage in which Satan had held her for eighteen years'.[4] And in the Acts we read of the way in which Jesus had healed 'those who were oppressed by the devil'.[5] This is one aspect of suffering we do well to take note of. There is a devil: and he is out to spoil.

Thirdly, there is the fact of human free will. This is a major cause of pain in the world. God cannot take away from men their freedom when they use it to reject his way for them. That would be to reduce them to robots – and he is Love. Love can't be satisfied with robots. No, God will not intervene to stop train accidents, wars, thalidomide babies and the other products of man's misuse of his freedom. Let's make sure we don't blame God for these things.

But that does not cover all pain: it does not explain hurricanes and earthquakes, and there is therefore *a fourth factor* we must take into account. It is *the interdependence of a fallen world*. The world is not as God meant it to be. The Architect's plans have been scrapped by his clients. Chaos has resulted. And it affects every aspect of our rebel world. In the picturesque account of Genesis, the act of human disobedience results not only in shame, alienation from God and banishment, but in the disruption of nature with thorns and thistles. We and our environment belong together, as we are all belatedly discovering. Human rebellion has affected our habitat. We are not just individuals: we are part of a common humanity, and it is tainted stock.

When you come to think of it, the sheer randomness with which suffering strikes is not so surprising after all. It is rather like smallpox. Once the virus has infected your bloodstream, the actual spots occur quite at random. There will be no rhyme or reason to their appearance. It is like that with suffering in the body of humanity. It does strike at random. It is no good asking, 'Why should this happen to me?' any more than we ask with smallpox, 'Why should this spot occur here?' In both instances the disease has to be met at its root. Suffering as a whole is linked with human sin as a whole: though individual suffering is not by any means necessarily related to individual sin.

What has God done about it?

Well, what has God done to meet the problem at its root? The cross is the deep and mysterious but wonderful answer. And from the cross these four beams of light shine out upon our problem.

Firstly, the cross shows that God is no stranger to pain. He does not allow us to go through what he himself avoids. He is the suffering God, the one whose royalty is displayed in suffering and in dying. 'In all their affliction he was afflicted,'[6] the Old Testament says of God, just as a father agonises over a sick child or a teenager's wild oats. But supremely he shared our agony on that cross. The cross shows he knows all about suffering. The cross shows he has been through it. And he still suffers in and with all the suffering of humanity. Ever since the incarnation he has remained one of us. Isn't that just like God? He did not give us an answer to the problem of pain: he shared it. He did not explain it: he accepted it.

Secondly, the cross shows that God loves on through pain. If you are ever tempted to feel that suffering is a sign God does not love you, remember that Jesus died on a cross, yet God still loved him. It was into God's hand that Jesus committed his spirit. We can do the same, for we are not left desolate and unloved when we suffer. We may not understand the experience we are going through, but the cross of Jesus Christ assures us that God still loves us.

Thirdly, the cross shows how God uses pain. Evil though it is, God makes good come out of suffering in a variety of ways. He does it in nature: think of the way an oyster uses the irritation of grit within the shell to turn it into a pearl. He does it in human character: think of qualities like courage, self-sacrifice and endurance which spring only from the soil of suffering. He does it in the spiritual life, too. Sometimes he uses pain to *reach* us: I have met several folk who would never have stopped to listen to God and would never have come to know him, were it not for some tragedy that halted them in their tracks and made them think. Sometimes he uses pain to *teach* us. 'Let God train you, for he is doing what any loving father does for his children. Whoever heard of a son who was never corrected? If God doesn't discipline you when you need it, as other fathers do, it suggests you are not his true children at all, but illegitimate!'[7] Sometimes he uses pain to *equip* us. Paul came to realise that a ghastly experience he had been through was intended by God to equip him to 'comfort others with the comfort by which God had comforted him'.[8] So just think of the wonderful way in which God blessed and overruled for good the tragic agony of the cross, and remember that he can and does use pain, though he does not will it.

Fourthly, since the cross can never be separated from the resurrection, *it points to God's triumph over pain.* We have seen that pain as a whole is due to sin as a whole. On the cross Jesus dealt with sin at its root. He fought Satan and won. He bore sin and drew its fangs. He drained the cup of suffering and won through. Good Friday was followed by Easter Day. And we can look with sober confidence to a final triumph over pain because Christ has triumphed over sin which caused it. Paul does so in a famous chapter of his Letter to the Romans:

Since we are his children, we will share his treasures – for all God gives to his Son Jesus is now ours too. But if we are to share his glory, we must also share his suffering. Yet what we suffer now is nothing compared to the glory he will give us later. For all creation is waiting patiently and hopefully for that future day when God will resurrect his children. For on that day thorns and thistles, sin, death and decay – the things that overcame the world against its will at God's command – will all disappear, and the world around us will share in the glorious freedom of the children of God.

For we know that even the things of nature, like animals and plants, suffer in sickness and death as they await this great event. And even we Christians, although we have the Holy Spirit within us as a foretaste of future glory, also groan to be released from pain and suffering. We, too, anxiously wait for that day when God will give us our full rights as his children, including the new bodies he has promised us – bodies that will never be sick again and never die.[9]

Such is the Christian hope. It is soundly based on the resurrection of Jesus Christ from the dead, the pledge of God's final triumph over sin and death.

A note of triumph

This means that we can face not only suffering but death in a new light. No longer will we see it as the worst thing that can befall us; no longer as the extinction of our lives. We shall see it rather as the door into a fuller life; a life which we shall continue to share with Christ as we share this life now. But a life which will not be marred by sorrow or suffering or decay. In his vision of heaven, St John brings this point out with matchless poetry. 'I heard a loud shout from the throne saying, ''Look, God shares his home with men. And he will live with them, and they will be his people and he will be their God. He will wipe away all tears from their eyes, and there shall be no more death, nor sorrow, nor crying, nor pain. All of that is gone for ever.'''[10]

Away, then, with the gloom which so often accompanies even Christian funerals. The Christian dead go to 'be with Christ, which is far better'.[11] Let us wear buttonholes – not black ties; and rejoice – not go round with hushed voices. Let those who have no hope of heaven, no expectation of life after death, treat death as the last enemy if they must. But for us it is a defeated enemy, ever since the first Easter Day. Of course there is shock. Of course there is loneliness for the one who is left. We must support bereaved people with great sensitivity. But for the departed Christian we can confidently rejoice. Let's have a bit more of this confidence and rejoicing as we grow older and face the sombre realities of pain and death. We Christians are the only people in the world who have something to shout about at this point. Our Lord Jesus has been through it all: he has overcome. And when we go through the valley of the shadow, he will be with us: he will receive us. He has promised.

3. Self-discipline

If the youthful years of our Christian lives show a silent revolution in our attitude to sex, and the later years lead to a similar revolution in our attitude to suffering and death, Christians are called to face the current of popular attitudes in the matter of self-discipline right the way through their lives.

It is an unwelcome subject. 'Do your own thing' is

the accepted norm. But if we love him, we shall be prepared to do his thing. Self-control is really Christ-control, because I certainly can't control myself. I need him to do that. And in view of all he has done for me, I am prepared to let him do so. Let's have a quick look at some of the areas it may involve.

Ambition

Some people aren't worried by this one at all, but others are eaten up by it. They must get to the top of their particular tree, whoever they have to tread on in getting there. Well, this attitude will change once we're Christians. In some ways it is no bad thing to have a driving ambition – provided it is redirected. I shall no longer be out to show how wonderful I am, but I can channel all that drive into living my life to the full for Christ. I think of a general, of a financier, of an actor, all of whom belong to Christ, all of whom have laid their careers at his feet, all of whom want above all to please him. Paul was like that. Once he had been ambitious for himself: now he was ambitious for Christ. Listen to him:

I was a real Jew if ever there was one! What's more I was a member of the Pharisees who demand the strictest obedience to every Jewish law and custom. And sincere? Yes, so much so that I greatly persecuted the church; and I tried to obey every Jewish rule and regulation right down to the very last point.

But all these things that I once thought very worthwhile – now I've thrown them all away, so that I can put my trust in Christ alone . . . I am bringing all my energies to bear on this one thing. Forgetting the past, and looking forward to what lies ahead, I strain to reach the end of the race and receive the prize for which God is calling us up to heaven because of what Christ did for us.[12]

Did you get that promotion? Then thank him for the wider opportunities of service it offers. Did you get passed over? Don't take it to heart. It means the Lord wants you where you are. You have only one life. You have given it over to him for his safe-keeping and his guidance. He knows what he is about. He will give you the sphere of work in which the talents he has entrusted to you will be best deployed. So what are you worrying for? You don't have to prove anything by trying to show what a fine person you are. He has accepted you even though you are not nearly such a fine person as you thought. He has a place in his plan for you to work for him. So pray about your work. Tell him that you are willing to stay where you are or move on, just as he wishes. You'll find that you are delivered at a stroke from the burning ambition that eats up some of your mates, and gives them a chip on the shoulder if they are not successful, or ulcers from overwork if they are. Make it your ambition to please him. Never selfishly seek, or refuse, a position of greater responsibility. Your life is in better hands than yours. He knows what you were made for, and he will give you fulfilment in your work.

Time

This is an area where we are incredibly wasteful. How much time do you simply waste each day? It must be phenomenal, even for busy people. Of course, the Lord does not want us to be tense, over-earnest and killjoy, all work and no play. But he does want to guide us in the use of our time. After all, we have only the one life. Each day is an unrepeatable experience. He lends us our time, just as he lends us our talents. And he wants to direct our use of it. Time for himself and deepening the friendship. Time for the job. Time for the family. Time for Christian service. Time for sleep is important: some of us have too much, some too little. Find what you need, and try to stick to it. There needs to be a balance, a wholeness about our use of time, so that we are not slothful on the one hand, or running around chasing the clock on the other. 'My times are in thy hand,'[13] wrote the psalmist. Let's ask his guidance on this important side of our lives every day, and his blessing on our use of it.

Leisure

This is worth a thought. The five-day week is universal. The four-day week is on the way. The amount of leisure will rocket. And masses of people won't know what to do with it. Stupefying boredom leaves millions gaping at the television for hours each evening. What will it be like in a few years time?

But the Christian won't be bored. We share our leisure time, just as we share our work time, with our Lord. And there is always something to be done for others. I remember how, in the last year of his long life, the saintly Bishop Houghton told me that he walked down the road to the bus stop at eight o'clock every morning with a schoolboy who lived opposite – simply out of love for Jesus and the desire to share

105

that love with the lad. That is the charm of the Christian life, or one of them. You never retire. You are never too old to be of use to your Friend . . . doing things for him, introducing others to him. The scope for Christian service in our leisure time is greater now than at any time in the history of the Church.

Perhaps as a Christian you will want to review your holiday arrangements. More and more people spend an ever-increasing amount on overseas holidays, when an equally restful time could be had nearer at hand at a quarter of the cost. At a time when world famine is greater than ever before, when missionary societies are more than ever pressed for funds, do we spend more on ourselves and our holiday arrangements than our Friend would wish? It may be worth talking over with him.

Cigarettes, drink and drugs

What is a Christian to do about these stimulants?

Nobody should rob us of our personal freedom in these matters. We have been called to liberty, and this is not the moment to reach for the rule book. Nevertheless, two limitations on our freedom are clearly given in the New Testament. 'All things are lawful to me, but all things are not expedient. All things are lawful to me but I will not be brought under the power of any.'[14] That was one crucial question Paul asked himself: are these perfectly legitimate things going to rob me of my freedom by bringing me into a new bondage, by gripping me in a habit I can't break?

The second question is this: what effect will the exercise of my liberty have on other people who may look to me for an example? 'But why,' you may ask, 'must I be guided and limited by what someone else thinks? If I can thank God for food [Paul's example is drawn from whether or not to eat food that had been offered to idols, but the principle behind it is widely applicable] and enjoy it; why let people spoil everything just because they think I am wrong?' 'Well, I'll tell you why,' says Paul. 'It is because you must do everything to the glory of God, even your eating and drinking. So don't be a stumbling block to anyone, whether they are Jews or Gentiles or Christians. That is the plan I follow, too. I try to please everyone in everything I do, not doing what I like or what is best for me, but what is best for them, so that they may be saved.'[15]

Now apply those two principles to drink and cigarettes and drugs. Are you master of them, or are they master of you? Spurgeon reckoned he could smoke the occasional cigar to the glory of God – but many Christians who smoke are enslaved by it. I suppose the Christian attitude here is either moderation or none at all. But then we have to take into account the second question: what would others think? Would it or would it not commend our Master? One friend to whom I was speaking recently told me that as a chain-smoking, hard-drinking man he had cut it out completely when he became a Christian. On the building site where he worked they were amazed to find a real Christian. But having found him, they would have been even more amazed if he continued to drink and smoke. For him, therefore, it would have been wrong to continue. With you in your circumstances it may be different. It is something to put to Christ, and let him guide you.

It comes to this, really: where do you reckon to get

your stimulus from? Christ – or drugs, alcohol and cigarettes? If we are high on reality, the reality of Christ as our friend, we shall certainly not allow ourselves to be enslaved by any of these things. We may occasionally use them when the circumstances are right. But we will derive our main stimulus from elsewhere. Listen to Paul again. 'Don't drink too much wine, for many evils lie along that path; be filled instead with the Holy Spirit, and be controlled by him as you sing and make melody in your heart to the Lord.'[16]

Language

'Men can train every kind of animal or bird that lives, but no human being can tame the tongue. It is always ready to pour out its deadly poison. Sometimes it praises our heavenly Father, and sometimes it breaks out into curses against men who are made in the likeness of God. And so blessing and cursing come pouring out of the same mouth. Dear brothers, surely this is not right.'[17] No, of course it is not. The cruel words, the foul talk, the backbiting, the white lies, the half truths and all the rest of it. Jesus Christ wants our language to bring credit to him. He is quite prepared to do the impossible and tame our tongue, if we will make it over to him. Paul expected to see the language of the converts at Ephesus change:

Don't use bad language. Say only what is good and helpful to those you are talking to, and what will give them a blessing. Don't grieve the Holy Spirit. Put all bitterness, anger and bad temper away. Quarrelling, harsh words and malice should have no place in your lives. Instead, be kind to each other, tender-hearted, forgiving one another, just as God, for Christ's sake, has forgiven you . . . Dirty stories, foul talk and coarse jokes − these are not for you. Instead, remind each other of God's goodness and be thankful.[18]

I like that last bit. Our minds are so constituted that we can't concentrate on two things at the same time. When the temptation to give way to foul talk hits you, try thanking God for his goodness, and you'll find the temptation withers away. Another thing I have found helpful is to pray the psalmist's prayer before each day begins − as I climb into my clothes, maybe. 'Set a watch, O Lord, before my mouth. Keep the door of my lips.'[19] You'll find he can tame even that intractable member, the tongue.

In all these areas of life the silent revolution goes on, once Jesus is welcomed into our lives and made at home. So long as we make it our determination to please him in all we do, we can safely leave the rest to him. He has the power to transform us, and transform us he will, provided we are willing to be changed. But not otherwise. He declines to force his way upon us if we refuse him entry to some area of our lives − if we say, in effect, 'Start the revolution without me.'

NOTES

1 Matthew 19:4−6
2 Romans 14:22
3 Lamentations 3:33
4 Luke 13:16
5 Acts 10:38
6 Isaiah 63:9 (RSV)

7 Hebrews 12:5–7
8 2 Corinthians 1:4
9 Romans 8:17–23
10 Revelation 21:3–4
11 Philippians 1:23
12 Philippians 3:5–14
13 Psalm 31:15 (RSV)

14 1 Corinthians 6:12
15 1 Corinthians 10:29–33 (LB)
16 Ephesians 5:18–19
17 James 3:7–10
18 Ephesians 4:29–5:4
19 Psalm 141:3

7

New Relationships

1. Personal Relationships at Home

It was a hot afternoon, and I was watching him chat to the large number of elderly people who had gathered for their regular informal Thursday afternoon meeting. I was struck by the way he seemed to care. Then I met his wife, and I noticed their relaxed trust in one another and their obvious harmony. I remarked to my friend the vicar that he had got a splendid new assistant, even if he was a bit older than most. Then he told me the story. Actually, I could not do better than give it to you in the assistant's own words:

> When I was in my early thirties, I became involved with another woman. I fell deep into sin – sin of the ugliest kind – which made me reject all thoughts of God and which very nearly broke up our family life. Five months in a neurosis hospital under the care of some of the finest psychiatrists made no difference to my attitude to life. I came out of hospital worse than when I went in. I had developed a terrible stammer; I took drugs at night to try to help me sleep; I took pep pills during the day to try to keep me going; I went out of my way to avoid contact with

anyone at all; I fainted in the streets and I jeered at anyone who tried to help me. I was determined to carry on with my selfish and sinful way of life, no matter what hurt it caused other people.

Then one Christmas, my son Alan (who was then just eight years old) gave me a picture of the Lord Jesus standing at the door, knocking. 'Behold, I stand at the door and knock; if any one hears my voice and opens the door, I will come in to him and eat with him, and he with me.'[1] For a long time I deliberately turned away from that picture. But the knocking became more and more insistent until finally, at 10.00 p.m. on the 26th June, 1961, in utter desperation and almost unbelief, I said, 'Lord, you say you can change people's lives – come into my heart and change mine.' At last I had taken that step of faith, and immediately my prayer was answered. There was a complete transformation in my life from that moment onwards.

Undoubtedly there was. It was perfectly obvious, even to the casual observer. Once devoted to self, he was now an ordained minister, giving himself for others. Once ruining his family life by another woman, he was now happily reunited with his wife, and at one with her in the work of the Lord. Once dependent on drugs for excitement, he was now alive with Christ's joy and love. Quite a change. And nowhere greater than in his relationships with others. It doesn't take much imagination to think what a different place his home is, now . . .

And home is the place to begin. Jesus once healed a man who had serious psychological trouble. The man wanted to accompany him as a disciple on a roving ministry. In a way that would have been much easier for him. But Jesus said: 'No. Go back home to your folks, and let them know what wonderful things the Lord has done for you.'[2] Christianity, like charity, begins at home.

It's the life that counts

I don't think it is wise to *talk* too much about Jesus at home to begin with. They know you too well! They will probably think you have got a touch of religious mania, and that given time it will blow over. So softly, softly, as far as talking goes. Begin with living. Let your allegiance to Jesus show itself in a new cheerfulness around the house, particularly when others are in the dumps. A new helpfulness when the wife is obviously getting tired – how about *you* doing the washing up and the cleaning and putting the kids to bed? Or maybe you are one of the youngsters in the family. One of the best things you can do is to see that your room is not so knee-deep in mess that Mum can't get in to clean. 'What, tidiness?' you say, 'A boring virtue.' Not when someone else has to come and clean up after you. It is a matter of Christian considerateness.

The scope for mutual considerateness in the home is enormous. We are called to 'bear one another's burdens and so fulfil the law of Christ'.[3] Nowhere is burden-bearing more sorely needed than in the home. Think of ways in which you can work out in family life that principle of pleasing Christ which lies at the heart of Christian living.

New depth to sharing

If both partners in the home have come to know Christ,

then this at once brings a new depth to their relationship. I vividly recall one evening when a couple, both of whom had given in, after a real struggle, to the claims of Jesus, said with tears of joy in their eyes: 'This is more wonderful than our wedding day.' At once they began to use their home for the Lord. They offered their place as a venue for one of the house meetings that was starting up in this parish, composed of some who had recently discovered the new life, and some who were still searching. It is a marvellous joy to use your home like that.

It is a wonderful thing for a Christian couple to go to sleep in each other's arms at night, having just shared the events of the past day, its joys and failings, with the Lord, and having committed to him their lives and programme for the morrow. It is a wonderful thing to be able to pray with your children – and they so often have a shrewder insight and clearer perception of right and wrong than we do. God cares very much about the family: he invented it. Moreover, it is the fundamental unit in society. What we do as a Christian family, therefore, is more important than any other Christian work we attempt for God. If we fail here, we fail comprehensively. Many Christians make the mistake of neglecting their family responsibilities, either as children or as parents, in the interests of Christian service outside the family. It's a snare and delusion. Don't fall for it!

Open house

A Christian family will be a happy place: Jesus is welcomed in, and 'in his presence is fullness of joy'.[4]

It will be a hospitable place: 'given to hospitality' was one of the characteristics of the early Christians, and it still marks out authentic Christianity. Our home is not meant to be enjoyed in lonely isolation: it is there to be shared. This is hard work, but it is most rewarding, not only to the parents but also to the children. Once our daughter, aged three, went to stay with her Granny (who lives alone) and when Sunday lunch arrived, said: 'I need more people.' She wanted to know where the students were. When Granny replied that no students were to be had, she piped up: 'Then let's go out and buy some!' That child had got some root of Christian hospitality planted firmly inside her!

I don't know what it is, but time and again people express their gratitude when they have been made to feel welcome in a Christian home. I would like to think it is something of the attractiveness of Jesus getting through. I remember an income-tax inspector's home I used to go to when I was in the army. It was years ago now, but I have never forgotten it. This delightful Christian family used to open their home assiduously. If ever I wanted to help one of my army friends to find Christ, I used to take him for a meal and a chat there. They did not talk to him about Christ (unless he raised the subject) but their home radiated Christ's presence, softened him up and generally led him to ask what it was those people had got!

No need to pretend

Of course there will be arguments and failures in the Christian home. But they won't last long, because as members of the heavenly Father's family they will quickly come to him and apologise, and apologise to each other as well. 'Do not let the sun go down on your anger' is sound biblical wisdom.[5] It applies to husbands and wives (how can they pray together at night if they are holding something against the other?) and to parents and children. How important it is, by the way, that parents should not be too proud to apologise to their children. Yet too few do it. As Christians it will come naturally: we don't have to pretend we are better than anyone else. The fact that we have come to Christ for pardon means we are sinners, we know it, and are not ashamed to admit it to even our nearest and dearest.

Halfway house

But how about the situation when the home cannot be called Christian – when one partner is committed to Christ and the other is not? Tact, not talk, is the crucial thing. Don't be ashamed of your Friend, but don't embarrass others by constant reference to him. There's a lovely piece of advice, in Peter's First Letter, for Christian wives married to unbelieving husbands. 'Wives, fit in with your husbands' plans; for then if they refuse to listen when you talk to them about the Lord, they will be won by your respectful, pure behaviour. Your godly lives will speak to them better than any words.'[6] Above all, pray on for your loved ones. The fact that God has put you, a believer, in the same family as them is an indication that he wants to reach the whole family through you, his bridgehead. Your consistent life, your persistent prayer is likely in time to undermine the stoutest opposition. I met in Canada recently the tough head of a building firm –

now a radiant Christian. But it had taken six years of wise, loving, prayerful behaviour on his wife's part before he gave in to Jesus. Or think of St Augustine – a licentious youth who traced his eventual conversion to the faithfulness of his mother's prayers. Pray on for those in your family who are strangers to Christ as yet. Ask him to shine through you as well as through your Christian friends who drop in. Expect things to happen. They will. I shall never forget meeting in Jerusalem an Arab girl who had been brought to Christ through the loving care of an Israeli Christian woman. The girl went back to her home, and said very little about her faith in Christ, but began to read the Bible and to pray. Her parents were curious to know what she was up to; they asked her, and before long they too had come to Christ.

Bleak House?

Some of you reading this may feel, 'It's all very well talking about the married in their homes. I'm not married – and I haven't got a home.' That may well be your position; but it needn't add up to a 'Bleak House' situation. In the first place, remember that there are many things you can do, and many places you can go for Christ as a single person which would be out of the question if you were married. That is why Paul wrote to the Corinthians in praise of the single state: 'An unmarried man can spend his time doing the Lord's work and thinking how to please him. But a married man can't do that so well; he has to think about his earthly responsibilities and how to please his wife.'[7]

Secondly, it may well be God's purpose for you to

be married and have a home later on, but not just now. Can't you trust him to bring the right person across your path, without fretting because friends of your own age have got their partners lined up? God's plans are often for those who are prepared to wait.

But, thirdly, it may be his will for you to be single. Paul wrote about 'some to whom God gives the gift of husband or wife, and others to whom he gives the gift of being able to stay happily unmarried'.[8] Both marriage and celibacy are a *gift* from the Lord. And though we may prefer the gift of marriage, that might not be God's perfect will for us. Jesus commended those 'who refuse to marry for the sake of the Kingdom of Heaven'.[9] That could be his calling for you. If it is, there is no need to lead an unfulfilled life. After all, Jesus remained a bachelor. Could anyone call him odd, unbalanced or unfulfilled? Several of my closest friends have remained unmarried for the Lord's sake, and their lives have been enriched by the sacrifice. Their hospitality to others and their talent for friendship have been enhanced by remaining single.

Others of my Christian friends have been bereaved at an early age, and have suddenly found themselves single again. This is how one young mother is coping, whose husband died five years ago from cancer at the age of about thirty:

I'm getting used to having to make it on my own, and the Lord has been marvellously good to me. I have received so much in so many ways.

I think now I'm teaching, and I've joined the local choral society, I feel more of a complete person, if you see what I mean, though I still long for the day to day companionship of give and take. But even

118

there I think I'm slowly learning to lean on God more.

Here is another letter, which shows the courage of a young clergyman whose wife died from an overdose of sleeping tablets, taken during a deep fit of clinical depression to which she had been subject for some years. He has continued in his parish, and writes:

The Lord has been very real to me in the last few months, and the fellowship and hospitality of his people are absolutely wonderful. It is great to know it in experience as well as preach about it. This has been a year I will never forget, but one which I can look back on with thanksgiving as well as heartache. I'm indeed grateful for the advice to extract every positive aspect from the illness and passing of dear Jenny. With the Lord's help I am beginning to do just that. Life is very full, rich, and satisfying – as only the Christian ministry can be.

With Christ in the house it need not be bleak, even if, humanly speaking, you are on your own.

2. Personal Relationships at Large

At work

It won't be long before the folk at work realise that something has happened. They may wonder what makes you so happy even on a Monday morning. They may be amazed that you actually turn up on time, that you treat your secretary with courteous consideration

119

and neither like a dictating machine on the one hand, nor a mistress on the other. You will get your leg pulled, and your good humour and patience will count for a lot. They will expect from you a standard of behaviour they do not expect from others. What a compliment that is to your Master! Your honesty in little things will be watched. Although the practice of 'knocking things off' from the firm may be universal, although going home half an hour early when being paid overtime may be done by all the rest, it hardly squares with your Christian profession, and your friends will be quick to point this out.

Are you an employee? Then your attitude will be to do your job not just to get your pay packet or to keep on the right side of the boss: you will be working for Jesus, and you will want to turn out work of which he could be proud. Can you imagine any shoddy workmanship coming out of his carpentry shop in Nazareth? 'You employees, put your backs into the job you do for your earthly employers, not only trying to please them when they are watching you, but all the time; do it willingly because of your love for the Lord and your desire to please him. Work hard and cheerfully in all you do, as men who are working for the Lord and not merely for the bosses, remembering that it is the Lord Christ who is going to pay you, giving you abundant wages from all he owns.'[10]

Are you an employer? Then your attitude to your labour force will not be to see how much profit you can get out of them, and how cheaply you can make wage settlements. No, 'you bosses must be scrupulously just and fair to all your employees. Always remember that you too have a Master in heaven.'[11] When both sides of industry relate beyond themselves to the Lord and what he would want, then you get real harmony in a firm. But when he is left out of account, and rival policies of greed govern business and industry, then it is not surprising that intransigence, suspicion and hostility often result.

Concern for others

One of the most distinctive Christian qualities is love for other people. This sounds trite, but it is not. It is unique: so much so that the New Testament writers had to coin a new word for it. For it is an attitude which came into the world with Jesus Christ. The ancients knew all about *philia*, friendship, which was determined by the mutual attraction, affection and respect of two people for each other – it depended upon the worthiness of the beloved. They also knew all about *erōs*, passionate love, and rated it as highly as we do: here again, the worthiness of the beloved was crucial. But what Jesus brought with him was *agapē*, and that love is determined by the generosity of the giver, not the worthiness of the object. Indeed, St John tells us that God so loved the world (which he assuredly could not like, feel attracted to or respect – still less could he feel passionate emotion towards) that he gave his only Son for us. This love was sheer self-giving. It was not determined by the worthiness of the beloved but by the nature of the Lover. He loves us not because we are lovable but because he is love. His love, like his sun, shines equally upon the just and the unjust. Now that is the love which has reached us. That is the love which has taken root in us, and must get through us to others. Therefore we shall care for people whether or not they are nice or attractive. We

121

may not like them, but we shall love them, as he loves them through us. This means that we shall not take the mickey out of the little man in the office who is the butt of everyone else; we shall not allow our weeds to blow into the next-door neighbour's garden, however un-neighbourly he is towards us. We shall not write someone off because he went to a public school – or because he didn't. We shall not stick exclusively to people of our own social group or our own colour. There will be no trace of snobbery or race discrimination in our behaviour towards other people. God made them as they are. Christ loved them enough to die for them. And he wants to channel his love towards them through us.

Service abroad

One of the ways you might consider showing this self-giving love for others, if you are young enough, is to offer to VSO or one of the missionary societies to go and work without pay for a year or two in a developing country overseas. You would be giving your youthful enthusiasm and such skills as you have, and you'd be doing it for Jesus. In the doing, you would be tremendously blessed and enriched yourself. Even a short period is much better than nothing. Many Christian university students spend the summer vacation in some sort of voluntary service in a developing country. Doctors in training do their electives in mission hospitals. But you don't have to be young or go overseas in order to find opportunities for service. There are plenty of them in your own town, your own street. The Lord will show you where you can be useful, if you are open to his suggestions.

Love in the church

There is one side to this love for others which is stressed above all else in the New Testament. It is the very special love Christians have for other members of the Lord's family. 'Love of the brotherhood', they call it. It is a remarkable and most moving thing: I know nothing on earth to match it. The fact that the same Lord has loved you, the same Father accepted you into his family, the same Spirit lives in you, the same motivation grips you – why, this binds you to other members of the Jesus family wherever they may be, in a way no words can describe. I have experienced it in Cape Town and Nairobi, in Toronto and Hong Kong, in Sydney and Accra. It is a deep sense of mutual belonging to the Lord. It means you can relate quickly to the other Christian; it means you want to give to him; it means you love to pray together; it means the two of you are prepared to stand together even if to do so is politically dangerous, or socially frowned on. The Church of Christ transcends all our barriers of race, age, class and colour. We must keep it that way!

3. Personal Relationships for Christ

It goes without saying that as Christians we will want our lives to count for Jesus Christ. Magnetised by his love, we shall want to magnetise others. Let me make a few suggestions as to how we may go about this in our relationships with other people.

NEW LIFE, NEW LIFESTYLE

Demonstration method

Without doubt this is the most telling way of all. Our
lives are very often the only gospel any of our friends
will read, and if the writing they see there is unattractive, they won't want to know any more. On the
other hand, if they are attracted by what they see, it
will not be difficult to lead them to Jesus Christ, the
author of the transformation which has impressed
them. I remember an Olympic swimmer who, after a
tough battle with herself, committed her life to Christ.
She had been amazed by the Christian life of a friend
of hers, and this disposed her to listen to the good
news about Jesus.

You don't need to have been a Christian more than
a few days to begin influencing people by this
demonstration method. But it is sadly possible, if you
cramp the Holy Spirit away in some forgotten corner
of your life, to be a Christian of sorts for years without
anybody noticing much difference or being attracted
to Jesus Christ. And when that happens it is more than
a tragedy. It is a slander on the name of Jesus.

Contribution method

There is another way in which we can help our friends,
and those whom we don't even know. And that is by
giving. It may be giving our time to planning a radio
programme or helping get a hall ready for a Christian
meeting. It may be providing the refreshments at a
home meeting. It may be giving our mind to planning
an evangelistic meeting in the youth group. It may be
buying Christian books to give or lend to others. One
man wrote to me some time ago to say that he had

come to faith largely through a Christian paperback. He wrote: 'You may be amused to hear that when I told a friend of my conversion his comment was, "Oh, that's nothing. Old So-and-So found it so useful that he bought fifty copies to distribute to his friends!"' That man was using the contribution method in order to try to share his relationship with the Lord among his friends.

But the most obvious and basic aspect of the contribution method is financial giving. Giving to Christian enterprises that you know are committed to declaring the good news. This means informed, discriminating, prayerful giving. Jesus once spoke about a crooked business man who was discovered by his boss and fired. But before he left, he went round his boss's creditors and knocked their bills down for them. This meant, of course, that when he was kicked out, he had collected a number of addresses where he would be a welcome visitor, on account of the financial help he had given them. Jesus commended the man for his shrewdness (though not for his honesty!) and wished that Christians were as far-seeing in their use of their money. 'Make friends by the wise use of your money, so that when the day of money is over there will be people to welcome you into an eternal home,'[12] he said. In other words, invest cash in evangelism: through it some may hear and respond to the gospel who would have remained ignorant of it, had it not been for your sacrificial giving.

Subterranean method

There is a fascinating verse in Paul's Second Letter to the Corinthians where he invites their prayerful support for his work of making the gospel known. Literally he says: 'You also helping together underneath in prayer.'[13] What could he have in mind? I suggest that he is thinking of the fortresses which were such a common feature in the ancient world. Evangelism involves storming strongholds like that in people's lives. But a frontal assault is often useless. What is needed is a tunnel. That requires hard work, sustained work, team work. Such work is unseen and unsung. But it is crucial if the fortress is to be taken. Prayer is like that. It assails the inner recesses of a person's will in a way that all our talking cannot.

Now let me confess to you at once that I am not much good at this. By temperament I would much rather storm walls than tunnel away in prayer. But I know, I know from constant experience, that it is the tunnelling which counts. I recall vividly a mission to Cambridge University some years back. We had seen large numbers coming night after night, between eight hundred and twelve hundred. But there was not much to show for it in terms of definite conversions. We were driven back to fundamentals, back to the tunnelling of prayer. Much of the last-but-one night of that mission was given to prayer by people all over Cambridge. On the final night of the mission we had a remarkable breakthrough by the Holy Spirit of God, and many people responded to Christ, both then and in the weeks that followed. It taught me once again that prayer is perhaps the most important aspect of evangelism, and the one I, at any rate, am most liable to miss out on.

Invitation method

If one sixteen-year-old schoolboy had not used the invitation method with me, I very much doubt whether I would be writing this. He invited me to a meeting where I discovered what a Christian life was all about. As I went along regularly for many weeks, I observed the other teenagers at work on the demonstration method. And I know now that there were folk in the background tunnelling away on the subterranean method. These factors, under God's good hand, combined to bring me to my knees. My friend who invited me had himself only discovered Christ a few weeks previously. He was very inexperienced. But he could say, 'Come and see.' And I shall always be thankful that he did.

That is precisely what you find people doing in the first chapter of St John's gospel. 'Come and see,' says Jesus to the first pair of disciples. One of them goes home in excitement and says, in effect, to his brother, Simon Peter, 'Come and see.' Shortly afterwards we come across a sceptical Nathanael: Philip counters his hesitations with precisely the same invitation, 'Come and see.'

The point is obvious enough. William Temple put it crisply:

It is quite futile saying to people, 'Go to the Cross.' We must be able to say 'Come to the Cross.' And there are only two voices which can issue the invitation with effect. One is the voice of the sinless Redeemer, with which we cannot speak. And one is the voice of the forgiven sinner, who knows himself forgiven. That is our part.

It does not require long experience. It does not require the ability to explain the good news. But it does require us to have found Jesus for ourselves. And it does require the desire to share him with others. Given those conditions, we will pluck up courage to ask people to the supper party, the house meeting, the church service, the rally or what-have-you where we know the gospel will be attractively and relevantly made known. The speaker on these occasions might be the Archangel Gabriel for all I care. He could do nothing whatsoever unless some faithful Christians had been doing a good job on the invitation method. And remember, they'll come if they like you, and if they respect you, and if they are impressed by the changes Christ has effected in you. But if they see no difference in you, they are not likely to respond to your invitation.

Testimonial method

It's not difficult to go one stage further than the invitation method, even when you are very green in the Christian life. It is to give Jesus a testimonial. To be willing to say, 'Yes, there is a difference in my life, and it is due to Jesus. I have discovered that he is alive.' Something quite simple like that. 'Make Christ supreme in your heart, and then if anybody asks you the reason for your confident belief, be ready to tell him, and do it in a gentle and respectful way.'[14] That was Simon Peter's advice – and he had had quite a bit of experience at it by the time he wrote those words. I love that passage in the story of the Samaritan woman who had encountered Jesus. She was so thrilled that she left her water pot by the well (oblivious of the fact that she had come to draw water in the first place!), rushed back to the village and gave Jesus an open and glowing testimonial. 'Come and meet a man,' she said, 'who told me everything I ever did. Can this be the Christ?' The men were impressed by her testimony. They determined to find out, and after Jesus had spent a couple of days in their village, they were convinced. 'Now we believe,' they told the woman – and how she must have thrilled to see the fruit her testimony had borne – 'because we have heard him for ourselves, not just because of what you told us. He is indeed the Saviour of the world.'[15]

It is difficult to overestimate the effectiveness of even the most halting testimonial to Jesus given by the most recent believer. In a parish mission in East Anglia one young man (a local villager to his toenails), who came from a grim home, was led to the Saviour on the morning of the last Sunday. That same evening he had the courage to get up in church and say a single brief sentence: 'I have today asked Jesus Christ into my life.' They all knew him, of course. He worked in the nearby slaughterhouse. His words made more impact than the sermon – such is the power of the testimonial method of reaching people for Christ. It is available for every one of us to use.

Conversation method

How did Jesus reach men like Nicodemus or Zachaeus? Not by preaching a sermon to them, but by engaging them naturally in conversation. This is something we shall want to become adept at. It is rewarding; it is stimulating; it is challenging and it is humbling. What a *reward* when you see someone else,

129

perhaps someone whom you have prayed over and cared about for ages, commit his life to Jesus. What a *stimulus* to you mentally and spiritually, when you have to think your way round the gospel and the common objections to it, so as to be able to share it effectively when opportunity offers – and offer it may, even when you sit down next to a stranger in the bus. The *challenge* comes from the complete honesty we must demonstrate – the willingness to strip away every shred of pretence, and really to put ourselves out for the other person, even if it means shortage of food or sleep, or months of waiting and battling in prayer. And it is *humbling*, because, when you stop to think of it, it is just fantastic that God should use the likes of you and me to, as St Paul put it 'open blind eyes, to turn men from darkness to light and from the power of Satan to God'.[16] But it happens. He does it, not you (once you start thinking you are rather a dab hand at this evangelism business you will be useless. God cannot and will not use a proud person). But although he does it, he expects the co-operation of our lips. The Lord of glory stoops to co-operate with us!

I always feel that a splendid object lesson in evangelism by conversation is given to us by Philip, the businessman from Caesarea turned evangelist. We find his story in Acts chapter 8. A modest man – why, he was the preacher in a great revival in Samaria; and yet, when he felt God was calling him to go down to the desert, to the desert he went, even though there would have been red faces from his team when he failed to turn up to preach to the waiting hundreds that evening! God had a job for him: an appointment with a single individual in the desert.

Philip spotted this man riding in his chariot, and

such was his enthusiasm that he *ran* after it. Just imagine him belting after a chariot in the desert at a temperature of 140 degrees in the sun! Had anyone been around to notice him, they would have thought he was mad. But he wasn't mad. He was obedient to the leading of God. And he found (as you will find) that God had already prepared the way. Of all incredible things, this Ethiopian in his chariot was not reading the *Jerusalem Echo* but the Book of Isaiah. Better still, he was reading that piece about the Servant of the Lord who was led as a sheep to the slaughter and did not open his mouth before the shearers. What a chance! Even so, Philip did not rush in tactlessly. He asked if he could be of any help to the gentleman. The man in the chariot asked if he could assist him over a difficulty he had with the meaning of the passage. Not surprisingly, Philip was invited into the chariot, and he began to tell the enquiring Ethiopian official about the Jesus to whom this prophecy looked forward. Before long the man professed his belief, and took the opportunity of being baptised in the only pool of water in that hot, deserted Gaza strip – a spring that is still there today.

Now you and I won't expect to find people reading Isaiah 53 each time we talk to them! Nor will instant baptisms often occur. But if we ask our Friend to guide our conversations each day, and to give us opportunities to speak on his behalf when he wishes, then we are in for an exciting time. He will certainly take us at our word; opportunities will come our way. We shall fail sometimes. Sometimes we shall make a little headway. Sometimes we shall get stumped by a difficulty to which we do not know the answer, and we will have to go away and find out. Sometimes, however, we shall have the joy of leading an enquirer right through to Jesus personally. And I know no greater joy in life than that. It is the crowning thrill of using our relationships as channels of his love. And every Christian is meant to engage in it. Don't rob yourself of blessing by holding back!

NOTES

1 Revelation 3:20 (RSV)
2 Mark 5:19
3 Galatians 6:2
4 Psalm 16:11
5 Ephesians 4:26 (RSV)
6 1 Peter 3:1–2 (LB)
7 1 Corinthians 7:32–3
8 1 Corinthians 7:7
9 Matthew 19:12
10 Colossians 3:23–4
11 Colossians 4:1
12 Luke 16:9
13 2 Corinthians 1:11
14 1 Peter 3:15
15 John 4:29, 42
16 Acts 26:18

8

New Society

1. On Being the Church

We have thought a good deal so far about the individual Christian. But God is not merely concerned with the salvation of the individual. He wants to forge new individuals together into a new community, which will in turn affect society, and indeed the very cosmos we live in.

There is an increasing tendency in many countries today towards centralising power in the hands of the government. People want to exert external constraints (be they political repression or financial involvement) to make others conform to a predetermined pattern which they have not chosen.

What Jesus wants to do is quite different. It is to change people from the *inside*, and to do it not by constraint but through setting them free from themselves and filling them with his love for others. His strategy is to change society by transforming individuals one by one, and uniting them into a dynamic counter-culture.

Celestial strategy

When you commit yourself to Jesus Christ in personal

allegiance, you join a world-wide family of those who have done the same thing. It is a family in which, according to the New Testament's very bold language, Jesus is the elder brother and we are adopted alongside him into God's household of faith. What a wonderful conception that is! No barriers of race, class, sex or age. That is what we are called into. Of course, we do not achieve it all at once. Indeed, we do not fully achieve it on this earth at all. But the whole thrust of New Testament ethics says to us: 'Become in practice what in Christ you already are.' You are sons and daughters – then live like that. You are justified – then live a just life. You are washed – behave in a clean way. You are all one in Christ Jesus – show your unity in your church life. You are accepted in the Beloved – make sure you accept other members of the family.

That is the heavenly strategy. Alas, we often frustrate it by our selfish tactics, by allowing sectional or personal interests to motivate us. We close our ears to the needs of others, and remain silent when we should speak. But of the heavenly Father's plan there can be no doubt. He wants to show to the world, and indeed, Paul says, to the very angels (who have never known either the awfulness of sin or the wonder of forgiveness) what he can do with a community of people from every background and type, who commit themselves to him and allow him to shape their personal and corporate lives. 'God has given me the wonderful privilege of telling everyone about this plan of his,' said Paul. It is 'to demonstrate to the heavenly beings how perfectly wise he is, when all his family – Jews and Gentiles alike – are seen to be joined together in his church'.[1]

The Christian family

The church, then, is no optional extra for those who like that kind of thing. It is absolutely essential. Without it we shall not develop as Christians. Without it God's purpose will be frustrated. In the Church of Christ there is available a quality of fellowship which will surpass any friendship you can find in the pub, or any community life shared by the drop-outs. Does the New Testament not talk about our all being sheep in the one flock, which Christ looks after and directs;[2] or stones in the one building which the Holy Spirit inhabits and shines out from?[3] Are we not branches in his vine,[4] soldiers in his army,[5] and, incredible though it may seem, limbs in his body?[6] It is impossible to exaggerate the corporate nature of the Christian life. It stares at us from every page in the New Testament. It is through this corporate life, this new society, that Jesus wants to reach the millions who are strangers to him – not merely through the changes made in individual lives here and there.

Alas, many Christians have not seen this. I once talked to someone who had been a believer in Jesus and a fearless witness for him at work for three years without linking up with any Christian community. He realised what he had been missing; the Church, too, had missed him. It is tragic when Christians fail to see that they belong together and need each other; as a result they tend to lose their zeal because of isolation, and the Church loses their freshness and warmth.

The body of Christ

Think for a moment about that metaphor of the Church

135

being Christ's body on earth today. It speaks of the necessity and interdependence of all the different limbs in the body. It points to the harmony and unity of purpose that should characterise their relationships. It reminds us that all the members are at the disposal and direction of the mind; and that the mind can only express itself through the limbs. In other words, your ascended and invisible 'mind', Jesus Christ, *needs* you, together with other members of the new society, in order to express himself to the world through the harmony and variety of the whole body's corporate life. If you are missing from your place in the family gatherings, then the whole family is impoverished and weakened. And so are you. Regular Christian companionship is absolutely necessary for mature Christian discipleship.

So join up with your local church if you have not already done so. Even if they seem a wet lot, you belong with them. By all means see what you can do to blow away the stuffiness. But you may well find that they have as much, or more, to give you as you have to give them. After all, they are more experienced members of the same family.

Church renewal

But what if the local church seems to you to be dying? You still belong, just as you do to the more antique members of your family, the great aunts and so on! It is very interesting to notice the way God has worked down the ages. You can see it happening time and again in the history of Israel. God does not scrap his Church when it goes down the drain (as it has made a habit of doing from time to time; it is composed, after all, of sinful men and women). He doesn't throw it aside and start again. No, as Jeremiah learnt down in the potter's house, God is like a potter who remoulds the lump of refractory clay when it gets spoiled.[7] He does not throw it away. The church of Ezekiel's day was like a valley full of the dry bones of a dead army. But God did not say, 'Right, we'll start again.' In his vision, Ezekiel saw God breathe his Spirit into those dry bones, and new life soon showed itself.[8] He continues to work like that. Perhaps he wants to use you, among others, to revive the sleepy church in your area. Time and again a church whose minister has lost his vision and whose congregation has lost what Keith Miller calls 'the taste of new wine' has been revived by one or two people who mean business with God. They have not separated themselves from their local church in search of one more lively miles away. They have heard the call to join God's people where they live, and their coming has meant renewal.

Of course, in the early days of your membership of the new society you will be in great need of building up. Therefore you will be particularly dependent upon the warm fellowship and sound teaching of a church that knows how to care for new believers and how to build a community on the New Testament pattern. Perhaps you should go there once a week for your own soul's good; and go to the local church once a week in order to show the flag! Then later you can transfer your regular membership to where it is most needed. God will show you, if you make it a matter of prayer. But don't be surprised if he calls you to join that branch of the family which is operating where you live. Give it a try, at all events, and get fully involved, not merely

137

in public worship but in the smaller, informal meetings appropriate to your age and particular interests.

The service Jesus left us

At the heart of Christian fellowship lies the Holy Communion, Eucharist, Mass, Lord's Supper – call it what you will. Incidentally, each of those names stresses one side of the central act of Christian devotion. 'Holy Communion' reminds us that we come there in order to deepen our communion and fellowship with a holy God and with other members of his family. 'Eucharist' means 'thanksgiving' and warms our hearts with gratitude for all Christ has done to bring us into the family. 'Mass' probably means either 'meal' or 'dismissal' of those who are not baptised into Christ – this intimate family meal is for believing members of the family and none others. And 'Lord's Supper' reminds us who is the host and celebrant at that meal, Jesus himself, the one who inaugurated it at the last supper he had with his disciples on earth.

We come then, looking back to the cross; the cross he was going to when he had that supper with them. He told them, as he broke the bread, that his body would be broken for them; he told them, as he distributed the cup, that his blood would be shed for them.[9] It happened the very next day. How we need to go back time and again to Calvary with grateful hearts in order to reappropriate the forgiveness Christ won for us there! That is where our adoption certificate into the family was issued, where our citizen rights in the new society were secured, at such tremendous cost. The Communion awakens us afresh to the awfulness of sin, the greatness of his sacrifice and the wonder of our forgiveness.

We should also approach the Communion with a good long look at our own lives, in the light of that love of Christ's. How far do we come short of his considerateness, love, purity and honesty? Now is the time to search our consciences, get right with him, and as we stretch out our empty hands for the bread and the wine, symbols of his self-giving, to remember that we are indeed empty in ourselves; we deserve no good thing from God. We come simply by right of his generous free invitation to receive what he offers us – himself.

A third side to the Holy Communion is this. The early Christians knew that 'the Lord is at hand'. It was no festival in honour of a dead Jesus, but a meal of companionship with a risen Lord. So thank him that he is alive, that he is at work in you and the rest of the community of the resurrection, as the Church might well be called. That is something to rejoice about.

Make a point, too, of looking around you. That old lady, that bluff shop-keeper, that lanky youth, that friendly bus-driver – you all belong together in the Lord's family. You all kneel or sit together to receive the bread and wine, the sacred emblems of his body and his blood given without distinction for you all. No place for pride before such self-giving love, is there? No need to have any chip on the shoulder! No excuse for keeping up a feud with any other member of the same family. You are all on a par: fellow-sinners, fellow-heirs of the same kingdom and fellow-guests at the same table.

And spare a thought for the future God has for his

new society. It may not bring in Utopia on earth. God never said it would. But each Lord's Supper should have a touch of the future glory about it. It should remind us of the Marriage Supper of the Lamb (as the Book of Revelation picturesquely calls it), the final consummation in joyous harmony of God's plan for all his people. *'Maranatha!'* cried the earliest Christians in their native Aramaic, when they sat at the Lord's Table. 'O, Lord, come!'[10] It is as if they said, 'Lord, you have come to this world, and lived and died for us. You have set us in this new society. We see many marks of your presence and of your renewing work. But, Lord, there's such a long way to go. Hasten the day when you wind up your plans for this world, and bring us all to the family table in heaven.' No escapism, there, you will notice. But just a foretaste of the future glory to give us perspective in our daily work, and the determination to be the best for him on earth.

Make room, then, for informal fellowship at home and at work; make room for meeting other Christians, especially on Sunday; make room for services of other kinds; but, whatever you do, do not neglect Holy Communion. It is the seal of your pardon, the food for your Christian life, the bond of your fellowship and the foretaste of heaven.

Corporate worship

While the Holy Communion is perhaps the most important act of Christian worship and fellowship – it was, after all, instituted by Christ himself – it is not the only one. The early Christians found it so important to meet together both formally and informally for mutual encouragement and service, for worship and prayer, for learning and sharing, that they broke the imperial law in order to do it, and were prepared to face execution rather than give it up. That is how highly they rated the fellowship of the new society. 'We ought to see how each of us may best arouse others to love and active goodness, not staying away from church meetings, as some do, but rather encouraging one another, and all the more so as the day of Christ's return is drawing nearer.'[11] Such was the advice given in the Letter to the Hebrews. The quality of discipleship which that fellowship engendered captured the Roman world. Ancient paganism had nothing to compare with the loving, useful, happy lives of the Christian communities in their midst. And modern paganism has nothing to compare with it, either.

But if the Church is to make that kind of impact in society, its worship must have, and be seen to have, three qualities. Without them, what is done in church becomes as empty and meaningless as a shell when the nut has been removed. Worship must be united: it must be shared; and it must issue in practical goodness.

1. *Real worship must be united.* Naturally, for the various limbs in the body are stretching up in unison to praise and thank and trust and learn from their head. But if it is well known that the minister can't bear the organist, that the choir eats sweets and plays games through the sermon, that the congregation never talk to each other afterwards, and that the church council meetings always develop into an unholy row between the minister and one of the members – well, it is hardly surprising if such a church cuts no ice with

the neighbourhood. It is useless preaching a gospel of reconciliation if it is perfectly obvious that the members of the church have not settled their differences. And that goes for denominations as well as churches. We all know that the Roman Catholics have for centuries unchurched all other Christians, but are now changing their tune. It has been equally true that many Protestants have unchurched all Roman Catholics, and have thought it impossible that anyone should continue a member of that church once he had come to a living faith in Jesus. This Protestant exclusivism is as wrong as the Roman Catholic intransigence was. Every believer in Jesus is baptised by the one Spirit into the one body of Christ, in which there is no essential difference between Protestant and Roman Catholic, black or white, Cockney or old Etonian. Work for that unity in your place of worship.

2. *Real worship must be shared.* The Lord does not expect us to file into an ancient monument once a week, try to cope with Elizabethan English, marvel at Gothic architecture and a choir in resplendent clothes, and listen to a professional in a dog collar. Where these conditions still persist, the church has got to change. There needs to be room for the mutual enrichment and encouragement of different members of the body. It simply will not do for one member to monopolise the service. There has got to be room for the discussion of Christian principles and their outworking in daily life, not just passive listening to a sermon from the preacher, however talented he may be. (This is not to knock the sermon: there must be proclamation of God's truth, no less than discussion of how to apply it. The two belong together.) There has got to be

informal discussion in the small group as well as in the Sunday service, to enable the members to get to know, trust and learn from one another.

3. *Real worship must be practical*. It has to issue in 'love and active goodness' as the writer to the Hebrews reminded us. Genuine caring for the needs of society round about. It may be the quiet visiting of the sick, or reading to the housebound. It may be mounting a campaign for better housing or for children's playing areas. 'Fellowship is all very well,' remarked one friend to whom I showed this manuscript in an earlier draft, 'but the dying, hungering, longing people on the housing estate or in the lecture room alongside me remain dying. We are damned if our lives are not pinned on that cross with our Lord. James rightly says that "faith" alone is useless: faith is not faith when it draws back before the sacrificial giving of everything we have and are.' He rightly points out the great disinclination to *work* among Christian people; we prefer to take refuge in a cosy little Bible study. But the two are intertwined. We shall only increase in understanding when we obey Christ, and engage in loving, active service for him. Otherwise we shall find dullness and apathy at the weekly Bible study, when the group meets and has to admit, 'Sorry we haven't actually managed to be the hands and feet of Jesus today, but bless us all the same!' Genuine worship and genuine work go hand in hand. They cannot be separated if either is to remain healthy.

Is worship a priority in your church? Is it united? Is it relevant? Is there scope for all to take a real part? Does it lead to action? If not, start stirring things up. It should be.

2. On Being the Church in the World

Club for non-members

The new society must never degenerate into an introspective club. It is, in the memorable words of Archbishop Temple, the only society in the world which exists for the benefit of those who are not members.

Christians will therefore be concerned not only with evangelism, which we have considered in a previous chapter, but with social and political issues, with the equitable distribution of wealth and power, and the preservation of our world for future generations. There is a great deal which Christians can do in these areas. The Church should assuredly not leave politics to the politicians or economics to the economists. The Church at large, and the individual Christian in particular, may not be well equipped in any detail to pronounce on these highly complicated issues. But we all have some influence: we can stand up and speak up when the will of Christ is plain. It is our duty as Christian citizens. And in so doing we shall undoubtedly affect society. Let us take a glance at some of the crucial areas where as Christians we should be involved.

Social concern

I remember being delighted, on a visit to Australia, to discover the tremendous social conscience of the diocese of Sydney. This has the reputation of being the most uniformly evangelical diocese in the whole Anglican Communion. Far from evangelistic emphasis being the foe of social involvement, the reverse is proved to be the case. It gives more money to social work than any diocese in the world, and the motivation comes direct from a strong sense of the new life brought by Christ. Therefore *of course* the Church must build hospitals for the aged, villages for the retired, homes for unmarried mothers, boys and girls on probation and when they come out of prison. *Of course* they must provide help for the down-and-outs and would-be suicides. It is as important as the missionary work in which they engage so wholeheartedly. Sydney's Archbishop Marcus Loane was a superb example of this balance. On the one hand he had just walked the fabulously wild Kadoka Trail, a route through the mountains and jungles which had a gruesome reputation in the Second World War, in order to help raise a million dollars for the impoverished diocese of New Guinea. On the other, he had just fearlessly accused the federal government of policies which were producing a hundred thousand unemployed and family hardship hurting half a million. Angry questions were asked in Parliament. One member requested the Archbishop to stick to sin while politicians handled economics. The Prime Minister patronisingly said he would have a chat to the Archbishop, who clearly did not understand these things. The result? Churchmen at large backed the Christian lead given by Archbishop Loane, and all the other diocesan bishops backed him to the hilt, to the great embarrassment of a government which was unwilling to grapple with a crying social problem because of a forthcoming election. Christian concern over the unemployment issue led to a national enquiry into the causes and cure of poverty in Australia.

Race relations

A word about race relations may not be out of place in a day when, sadly, they are often a major disruptive force in societies across the world.

Many years ago in America a Civil Rights Commission came out in support of claims by black people for equality in citizenship rights, and yet absolutely nothing was done to carry those recommendations through. The magnetic leadership of Martin Luther King, with his policy of non-violent protest allied to civil disobedience, forced both President and Congress to act. Though assassinated in the cause of winning justice for black people, Martin Luther King's life and ideals still live on and have influenced the cause of freedom the world over. In his Christmas Eve broadcast, shortly before he was killed, he outlined his vision for humanity. It shows not only the greatness of the man but the Christ-centred motivation for his social concern:

I still have a dream this morning that one day every Negro in this country, every coloured person in the world, will be judged on the basis of the content of his character rather than the colour of his skin, and every man will respect the dignity and worth of human personality. I still have a dream today that one day the idle industries of Appalachia will be revitalised and the empty stomachs of Mississippi will be filled, and brotherhood will be more than a few words at the end of a prayer, but rather the first item on every legislative agenda. I still have a dream today that one day justice will roll down like water, and righteousness like a mighty stream. I still have a dream today that in all of our state houses and city halls men will be elected to go there who will do justly, and love mercy and walk humbly with their God. I still have a dream today that one day war will come to an end, that men will beat their swords into plowshares and their spears into pruning hooks, that nations will no longer rise up against nations, neither will they study war any more . . . I still have a dream that with this faith we shall be able to adjourn the councils of despair and bring new light into the dark chambers of pessimism. With this faith we will be able to speed up the day when there will be peace on earth and goodwill toward men. It will be a glorious day, the morning stars will sing together, and the sons of God will shout for joy.

Such was the vision behind the practical action of one of this century's truly great Christians. Yet he was shot. Does this mean that Christians are mistaken in renouncing force and rejecting violent revolution in a world that seems to be becoming increasingly violent?

Revolutionary violence

This is a difficult issue. It is hard, on the one hand, to see how the Church, committed as it is to love and peace, could be involved in violence and revolution. But what is it to do, on the other hand, when the surrounding society is utterly corrupt, when justice has been banished, and oppression is the order of the day? The temptation to violence is almost irresistible in those circumstances, and yet for the life of me I cannot see violent revolution squaring with the example of Jesus. Though he had some Zealot revolutionaries among his

147

disciples, he would not accept the option of violent revolution in the interests of either nation or ideology. Ironically enough, he was crucified as a revolutionary leader ('King of the Jews'), and yet he refused to allow the ideological cause of the Kingdom of God or the political cause of throwing off the Roman yoke to tempt him to sanction arms. Force is not exorcised by force. Violence breeds violence. And that will give the Christian pause before considering it, even under extreme provocation. For the cross of Jesus shows us clearly that violence is disarmed not by retaliation but by patient, innocent suffering.

There have been Christians of the utmost spirituality and integrity who, goaded beyond endurance, have accepted the option of violence for the sake of helping other people whom it seemed impossible to defend in any other way. One thinks of Camilo Torres, the Roman Catholic priest, who was so appalled at the conditions of the peasants in Colombia that he sided with the guerillas in the mountains in the attempt to improve their lot by violent revolution. This brave man joined the revolution out of love for his neighbour, and we must salute him. He was shot in action in 1966. And many Latin American hoardings carried the legend *Camilo viva!* for years afterwards.

Or one thinks of Dietrich Bonhoeffer, the lifelong Christian pacifist, who eventually was so appalled by the atrocities of Hitler's Germany that he took part, out of Christian love for the German people, in an attempt to kill Hitler – and paid the extreme penalty. These great men reluctantly took the way of violence, but only when, evil as they saw it to be, it seemed less evil than the *status quo*. They may have been wrong. But we certainly cannot judge them. They had the courage to give practical proof of their sense of justice and their Christian love for others, knowing that they were risking their lives by so doing. Equally great men, such as Martin Luther King in USA, Bishop Helder Camara in Brazil and Bishop Wilson in a Japanese Prisoner of War Camp in World War Two, have followed Jesus in meeting violence by suffering, and in the long run their judgment may well prove the sounder. 'Christians,' said Jacques Ellul, at the end of his careful book, *Violence*, 'will be sufficiently and completely present in the world if they suffer with those who suffer, if they seek out with those sufferers the one way of salvation, if they bear witness before God and man to the consequences of injustice and the proclamation of love.'

Reactionary violence

But there is a reactionary as well as a revolutionary violence. In the South American scene, revolutionary violence is understandably sparked off by the violent oppression, rapacity and ruthlessness of the tiny ruling class. In South Africa the black majority has for many years been shamelessly maltreated and kept down by the wealthy white minority. In Eastern Europe it has been the same story, as Communist regimes have silenced all opposition with the gun and with the gulag. What attitude is the Christian is adopt?

It is tempting to join the guerillas and match violence with violence. But that is not Christ's ideal for us. The way of reactionary violence is bound to fall apart from its own dynamics of hate. We have seen that happen with graphic suddenness in Eastern Europe in 1989. The only thing in the world that will last is love. And love is the political option which has for so long remained untried. Michael Cassidy wrote a fascinating book in 1990 entitled *The Politics of Love*, where he applied these four principles of love in politics with clarity and power to the South African scene which he knows so well, and where he has for so long been a powerful advocate for the ways of Christ. Here are his four 'laws of love':

Love sees politics as all about people
Love deals with its own heart first
Love loves, humanises, and forgives its enemy
Love hears and sees the other side

Whether the people of South Africa will heed this powerful appeal remains to be seen. But there can be no other cure for violence, reactionary or revolutionary. The only way to change your enemy is to love him: it is costly, sacrificial, humbling, but the only way, so Jesus tells us. He ought to know. He trod it himself.

The environment

In recent years, leading scientists the world over have been warning us that unless we change our priorities radically, the earth is heading for destruction within two generations. The threat to human survival comes from a variety of sources. There is the spectre of the hydrogen bomb; and an increasing number of nations join the Nuclear Club every year. There is the stock-piling by many nations of germ weapons which can wipe out a whole country overnight. There is the unsolved problem of hunger; nearly two-thirds of the world's population is underfed. There is the appalling threat of overpopulation. The world population took two centuries to double between the seventeenth and the nineteenth century. But now it doubles every thirty years! By the year two thousand there will be twice as many people on this overcrowded planet as there are now. Most of them will be born to starvation, since food supplies cannot even support the present population, and almost all the cultivable land in the world has already been used up. There are plenty of other problems. We are depleting the natural resources of our planet at a shattering rate and cutting down the rain forests. Furthermore, the world is being polluted to an incredible extent and the ozone layer is eroding at an alarming rate. We are like rats, fouling our own cage. We pollute the atmosphere with carbon dioxide, poison the seas with oil and chemicals and inundate the land with garbage. Add to this the gross inequality between the 'haves' and the 'have-nots' and the critical nature of the world situation comes into even sharper focus. Americans eat fifty times more food in their lifetime than do people in India. The inequality which exists between industrialised and non-industrialised nations to so marked a degree is a massive irritant to war.

As Christians whose lot it is to live in such a significant and indeed terrible chapter of the world's history, how are we to carry out the Lord's command to love our neighbour? Bishop Hugh Montefiore, who has consistently pointed out the seriousness of these issues, wrote this selective adaptation of the Ten Commandments:

I am the Lord your God; you shall have no other gods but me.

You shall not make to yourself any graven image or idol,

such as the Gross National Product or possessions or riches, *whether in the heavens above or in the earth beneath or in the waters under the earth: you shall not bow down and serve them.*

You shall not take the name of the Lord your God in vain by calling on his name but ignoring his natural law.

Remember that you set apart one day in the week for true festivity, or you will be bored stiff in the technological age you are bringing on yourselves.

Honour your father and mother, but do not seek to prolong their natural term of life so that they are miserable.

You shall not murder future generations by your present greed.

You shall not commit sexual sin by producing more children than is your right.

You shall not bear false witness against your overseas neighbours by lying to yourself about the extent of their needs.

You shall not covet an ever-increasing standard of living.

Secular assumptions – and Christian attitudes

As Christians we shall want to contest the assumptions of most of our contemporaries in the industrialised West; namely, that we have a right to an ever-increasing standard of living, that increased wealth brings increased happiness, that governments should make material prosperity their chief aim and that man is autonomous over his environment. We believe that we are not autonomous here on this earth, but responsible to the God who put us here for our stewardship of the resources of his world. We believe that we are inter-dependent with the natural world, of which we are a part, and that flouting natural ecological law will destroy the world and ourselves. We believe that happiness does not consist in the multitude of things that we possess: it is not wealth, but relationships that bring the greatest joy. We believe that this world is not the be-all and end-all of life, but the foretaste of eternity, and our readiness for God's future will be determined by the way we have lived here on earth. Our character is the only thing we can take out of this life with us – and our character is developed by the responsible choices that we make on just such issues as those we have been discussing. We believe that nature is God's handiwork. Its beauty is his beauty, and when we spoil it we hurt him. We believe that we cannot love God if we do not love our neighbour; and our neighbour consists not only of the poor and needy at the other end of the world, but the generations yet unborn. We shall reflect on those principles, and act on them.

Christian attitudes

We dare not, therefore, as Christians in today's world, be bound by nationalism, by prejudice based on race, colour and class, or by considerations of personal gain. We dare not assume that because we do not see the sixty thousand homeless sleeping at night on the streets of Bombay we are not involved. We are involved. They are our brothers and sisters. No longer can we assume that it is our right to have a rise in income each year, a car (and preferably a new one every two years), satellite TV and an expensive annual holiday. It is not our right. It is salutary to recall that even the person on State Assistance or Social Security in the West lives like a prince compared with the average citizen throughout the Two-thirds World. We Christians must show ourselves masters over the greed, selfishness and irresponsibility that are taken for granted in our society. Our Christian allegiance must affect our pocket and our politics – no longer will it do to vote according to our class or according to what will benefit us most. We shall seek to discover which party as a whole is more committed to dealing equitably with the problems which bedevil our world; which party is committed to values beyond mere increase of wealth; which party cares most about the future of the world and about our neighbours in the Third World. And we shall vote for that party.

Workshop here: residence above

'Workshop below. Residence above.' You may have seen a notice to that effect by the doorbell of someone who lives over the shop. Well, read that in a Christian sense, and it will give a proper perspective to what has just been said. Christians ought to be very clear that no 'man-made' society can ever be a Utopia. All Towers of Babel get short shrift in Scripture, because it is made abundantly plain that any lasting building is God's work, not ours, and that the kingdom which we seek is the Kingdom of Heaven, not of men and women. We cannot bring it in. What we touch we spoil. The Christian hope for the future is built fairly and squarely upon God and what he will do; just as the Christian assurance about the past is built on God and what he has done through the incarnation, death and resurrection of Jesus. Incidentally, the events that took place in Judaea over nineteen hundred years ago are the pledge that we Christians are not kidding ourselves about the future. We live 'in between the times', marked as they are by the first and last comings of Jesus. 'God's gracious intervention, bringing rescue for all mankind, *has* appeared,' writes Paul to Titus; and from the certainty of that fact in the past he can look forward with assurance to the day when 'our great God and Saviour, Jesus Christ, *will* appear in majesty'. Christ's first coming was in humility and as Saviour. 'He gave himself for us in order to rescue us from every lawless way, and cleanse us as a people for his own possession, eager to do good.'[12] Christ's second coming will be in majesty, no longer as Saviour but as Judge, when, at the end of history, he will bring in the fullness of the Kingdom which was inaugurated at his first coming to our world. We live between those two great comings. Our goal is nothing that man can construct, but as the poet who wrote the Book of Revelation conceived it, in a fusion of metaphors:

The Holy City, the new Jerusalem, coming down from God out of heaven. It was a glorious sight, beautiful as a bride at her wedding. I heard a shout from the throne saying, 'Look, the home of God is now among men, and he will live with them, and they will be his people; yes, God himself will be among them. He will wipe away all tears from their eyes, and there shall be no more death, nor sorrow, nor crying, nor pain. All of that is gone for ever.'[13]

Such is the Christian hope. It is a hope based on the reality of the resurrection of Jesus Christ. That does

155

not, however, mean we are to sit and wait for the end.
Christians down the ages have tended to make one of
two mistakes at this point. Either they have neglected
the future hope, and put all their efforts into working
for an earthly Utopia: or they have refused to get
involved in the social and political intricacies of the
world of their day, waiting for the Second Coming of
Christ. How different the balance of the biblical writers!
They believed passionately in the reality of God's
future, when Paradise Lost would become Paradise
Regained. But for that very reason, and imbued with
that hope, they were committed to working at earthly
problems like race and labour relations, care for the
widows and relief for the famine-stricken. It is no
coincidence that the passage I have just quoted from
Paul's Letter to Titus has several phrases between the
mention of Christ's first and second comings. They
concern the life we should be living now, in between
the Advents, a life marked by practical honesty and
goodness. We Christians, therefore, should be allying
ourselves with every effort that is made to increase
justice, humanity, equality and peace among men: but
we should be very clear that the best mankind can
achieve will be a very provisional order until the day
when Christ returns to right all wrongs and bring in
the fullness of his Kingdom.

Meanwhile, he has given us his Spirit, the first
instalment of heaven. Equipped with that Spirit the
Christian Church, the new society, has a vitally
important part to play in moulding the attitudes of
society in the coming decades, when the destiny of the
world, for doom or for deliverance, may well lie in the
balance. Our lifestyle, moulded by that same Holy
Spirit (as we make Christ King in our individual lives

and in the Christian Church at large), will show that new life really is available for an old and jaded world. Life which begins now and stretches beyond the grave. Life which affects society now, and culminates in the community of heaven. This life is available – for anyone who is prepared to pay the price. And though costly, it is infinitely satisfying, for it is what we were created for: to know God and enjoy him for ever.

NOTES

1 Ephesians 3:7, 10

2 John 10:16

3 1 Corinthians 3:16,
  Ephesians 2:20–2,
  1 Peter 2:5

4 John 15:1ff.

5 2 Timothy 2:3–4

6 Romans 12:4ff.,
  1 Corinthians 12:12ff.

7 Jeremiah 18:1ff.

8 Ezekiel 37:1ff.

9 Matthew 26:26–8

10 1 Corinthians 16:22,
   cf. Revelation 22:20,
   Didache 10

11 Hebrews 10:24–5

12 Titus 2:11–14

13 Revelation 21:2–4